TOURING
With Stalin

A Tale of Two Worlds by
NORMAN BEIM

NEWCONCEPT press, inc.

New York   New York

NEW CONCEPT PRESS
425 West 57 Street-Suite 2J
New York, NY 10019
212-265-6284/ Fax: 212-265-6659
newconpres@aol.com

Library of Congress Control Number: 2011903582

Beim, Norman
        Touring with Stalin/Norman beim
                p.   cm
ISBN: 978-0-931231-18-6   0-931231-18-3 (trade paperback: alk. paper)
1. Theatre tour: Darkness At Noon 2. Stalin biography
Title: Touring with Stalin
Fiction...based on Fact, plus non-fiction
813'.54-de21

Special thanks to LARRY ELRBAUM, FRANK BARA, RUTH ELY

FRONT COVER DESIGN: HOMER GUERRA, New York City

Printed in the United States

10 9 8 7 6 5 4 3 2 1

FOR MARTY BEIM,
who has a way with words

BOOKS BY NORMAN BEIM

NOVELS
Touring With Stalin
Zygielbaum's Journey
Hymie and The Angel

PLAYS
Bitter & Sweet: Three New Musicals
The Wrath Of God, Plus 5 Additional Dramas
Six Ironic Comedies
Three Dark Comedies
Women Laid Bare
Comedy Tonite!
Infamous People
Giants Of The Old Testament
My Family The Jewish Immigrants
Plays At Home And Abroad
Six Award Winning Plays

AUTHOR'S NOTE

For the chapters on Stalin I consulted the following:

Darkness At Noon by Arthur Koestler

Conversations With Stalin by Milovan Djilas

Twenty Letters To A Friend by Svetlana Alliluyeva

The Autobiography of Joseph Stalin by Richard Lourie

Stalin, Breaker of Nations by Robert Conquest

Stalin by Leon Trotsky

Stalin, The Court of the Red Tsar by Simon Sebag Montefiore

And finally a most fascinating volume,
Stalin by Edvard Radzinsky,
on which I relied most heavily.

PRISONER 402

STALIN

On March 2, 1953 the Russian people were stunned by the news that their legendary leader was seriously ill. Moscow Radio's chief announcer read the official bulletin on Stalin's illness. Apparently the Boss had a problem with his white blood-cell count. Did this mean the end? Was our immortal leader actually made of flesh and blood? The newspapers, the radio were flooded with all sorts of suggestions to save the legendary ruler. People offered their own lives out of patriotic fervor. On March 5, 1953 the unheard of actually occurred. Stalin was dead.

Untold stories have been circulated about the Boss's death. He did not die in the Kremlin, where he was supposed to have died. Nor did he die on the day that was given. "On the night of February 28," one story goes, "Stalin's guards summoned Beria, the head of the notorious NKVD, to the Boss's dacha in the suburbs. Beria was informed that Stalin had not left his room for a suspiciously long time. Beria phoned his assistant, Malenkov as well as Kruschev.

"Together they entered the Boss's room. He lay on the floor unconscious. Suddenly Stalin moved. Kruschev, the First Secretary of the Communist Party, ran over to him and began to strangle him. Beria and Malenkov joined in, and the three of them choked the man to death. Afterwards, that same night, Beria ordered all the Boss's guards shot. So actually when the Boss's illness was announced the man had been dead for days." At least that's one version!

Stalin was embalmed. He lay in state in the Hall of Columns. The streets of Moscow were choked with mourners. Thousands arrived from all over the country. Crowds were shoved about by the police. People were trampled to death trying to get one final glimpse of their great leader. On March 9 Molotov, Beria and Kruschev spoke at his funeral. He was then laid in the Mausoleum beside Lenin.

On March 5, the day of Stalin's death, another death took place. That of the famous composer Sergei Prokofiev. When his widow tried to get flowers for his funeral every shop was closed. A neighbor took cuttings from some indoor plants to place on the grave. Prokofiev's favorite pianist, Svyantoslav Richter, who was flying in to play beside Stalin's coffin reported that the plane was so crammed full of flowers that the scent was suffocating.

After the funeral the Boss's son's apartment was bugged. His conversations have been preserved in the President's archives. Speaking to his chauffeur in regard to his father's funeral, Vasily said, *All those people crushed...it's terrible! I had a row with Kruschev about it...Something terrible happened in the House of the Unions. An old woman with a walking stick came in. Malenkov, Beria and Molotov were standing in the guard of honor...and suddenly the old woman says, 'You killed him, you swine, now you can be happy! May you be damned."*

Three weeks after the funeral Vasily, who was the Lieutenant General of Aviation, was discharged from the army. He was not even allowed to wear an army uniform. A month after that he was arrested. He wasn't released until the spring of 1961, when he was banished to Kazan. He died one year later, possibly helped to his death the same way his father was. Of course, that's only rumor. The official verdict was alcoholism.

Shortly after having jailed Vasily, Beria wound up in the same prison, where he also met his death. The archives contain a description of his execution. "They tied his hands behind his back and attached him to a hook driven into a wooden board. Beria said, 'Permit me to say...' but the executioner said, 'Gag his mouth with a towel.' One protruding eye glared at them wildly over the blindfold. The officer pulled the trigger and the bullet struck him in the middle of the forehead." He was cremated.

Stalin remained in the Mausoleum for eight years. Finally it was decided to remove him. A commander of the Kremlin Regiment remembered the event.

"October 31, 1961. Militia squads cleared Red Square and closed off all the entrances. When it was completely dark, they dug up a grave by the Kremlin wall. They then transferred Stalin's body from the sarcophagus to a coffin lined with red cloth. 'He looked as if he was alive', it was said. The Mausoleum staff wept, it was reported, as they replaced the gold buttons with brass ones, and also removed his golden shoulder boards. Then they covered the body with a dark veil, leaving only his lifelike face uncovered. After the Reburial Commission arrived there was a minute's silence as they lowered him into the grave. 'We had orders to cover him with two concrete slabs, as if they feared that he might return from the grave, but we just shoveled earth onto him.'"

1995 Russia celebrated the fiftieth anniversary of its victory over Germany. There was a victory parade and the man standing on the Lenin Mausoleum, where Stalin once stood, was President Yeltsin. The veterans of the army that had defeated fascism, the army that had been destined to conquer the world, marched by. A little green curtain hid the word "Lenin," and no sign of the Boss was to be seen. The Boss was merely part of history now.

Or was he?

Not far away, at the very same time, another demonstration was being held. A group of fifty thousand marched down the main streets of Moscow singing songs from the Stalin era. For the first time since his death dozens of portraits of Stalin were displayed. Communists, monarchists, even Russian fascists marched side by side honoring the memory of the Boss.

After forty years the details of the legendary leader, the famous show trials, the bloody executions, the fear, suspicion, the arrests in the dead of night, men and women pulled off the streets, pulled out of their bed and landing in jail...or worse, those memories had all but faded away. Along with pictures of Stalin placards reading "Jews Beware! Stalin Will Soon return" were now being waved. Included in this procession were priests in cassocks.

Despite all the horrors this man was supposed to have committed, despite the stranglehold this despot had on his domain, despite the heartbreak he wreaked on the people he governed, there must have been something about the man, something to admire, something to look up to.

APRIL 1951

Hungary releases Robert Vogeler, who had been convicted of spying for the United States. Five U.S. soldiers stationed in the Philippines are killed in an ambush by communist Huk insurgents.

HERB VOLPE

Let's go back to Paris, said Herb Volpe.

I wish, said Helen.

Helen was nine years younger than her husband, but there were times when she felt like his mother. She often wondered if that was the reason she fell in love with him, because of his childlike quality. It certainly wasn't because of his looks.

Herb was a beefy man; beefy body, beefy face with a prominent nose and squinty eyes. But there was this gentleness, surprising in a man so cumbersome.

You look very thoughtful this morning, said Herb. *What are you thinking?*

I'm wondering why I married you, said Helen.

Herb wanted to respond with something witty, something clever, but his wife's remark cut too close to the bone. He adored that woman, that gorgeous, sexy, voluptuous enchantress, so beautiful, so talented. He was so grateful that she'd chosen him above those other handsome, dashing suitors. If he were to lose her... But two show-business careers in a marriage... What were the chances?

No, seriously, said Herb, getting back to the subject of Paris, *I could get work dubbing.*

What about your stage career?

I'll learn French, said Herb. *If you can, so can I.*

Herb wanted to go back to Paris, not because he loved Paris that much, which he did, but because Helen was so happy there, having won that fellowship and studying with Madame Lewenska, and making all sorts of contacts in the concert and the opera world. But Helen had made up her mind when she married Herb. He was a good actor, and his career came first.

Breakfast was the best time of day for the happily married couple. Still warm from the bed they shared, they would review the past, the present and the future; family matters, career matters, household matters. This was Monday morning the time to come back to earth. They'd spent the week-end unpacking, shopping and putting the apartment back in order. The people who'd sublet the apartment during the summer they'd spent in Paris, had left a mess.

It's true the couple had paid handsomely, but most of that money had been spent in Paris. Helen's fellowship had not covered their expenses, and the two dubbing jobs Herb managed to get were minor ones. The couple faced a cold, hard winter.

What are you going to tell Stanley? asked Helen.

I'm not quite sure, said Herb. *I don't want to go out again. I know that. I've got to bite the bullet. Don't you think?*

Helen didn't answer.

Living separately for six long months was certainly no fun, but Herb was well paid for those tours, and he was able to save quite a bit each year. In addition to that Stanley offered Herb leading roles in good plays. Of course, career-wise those trimmed down productions traveling in a van, with Herb as driver, company manager and leading man led nowhere really.

He'd been told by agents that there would be work for him in television if he stayed in town, as well as auditions for Broadway shows. The prospect of auditions, however, did not pay the bills, and there was no guarantee of television work. The winters he had spent in town were frustrating and depressing. Going on tour he was an actor, not just a guy looking for a job. But he was now in his mid thirties, not a kid anymore, and if he was going to get somewhere it would have to be now.

No, said Herb, *I've made up my mind. I'm going to stay in town. But how are we going to manage?*

Maybe I can get some more pupils, said Helen. *And there's always a wedding or some church service. We'll manage. Don't worry.*

We were supposed to start saving up for your concert.

The concert can wait, said Helen.

I'll make the rounds today, and see what kind of reception I get, said Herb. *What are you gonna do?*

I'll make some phone calls, said Helen. *See how many pupils I still have. And I'll call some agents...and see if I can still cook. No more restaurants.*

She said nothing about going to see the doctor. She was almost sure, but she didn't want to say anything until she was positive. There was that one time, a few weeks ago, when they were carried away and she realized afterwards, that she wasn't wearing her diaphragm. She cursed herself, but said nothing to Herb. There was no use alarming him unnecessarily. Ah, yes. Paris was, indeed, a romantic city.

Herb put on his good suit and wore the elegant tie Helen bought him in Paris.

If Stanley calls what shall I tell him? asked Helen, as Herb got ready to leave.

Don't tell him anything. Just put him off.

Suppose he invites us to dinner?

I'm certainly not gonna close the door, said Herb. He studied his wife's face. *Are you all right?*

Yes, said Helen, *I'm fine.*

You look...

What?

Very thoughtful this morning, said Herb.

Well, said Helen, *it's back to reality.*

Love you, said Herb.

He kissed his wife and was out the door. And there he was, pounding the pavement again.

He decided to walk. It was over thirty blocks, but it was early, and it was a beautiful Autumn day.

His spirits rose with every step. He was on Broadway. Well, upper Broadway, the not very elegant side of town. But this was still New York City. Mecca! Why shouldn't today be the day? It's true he'd missed out on all the Broadway casting that went on during the summer, but there was television. There was always television. There were the "soaps," the dramatic shows. There were the commercials. All sorts of work. Why shouldn't some of it come his way?

He sat down on a bench in the little square on Sixty Fifth Street and Broadway. He opened his portfolio, took out his eight by ten glossy and studied his picture. He really should get new ones. The quality of the photography was not that great. The picture looked faded. Of course, it was a reproduction, but even the original had not been very impressive. Studying it more closely he decided that the expression wasn't too bad. It had warmth. It had character. Well, it would just have to do for now. He sighed, put the photograph back in his portfolio and continued on.

When he reached Sixtieth Street and Broadway he walked around Columbus Circle and sat on a bench on Central Park South, the magnificent Central Park behind him. It was still early. No one was in their office till at least ten o'clock. He thought about Helen. Her curvaceous naked body swam across his mind. He thought again how lucky he was, how complete he was, how nothing else really mattered...well, almost nothing else. He gazed at the elegant apartment buildings, the classy hotels.

What a rich country this was! Anyone could be a star, couldn't they? Not that he saw himself as a star...a major leading character actor perhaps. Character actors worked all the time. Beauty faded. Character only deepened. Well, it was true! All the great actors were character actors. Ralph Richardson. There was an actor for you.

He looked at his watch. Five to ten. Close enough. He walked slowly down Broadway, entered an office building just above Fifty Seventh Street and took the elevator to the twelfth floor. The Jules Ziegler office was always busy. The outer room was empty. He walked up to the window leading to the inner office.

Hello? he called.

Lillian, Ziegler's assistant (weren't all assistants called Lillian?) appeared. *You're early today,* said Lillian.

Well, I'm just back in town. I thought I'd get an early start.

Out on tour? asked Lillian.

No, I spent the summer in Paris. As a matter of fact, I did some dubbing there.

Really? said Lillian. *It's too bad you're not fifteen. We need a boy, fifteen, to do some narration.*

My voice is very flexible, said Herb. *I've done some radio work, you know, and played much younger.*

I don't think so, said Lillian. *Come back later. You never know.*

I really am flexible.

So am I, said Lillian, *only I creak a little. Come back later.*

Thank you, said Herb and started to leave.

Oh...., Lillian called. *I've forgotten your name.*

Herb. Herb Volpe.

Do we have your picture?

I don't know. I'll give you a new one. Herb handed her his eight by ten.

She studied it. *You need new pictures,* said Lillian.

Yes, I know.

Lillian handed him a card. *He's very good,* she said.

Herb looked at the card. *Yes, and very expensive.*

Tell him I sent you. He might take a little off.

Thank you, said Herb. *By the way, do you need any singers?*

You sing?

No. My wife does.

Tell her to drop by and leave her picture.

I just happen to have one with me, said Herb, and presented the woman with Helen's eight by ten.

She's very pretty, said Lillian.

She's beautiful, said Herb.

Lillian laughed. *Good luck,* she said, and watched Herb leave the office with a mixture of pity and envy.

Life seemed just a little less rosy, a little less promising as Herb left the building. How humiliating it was to go around begging for work. He was an artist, not a peddler.

He walked over to the NBC building at Rockefeller Center, took the elevator to the casting office on the second floor and left his name and phone number on the sign-in sheet. He started to greet the casting director who was sitting inside nearby. *Nothing today,* came the curt reply even before he opened his mouth. Thanks a lot, thought Herb, and left, a little more bruised. He walked to the office building on Fiftieth Street off Seventh Avenue.

There were many agents on the tenth floor. Two doors said, DO NOT ENTER. He entered a third office.

Do you sing? a young man called out.

No, said Herb. *But my wife does.*

When she has a sex change, send her in.

Would you like her picture?

Yeah, sure, came the gracious reply. *Leave it on the table.*

Herb hesitated. Would they hold onto it or drop it into the "round file"? What the hell, that's what they got the pictures for. He placed Helen's picture on the table.

Close the door, the gentleman called out as Herb exited.

Herb sighed and closed the door behind him.

It was twelve fifteen by now and he was beginning to feel hungry. He thought about calling the apartment, but since he had nothing cheerful to report he decided not to. He walked over to the Horn & Hardart Automat on Broadway and Forty Sixth Street.

The same faces were sitting around the same table. Vegetables were still five cents; a healthy meal, real cheap. As he set down his tray and joined the familiar faces he debated about creating lemonade with the cold water, free lemons and the sugar that were available. Everyone did. But was he really that poor? He decided he was, took a glass of cold water from the tray, collected the necessary ingredients and sat down at the table in front of his frugal, but tasty lunch.

He was greeted with a couple of guarded nods from the all male gathering. The conversation continued uninterrupted as he prepared his lemonade.

Jack had an audition for the Actors' Studio.

So did I. So what? Did he pass?

He doesn't know yet.

Big deal!

The neatly dressed black actor sitting next to Herb said, *Have you been over to the Martin Beck?*

What's happening there? asked Herb.

"The Crucible," the new Arthur Miller play, is replacing one of the men. I think you'd be right for it. Leave your picture with the stage manager.

Don't bother with the stage manager, came further advice. *Elsie Brenner is the one that's doing the casting.*

Thank you, said Herb.

There then ensued a debate, which developed into a rather intense argument about the pros and cons of The Method.

Elia Kazan is being called up by the Committee. Did you read about it?

Who wants to read about that shit?

There was an uneasy silence. The "Red Scare" was a subject better left untouched. As Herb finished his lunch, the conversation turned to the movies and Marilyn Monroe. *She's a comedienne,* was one comment.

Herb finished his frugal lunch. He rose and nodded to the black actor next to him. *Take care,* said one of the actors across from him. Herb was surprised at the friendly smile. But then again, why not? They all shared the same dream. It was understood. There was no need to discuss something so deeply felt.

Herb walked over to the Paramount Building at Broadway and Forty Third street. He took the elevator to the eighth floor and walked down the hall to Elsie Brenner's office. He knocked softly on the door, then opened it.

Well, don't just stand there, snapped Elsie. *If you're going to come in, come in.* Elsie was known for her eccentricity.

Herb closed the door and approached the desk. Elsie peered at him over her glasses.

You've been out of town, she said.

Yes, said Herb. *I was in Paris.*

What were you doing in Paris?

I did some dubbing work.

That's a long way to go for a dubbing job.

Herb decided not to go into a long explanation, and came right to the point. *I hear someone's being replaced in "The Crucible."*

Where'd you hear that? Well, that's all set. But I do have something you'd be right for. Henry Fonda's doing "The Caine Mutiny Court Martial." Someone may be leaving the company, and they're casting understudies. Would you be willing to understudy?

Herb hesitated.

You can say "no," said Elsie.

Herb thought quickly. Henry Fonda. "The Caine Mutiny Court Martial." The novel had been a best-seller, and the film was very successful. A year for sure.

For a Broadway show I would be willing to understudy.

And as the show goes on people do get moved up, said Elsie. *Good.* She made a note and looked up. *Friday. Ten o'clock. The Alvin Theatre.*

I'll leave my picture with you, said Herb.

I have your picture, and you need a new one.

Thank you, said Herb.

You really should stay in town, Herb.

For a moment he wasn't sure he'd heard correctly. Did she really say his name? Did she really remember him?

Thank you, said Herb.

And, oh yes, said Elsie.

Herb stopped at the door, and turned back.

Don't put on anymore weight, Elsie continued. *You're just right as you are.*

Herb was about to say "thank you" for the third time, checked himself and said, *Okay.*

He decided he'd done enough for the day. He stopped by Ideal Photography, the outfit that did his reproductions, and picked up some information about various photographers. Then he looked in at Actors' Equity. There was no one he recognized, and left. He decided to walk home, even though his feet protested. There was no good reason to spend the carfare. He wasn't really that tired physically. Actually it was the emotional roller coaster that left him weary.

The apartment was empty when he got home. He shed his jacket, tie and shoes and poured himself a glass of wine, a habit he'd gotten into during the summer. He'd picked up a copy of The Times on the way home. He turned to the entertainment section and studied the Events column. "The Caine Mutiny Court Martial" had racked up a huge advance. He set down the paper, closed his eyes and sat dreaming about the possibility of a year on Broadway. He opened his eyes to find his wife standing in front of him.

I didn't hear you come in, said Herb.

You were fast asleep.

Helen sat down on the sofa beside him, took his hand and rested her head on his shoulder.

What have you been up to? asked Herb.

I don't know how to tell you this, said Helen.

What? You're not sick, are you?

No, said Helen. *I'm fine. I'm also pregnant.*

Herb's heart stopped beating for a second or two. At least it felt that way.

Are you sure? asked Herb.

Helen nodded.

That's wonderful, said Herb, just a little too cheerfully.

I'm glad you think so, said Helen.

Aren't you? We do want kids, don't we?

Eventually, yes.

They sat silently contemplating the radical change their life was about to undergo.

We don't have to have it, Helen found herself saying, regretting the words as she spoke them. Herb said nothing, which alarmed her. Had he heard what she'd said, or was he just ignoring the idea...she hoped.

Stanley, called, said Helen, changing the subject.

What's that? asked Herb. *What did he say?*

He seems to be under the impression that you're going out again.

Herb sighed. He placed his arm around his wife and held her close.

He's gotten the rights to "Darkness At Noon," said Helen.

You're kidding, said Herb.

That's what he said.

Herb had seen the production on Broadway with Claude Rains shortly before he'd left for Paris, and suggested it to Stanley. It was a powerful play about the Soviet Union under the despotic rule of Stalin, and a magnificent vehicle for a character actor.

I'll get it for you, said Stanley.

Right, right, laughed Herb, never dreaming that the American Drama Guild would be able to get the rights to the first national tour of a show fresh from Broadway.

Just then the phone rang.

I'll get it, said Helen.

She picked up the phone. It was Elsie Brenner. She handed the phone to Herb. Elsie had another audition for Herb, a day player on the "soap," "Search For Tomorrow." Herb thought quickly. He didn't have the understudy, and what really were his chances of getting it? And Stanley went out of his way to get that magnificent play, with that magnificent role. He thanked Elsie and told her that he'd be going out again. Before he could finish speaking she slammed the phone down.

It's all my fault, said Helen, on the verge of tears.

I had something to do with it, said Herb.

Helen debated about telling Herb the sordid truth. Of course, he had been so accepting. Not a word of protest, not even a question, and it certainly wasn't deliberate on her part. She just plain forget to put in the diaphragm. She thought it best not to say anything; not yet, at any rate. They returned to the sofa, sat down and held hands.

I guess I'll be going out again, said Herb, repeating the information for Helen's benefit, as if she hadn't heard him on the phone.

Helen would have liked to protest, but it would have been pointless. They would need the money now.

I'm going to try to get more money out of Stanley, Herb continued.

You think you can?

I think so. He's got a workhorse he can count on, and I am one of his favorites.

They sat silently, each lost in their own private thoughts.

Helen called up the lonely nights and the deadly week-ends and the Sunday morning phone calls, so eagerly awaited and such a painful reminder of the empty hours that lay ahead. Of course, this time there would be something else to occupy her mind.

Herb sat reliving the Broadway performance he'd seen of "Darkness At Noon." He wasn't Claude Rains, but he did have something different to bring to the leading role of Rubashov, the conflicted Communist leader condemned to prison, possible torture and death, condemned by his former crony, his drinking buddy, his faithful comrade, the inscrutable Stalin.

STALIN

He wasn't born Stalin. He wasn't born in Russia. Joseph Vissarionovich Dzhugashvili was born on December 21, 1879, the day of the longest night, in the town of Gori in nearby Georgia. The child was swarthy and his eyes were yellow, like the eyes of a tiger. The medical records report "webbed toes on left foot." Soso (Stalin's Georgian nickname as a boy) was christened on December 17. It's an old Persian superstition that any child born on the day of the longest night should be killed at birth. Soso was spared. He was also luckier than the two brothers who preceded him, both of whom died in infancy. His mother, grateful for his survival, vowed that he would devote his life to the church and become a priest.

His parents were peasants, emancipated serfs. His father Vassarion (Beso) Dzhugashvili, an Orthodox Christian, aged twenty four, was a shoemaker. He was a dark angry man of medium height with mustache and beard, a bellicose and frightening drinker. His mother, Ekateria Geladze, known as Keke, was sixteen. She was pretty, light complexioned and freckled. She was religious, literate, loved music and had no dowry.

The family lived in one room in the poorest section of the town. Beso plied his trade at home, providing shoes for a factory in nearby Tiflis. He was often drunk, abusing his wife and child. One time he picked up Soso and hurled the boy across the room. There was blood in the boy's urine for days. Keke took the boy, fled and hid in a neighbor's house. She returned eventually and, as time went on, she became defiant and stood up to her husband. The boy became daring enough to hurl a knife at his father. Beso moved to Tiflis and worked in the shoe factory there.

Georgians are often described as chivalrous, nimble, generous and pleasure loving. A neighbor described Soso as *embittered, insolent, rude and stubborn, with an intolerable character.* The neighbor went on to say that after Beso left, Keke *was head of the family now, and the fist which had subdued the father was now applied to the upbringing of the son. The mother beat him unmercifully for disobedience.*

To support herself and the boy, Keke did housework for the wealthy families in town, especially for one rich Jewish family.

The boy resented his mother's humiliating position, which was possibly the initial source for his anti-Semitism though, in later years, a number of Jews figured prominently among his close associates.

Even as a child he was a good organizer, remaining behind to let others do the job. He once persuaded his little friends to let a pig loose in a synagogue. The boys were found out, but did not give Soso away. When told about the fate of Jesus the boy did not understand why the son of God didn't draw his saber.

At the age of eight, to the delight of his mother, he entered the Gori Church School. At a church fast Soso was one of three singers with the best voices chosen to sing the Penitential. The three angelic looking boys in surplices chanted the prayers on their knees. Soso, however, was no angel. His favorite game was "krivi," a collective boxing match. There were two teams, one from the upscale part of town, the other from the poorer section. The well fed, upscale boys were stronger and always won. They invited Soso, a real scrapper, to join their team. He preferred to remain where he was, where he was number one.

Beso would turn up from time to time. He scoffed at the idea that the boy would enter the church. Beso insisted that Soso should be a cobbler like his father. During one visit Beso snatched the boy and carried him off to Tiflis. The father got Soso work in the shoe factory, doing odd jobs for the workmen. Keke journeyed to Tiflis, reclaimed the boy and put him back in school. Beso was never heard from again. It was rumored that he was killed in a drunken brawl.

Gori was a quiet town so a public execution of two criminals on February 13, 1892 was an occasion. An audience gathered around the scaffold. The Gori Church School pupils were given a prominent place. The thirteen year old boy and the author, Gorki, who was also present, watched as the rope broke and the criminals were hanged for a second time, an event certain to leave a mark on any young mind.

Soso grew to the height of five feet four inches. At one point he developed a serious infection as a result of being hit by a carriage. The illness left his left arm shortened and stiff. As a result of small pox at the age of six, his face became pock marked.

He graduated the Gori Church school a star pupil and received a modest scholarship which enabled him to enter the Tiflis Theological Seminary. Clothes were also provided, but Keke had to work and scrimp to pay his way. At the Seminary he was exposed to the best education available in the country. He received lessons in Liturgy, Scripture, Church Slavonic, Greek, Latin and Russian, though he would always speak with a strong Georgian accent.

The young man loved to read, especially Georgian literature. One of his favorite books was "The Parricide" which featured a dashing national hero named Koba, a name which Soso was soon to adopt. At the age of fifteen the magazine, "Iveriya," published six of his poems. The poetry was romantic:
"The rose opens her petals
And embraces the violet.
The lily has awakened.
They bare their heads to the zephyr."
The poetry was rebellious:
"Know that he who fell like ash to the earth,
Who long ago became enslaved,
Will rise again, winged with bright hope
Above the great mountains."
In his first year the boy did well, scholastically and socially. In his second year, however, at the age of sixteen, he became bitter and rebellious. The school banned certain books, not only suspect Western literature but Dostoevski, Tolstoy and Turgenev as well. The students would get books in town from the local "cheap library," take them back to their rooms and read them secretly. There was Victor Hugo, the romantic rebel with "Toilers Of The Sea" and "Ninety Three." There were books on marriage, property, politics, religion. There was Darwin. *There is no God. They are deceiving us,* said the young man.

Ivan The Terrible was the boy's idol. Ivan created the secret police. He created Terror. Accompanied by his son, the monarch witnessed torture and executions. He commissioned an architect to build the magnificent St. Basil's Church on Red Square, then blinded him so that he couldn't create anything so beautiful for anyone else.

The young man took up the theory of Socialism. He was greatly influenced by Peter Tkachev, an early advocate who, interestingly enough, died insane at the age of forty one. Tkachev proposed that the road to Socialism could be accomplished by a narrow conspiracy group who would transform a country accustomed to slavish submission, but must then exterminate the majority of the population or, because of their roots in a slavish mentality, would hinder the entry into a social paradise.

The young man discovered Marx. He became the leader of his group. He would lead discussions and anyone who tried to rival him was shouted down. He was put on report for gathering groups and holding readings of books that were not sanctioned. His locker was broken into and the illicit books were confiscated. He was confined to a punishment cell for five hours.

He entered discussion groups with railway workers, and joined the Social Democratic Party called Mesame. After five years, much to his mother's dismay, he left the Seminary. Actually he was expelled for failure to attend his examinations. He was given an opportunity to defend himself but never showed up.

What he did immediately after leaving the Seminary has been in dispute. It's rumored that he took up with thieves and took part in robberies. At any rate, after a few months he got a job as observer-calculator at the Tiflis Observatory. He recorded meteorological data, while continuing to pursue his revolutionary interests. There was room at the Observatory to hide illegal literature, leaflets for the Russian Social Democratic Workers Party.

At this time Vladimir Ulyanov, an advocate of Marxism was an exile in Siberia. Eight years older than the young man, he became a revolutionary because of the execution of his older brother for taking part in a plot to assassinate Alexander III. Ulynaov's revolutionary pseudonym was Lenin. Though Lenin was a member of the gentry, the son of an intellectual Russian family, the two men were alike in many ways. They were both rude, arrogant, quick tempered and charismatic. An agent of Lenin appeared in Tiflis introducing his central ideas. "The party must be organized on the strictest principles. No broad discussion, no freedom of opinion." It was a militant organization, with revolution as its aim. "One must be merciless. Not afraid of blood. Any attempt to revise any Marxist principle must be condemned as the work of enemies." The young man became a Leninist.

He was visited by his mother who tried to persuade him to return to the Seminary. She realized it was hopeless and returned to Gori, heartbroken.

The Tiflis committee planned a workers demonstration which was meant to end bloodily. Arrests began before the demonstration even got started. On the eve of the demonstration the young man handed in his resignation to the Observatory. Two thousand demonstrators gathered shouting *"Down with autocracy."* The young man spoke as representative for the Railway Workers Circle. The police began breaking up the demonstration and the blood began to flow. The Observatory was searched and the revolutionary material was confiscated. Many people were arrested, among them many Social Democrats. There were house to house searches.

The young man escaped, became a part of the underground and began to lead the life of a professional revolutionary. He now called himself Koba, after the Georgian Robin Hood, who robbed the rich to feed the poor.

MAY 1951

A communist attack forces South Korean troops on the east coast back across the 38th parallel. UN troops repulse an assault on the northwest front near Seoul.

BETSY LANDERS

Betsy Landers wasn't exactly pretty. She had a blunt, honest face with soft blue eyes. But when she appeared on stage her inner beauty shone through. There was an innocence about Betsy that was most appealing.

There was also a strong sense of determination. She was continually honing her craft. When she came to New York from Lawrence, Massachusetts seven years ago she studied with the famous Stella Adler, the teacher who was responsible for helping to shape Marlon Brando.

You're very talented, my dear, said Stella, *but I'm much better with men. Go study with Herbert Berghof.*

So Betsy studied with Herbert Berghof. She also took dance lessons, ballet and modern dance. She made the rounds of agents and producers' offices assiduously. She played bit parts on soap operas. She auditioned for commercials. She devoted her life to the theatre, more intensely so since her divorce. It was the story of a number of women in the arts. Her husband turned out to be gay. The divorce was amicable, but it left her with an open wound.

It was on a Monday evening that she received a call from Herb Volpe. She'd spent a long day at the television studio playing Nurse Drummond on "One Life To Live." Nurse Drummond appeared on the show about two or three times a month, not often enough to bring in the bacon, but it was a step up, a running role on a well established show.

Hi, said Herb. *How are you doing?*

Betsy's heart skipped a beat. She couldn't help it. Of course, he was married, happily married. She knew that. They were only colleagues, that's all. But how many men were there like Herb?

I'm fine, said Betsy. *When do you go to Paris?*

We've been to Paris, said Herb. *We spent the summer there. Look, can we meet for coffee tomorrow? Say around one?*

Let me check, said Betsy, and she looked at her appointment book. *Can we make it two thirty? I've got an audition at one.*

Fine, said Herb. *The coffee shop at NBC?*

Fine, said Betsy. *I'll see you then.*

Right. I'll see you then, said Herb, and he hung up.

Maybe he was making a mistake. He knew that the two of them were on dangerous ground. There was one moment last year when they were on tour in "The Heiress," if it hadn't been for Helen... But that moment was safely passed, and there was now the understanding that they were friends, that's all. And the thing was, if he was going to play the leading role of Rubashov in "Darkness At Noon" he had to have, at least, one actor in the company he knew he could count on.

Career-wise the only lure a tour with the American Drama Guild offered was the artistic satisfaction and, perhaps, an impressive credit. "The Heiress" was an adaptation of a novel by Henry James, and not that current. But "Darkness At Noon," was hot off Broadway with Claude Rains, a major star. It was an adaptation of a famous novel by Arthur Koestler, a highly respected author. The only trouble was the role of Luba, Rubashov's mistress, was definitely a supporting role, and Betsy played the lead in "The Heiress." Of course, there was that steady pay check, and a tour sure did come in handy if you really needed the money, but he wasn't sure whether Betsy was particularly hard up or not. At any rate, Herb would really have to plead his case.

Betsy was trembling when she hung up, and she was angry at herself. She made herself some hot milk and had some Oreos, dipping the chocolate cookies with the white cream center into the milk the way she used to as a child. This usually calmed her down. Nevertheless she didn't sleep well that night. In the morning she was glad she had a dance class and an audition to concern herself with. The audition was for a voice-over for a television commercial for Country Margarine. She thought she did well, but that didn't mean a thing. It was a "certain quality" they were always looking for, whatever the word "quality" meant.

Herb was early and he was nursing a cup of coffee. *How'd the audition go?* he asked.

Fine, said Betsy. *How was Paris?*

Unbelievable!, said Herb. *Have you ever been?*

No, said Betsy, with a finality that indicated that she was not in the mood for chit chat. Since Herb was reluctant to get to the point, she asked, *What's up?*

That was Betsy for you, right to the heart of the matter. As a matter of fact, that was one of her most endearing qualities, so ruthlessly honest, so pure.

Helen's pregnant, said Herb.

That's wonderful, said Betsy.

Yes, of course, said Herb. *It also means that I've got to go out again.*

Yes, of course, said Betsy. She sat waiting for the axe to fall.

We're doing "Darkness At Noon."

Uh, oh, thought Betsy, the Kim Hunter role. *Really?* she said to Herb. *Isn't it still running?*

No, it just closed.

That's quite a coup, said Betsy.

Yeah, said Herb. *It's a workhorse of a role.*

Betsy sat waiting.

Herb took a deep breath and said, *How'd you like to play Luba? That's the Kim Hunter role.*

Yes, thought Betsy, I know its the Kim Hunter role. *I don't know,* she said to Herb. *I have this running role on "One Life To Live."*

Oh?

Yeah, said Betsy. *I've had it for a few months now.*

How often?

She knew he was going to ask that, and she had to answer honestly. *Actually it's just two or three times a month. But then, Arthur, Arthur Hammond, said he's working on a new soap and there would be a major role for me.*

Oh?

Yeah, said Betsy. And then, to her amazement, she heard herself saying, *Let me think about it. I'd have to talk to Arthur first.*

Yes, of course, said Herb, and he couldn't believe his luck. She would actually do it. *When...?*

I don't know, said Betsy. *He doesn't know. You know how these things are. Can I get back to you?*

Yes, of course, said Herb. He insisted on paying for the lunch.

You go on ahead, said Betsy. *I've got some phone calls to make.* She didn't really. She just wanted to sit and think.

Okay, said Herb. *Let me know as soon as you can.*

Betsy nodded and Herb left.

The son of a bitch, thought Betsy. He knew I wouldn't turn him down. Of course, she could still get out of it. She didn't say she'd go. But she did enjoy acting with Herb. And she wasn't really in love with him, was she? He was more like a father figure...with sex appeal. Of course, she could save, and the money would come in handy. I'll leave it up to Arthur. If he says go, I'll go. That's it. I'll leave it up to Arthur.

When Jenny left Nat...well, at first he couldn't believe it. She adored him...once. Of course, that was before she got her nose job and came into her own. It's true the marriage was rocky. He was trying to find himself as a playwright. She had a full time job, plus studying with Jasper and an occasional role at Hedgerow.

So, okay, I'll wait till she thinks it over and decides to come back. The thought of her leaving him was inconceivable. He was good looking, well maybe not handsome, but nice looking and sexy and talented. Hadn't he won that play contest with his very first effort? I mean, come on, what more could she ask for? Okay, so he wasn't a breadwinner. And he did have his moods. He was fragile. They were both frustrated. But they finally broke through. There was that unbelievable summer at the Provincetown Playhouse on Cape Cod. He was beginning to come into his own as an actor and Jenny had one triumph after another.

It's true he did neglect her that summer. But he was really in a daze...all those lines to learn, plus writing publicity articles. Come on! And what about that night, the night before they left, the night she initiated the sex, selfishly left him unsatisfied, and he had to got into the bathroom to finish the job. Okay, okay. That's part of the past. But he would never do that to her.

So while waiting for her to show up Nat went to that theatre school in Washington, DC for a year. He still had the GI Bill. He wrote some sonnets about a broken heart. He wrote a verse play based on a Greek myth. He worked on his voice. On the Cape he'd been accused of not projecting. So he locked himself up in a room and read Shakespeare as if he were performing in a huge arena.

But not a word. Where was she? What was she doing? At the end of the year he went back to Philadelphia, the site of that fateful marriage. He got together with a fellow actor and they produced three plays that summer on the roof of the "Y." A small envelope reached him there...FROM HER. He tore open the envelope. No note, no nothing. Just pictures of Jenny in costume in the role of Candida, the Shaw play that they had both worked on at the Hedgerow Theatre School. Pictures of Candida in all these different costumes. What the hell was that? What was that supposed to mean? Am I supposed to get excited about her different costumes? What's going on with that woman?

At the end of the summer he decided to face the Big White Way, alone. They had always planned to face it together, but he couldn't wait any longer. He was ready now. He had a season of stock and the year in Washington and the summer in Philly in all those great roles, Strindberg's The Father, and Anatal in The Affairs of Anatol. He was more secure as an actor now, and now he had a voice. And she might never show up, for all he knew. So this was it. It was sink or swim.

He took the train to New York. He got himself a room on the upper West Side, not too far from the Broadway area. He got his eight by ten glossies with his resume on the back. He did have a resume now. He got a part time job loading trucks. He made the rounds. Meanwhile he was writing away and bleeding inside. Without her, he was half a man.

The full realization hit him. He couldn't believe how much that marriage meant to him. He'd only married her because that was the only way he could get her into bed. But now he was the one that took it seriously...apparently. It was over a year now since he hadn't heard from her, but he still couldn't believe it. And then came the letter, finally, a letter. "I'd like to meet you, and talk to you," she wrote. And she set a time to come to his room. What did she have in mind? Was she coming back to him? At this point, did he want her back? Well, of course, he did. She was his wife. He was married to her.

And then there was that unbelievable meeting. She didn't look that hot either. She was still a little too heavy, but she was his wife.

I want a divorce, said Jenny.

They were walking down a stairway in Central Park and he had to take hold of the railing to keep from falling.

Are you all right? asked Jenny.

All right? My world has fallen apart. I'm a lost soul. Am I all right?! *I'm fine,* said Nat.

Will you oppose the divorce?

Yes, of course, I will. I'm not going to give you a divorce so you can marry someone else.

I'm not going to marry someone else.

Then why do you want the divorce?

Don't you wanna be free?

No, I don't wanna be free.

So you'll oppose the divorce?

Yes, he said, then added, *I'll get a full time job.*

She hesitated then said, *It wouldn't work.*

And he knew she was right. What kind of a man was he? He wasn't a man. A piece of driftwood. That's what he was. A piece of driftwood. He watched her walk away and probably out of his life. He decided not to oppose the divorce.

He pursued the acting and he wrote, wrote, wrote. He worked part time loading trucks and he made the rounds and he wrote, and his life was empty. Oh, there was one pretty blond he had his eye on, but he'd had his lesson. Success first and then love. Once burnt, twice shy. Oh, he was drawn to the blond all right, but he played it cool. Friendship. Colleagues. Two actors. That's all. But he kept an eagle eye out for competition.

And actually freedom did have its rewards. No responsibility. He didn't have to answer to anyone. He was his own man. He walked down the streets of the Great White Way, Broadway, the Street he was going to conquer or die trying. He was young and talented and the world was his. Why, his one act play, his prize winning one act play actually had a production at the Provincetown Playhouse in the Village and got an excellent review. Maybe that was an omen, the Provincetown Playhouse on the Cape and the Provincetown Playhouse in the Village. Maybe he was following in the footsteps of Eugene O'Neill who got his start in both of those theatres. No maybe about it, he was. And after that summer on the Cape and his work in Washington, DC and the summer in Philly he was a good actor. He was confidant, even more so in his acting than in his writing. Why he'd studied with Jasper Deeter at Hedgerow Theatre, and Jasper was a genius. All he needed was one good break.

And then there was that ad in Show Business, the actors Bible. The Stanley Warren Players were casting six plays for the summer in the Catskills. They were Equity productions. Maybe he could even get his Equity card. Actually become a member of the Union! A dream come true. What would Jenny think of that?

He went up to the Stanley Warren Office on Broadway and Fifty Seventh Street, signed in and scanned the list of plays and the roles that were available. The Jean Paul Sartre play, "The Respectful Prostitute," was the one that interested him the most. He decided to read for the role of the Senator, the father of the leading man, for which he was really right physically. But then all the young actors would be reading for that. There'd be less competition for the older role. After all, he did his best work in character roles. The Southern accent came easily, even though he'd never used one before, and he read with confidence. He actually enjoyed the audition. He knew he read well. They had him read a second scene, and he felt that the role was his and, by God, they offered it to him.

You'll put some grey in your hair, said Stanley.

Yes, sir.

See Miss Cotton in the office. She'll make all the arrangements.

Yes, sir.

He walked quickly into the office before Stanley changed his mind.

You are Equity, aren't you? said Miss Cotton.

Yes, of course, Nat said as casually as he could. Now that was acting for you.

He signed the contract, ran down to Equity, laid down a deposit for his entrance fee, and joined the union. He was now a professional actor. He couldn't believe it. He was a professional actor. Nirvana! That's what is was, Nirvana. His feet barely touched the pavement. He was walking on air. He looked about. He had to share this with someone, so he walked over to Horn & Hardart and headed for the table his crowd usually sat at, and he made the announcement.

I just made Equity, he announced.

It was not received as a bombshell. *Great,* someone muttered...grudgingly, Nat thought. One guy smiled and nodded...condescendingly. What a great reception. And then he came down to earth. His mind now turned to the sum of money he would have to borrow to pay the other half of his entrance fee. Reluctantly he called home. His mother sighed and sent him what she could manage. What could she do? Maybe he'll come to his senses. An actor yet!

The tour of "The Respectful Prostitute" up in the Catskills was a blast. Going from hotel to hotel, large auditoriums, small spaces, even an outdoor theatre. What a great learning experience! And then there was the food, endless food. And the leading lady was fresh from a Broadway production. And Stanley came to see the show and complimented him. Then bang! The station wagon bumped into the car ahead of it and the leading lady hit her head. She was out of the show. The show closed down. Nat's heart sank. But Stanley came to the rescue.

I've got a company called the American Drama Guild. I send out shows across the country during the winter, said Stanley. *Would you be interested?*

Yes, of course, said Nat.

So to keep Nat busy Stanley found a place for him in the summer package of "Come Back, Little Sheba." These shows were pared down versions of the original production and Stanley had cut out the role of the milkman. The role of the milkman was put back in and Nat finished out the summer in the Catskills.

And then it was back to town and wait. Would Stanley call him or wouldn't he? Stanley liked him, he knew that, but people forget. And suppose there was no role for him in the shows he was sending out. And how many shows was he sending out? If it was just one, maybe his chances weren't that good. It was back to loading trucks, and looking for stage work. There was television, of course, but that didn't really interest him. Television! Bit parts for peasants! Oh, he'd do it if a job came along, but he wasn't going to knock himself out there. He was interested in THE

THEATRE. Broadway. His standards were the standards of Hedgerow Theatre and Jasper Deeter. The classics. Fine roles in fine plays. Some of which he would some day write.

He received a call from a casting director. *Sidney Lumet is directing his first film and there's the bit of a soldier playing "craps" on a train. He's asked for you. Are you interested?* asked the casting director. Nat had met Lumet at a casting session, and the director seemed very cordial. *I'll keep you in mind,* said Lumet. Right, thought Nat, and promptly forgot about it. And now he actually called him.

Would I have to join SAG? asked Nat.

Yes, of course.

No, thanks, said Nat. It wasn't that he didn't want to play the bit, but he didn't want to get any deeper into debt. He'd borrowed enough money from his family to pay for Equity, and another five hundred dollars was out of the question; and the movies wasn't where it was really at, not at the moment, at any rate. So he went back to his truck loading duty.

Finally the call came from Stanley. *I'm sending out a production of "Darkness At Noon." There's a part for you,* said Stanley. *I don't know what part yet. Come by and pick up a script.*

Nat was ambivalent. Not about the job, God knows. He was delirious about that. Eight months on the road from coast to coast in an Equity production. What a fantastic credit, a recent Broadway show which starred Claude Rains! What an addition to his resume! He'd come off the tour a seasoned pro. The inexplicable qualms vanished. He picked up the script.

It turned out that "Darkness At Noon" was a dreary play that took place in a Soviet prison, where Rubashov, an old comrade of Stalin, was being held and interrogated. Eight months in that depressing play. But wait a minute. He hadn't been cast yet, and there was that juicy role of the ruthless young officer. Age-wise it was the most suitable. He set to work preparing to play the role of that wonderful monster, Gletkin, the villainous, ambitious jailer. He sat thinking about Stalin, trying to remember what he knew about the man.

After having left the seminary, after having become a Leninist and escaping capture, after having helped foment a bloody demonstration, Stalin now entered enthusiastically into the underground life of the revolutionary; a life of intrigue and ideological bickering, politics and love affairs; a life of strikes, forged documents, print shops hidden in cellars; a life populated by Russians, Armenians, Georgians, Jews, workers, noblemen, intellectuals like Lenin and more earthy aggressive types (like Koba?); a life threatened by certain arrest during which it was de rigueur to defy the gendarmes before being sent into exile. The trick was to remain at large as long as possible.

At first Koba, as he now called himself, fled Tiflis and took refuge at home in Gori, but life at home, plagued by the disapproval of his mother, was unbearable, so, dangerous as it was he returned to Tiflis. He found a dingy little room in an obscure section of town. He now wore the uniform of the true Social Democrat, the black Russian blouse with the red tie. The blouse, of course was dirty and his shoes were scruffy and unpolished. He wrote articles that were published in the first illegal radical Georgian newspaper. He frequented workers groups teaching the theories of Karl Marx, honing his skill of speaking the language of the worker. He was galvanized by the publication of Lenin's new tract, "What Is To Be Done?" He identified himself so closely with his idol, Lenin, that he was jokingly called "Lenin's left leg." The revolution was no longer relegated to the dim future. No longer must Russia be submissive. We've been waiting too long. The time is now. The autocracy must be overthrown by a coup.

The Social Democrats in Tiflis were uncomfortable with this firebrand, and the party sent him off to the southern port of Batum, a cool, peaceful town. Some of his comrades there fell in love, married and started a career. But Koba moved from one apartment to another, continuing his underground work. Now high on the police's wanted list he became the fervid leader of a small group of Lenin's supporters in Georgia. One police report read "the Batum organization is headed by Dzhugashvili. Dzhugashvili's despotism has aroused the indignation of many members, and there is a schism within the organization."

Wanted or not, schism or not, Koba was eminently successful. A strike took place and there were a number of arrests. This was followed by a demonstration protesting the arrests, which led to the arrest of three hundred more, which was followed by a massive demonstration. In the peaceful Southern port of Batum two thousand workers marched demanding the release of their comrades. There was a bloody clash with the police. Fifteen people were killed and fifty four people were injured. Arrests were made and again Koba escaped.

He fled to the mountains where he was sheltered by a peasant woman. Life was pleasant there, but life on the sunlit mountain was not for him. But where was he to go? Tiflis was too dangerous, and besides, the party there would definitely not welcome him with open arms. The police were on the lookout for him in Gori. He took the bold, unexpected step of returning to the scene of the crime. In Batum he was welcomed by the Party and elected to the All Caucasian Committee of the RSDRP (Russian Social Democratic Workers Party.) His triumph, however, was short lived. Attending a secret meeting one night in the apartment of a comrade, the building was surrounded by the police. The entire lot was escorted to the Batum jail.

The Batum jail was notorious for physical abuse. There were beatings from the guards. Criminals beat up political prisoners. There was filth and loss of rights and, at first, the young man was terrified. In desperation he managed to write a note to his mother and threw it out the window. "If you are asked when your son left Gori, tell them he was in Gori all the time." read the note. It was discovered, of course, by one of the guards, and Koba gave way to despair.

There wasn't much of an option, however. You either sink or swim. Maybe he lacked strength, but he was able to exhibit defiance. Hadn't he stood up to the violent abuse of his father? Hadn't he found strength in defiance?

The authorities decided to teach the political prisoners a lesson. They were lined up and forced to file through a passageway surrounded on either side by guards who beat them with their rifle butts. Koba walked the line, book in hand, and refused to bow his head, earning him the respect and admiration of his fellow prisoners. Before long the young man with the pockmarked face and the eyes of a tiger became a leading force in the prison. He made friends with the criminal element. He learned to speak their language, and he was well aware how useful the criminals could be to the revolution.

The Batum jail soon became a home. He found a time and place for his morning exercises. He studied German, since a true revolutionary read Karl Marx in the original. He became so powerful during his stay that anyone who defied him was beaten by his criminal friends. At the end of eighteen months he was sent to the Siberian village of Nizhnyaya Uda in the province of Irkutsk. He may have been exiled, but Koba left that jail tough and resilient.

JUNE 1951

Following a Supreme Court decision 2 weeks earlier that upheld the constitutionality of the Smith Act, under which 11 top leaders of the American Communist Party were convicted in the 1949 Foley Square trial, a New York Federal grand jury indicts 21 more party leaders for conspiring to forcefully overthrow the government.

THE FIRST REHEARSAL

You've got to eat something, said Helen.

I'll pick up something on the way down, said Herb.

Herb was angry and nervous. He was angry at Stanley because he was so cheap. Yes, he did give him more money when he threatened to back out of the tour. But Stanley refused to hire a director, and Herb was not a director. He never pretended to be a director, but he was forced to undertake the job of directing in addition to playing that workhorse of a leading role, in addition to driving the van, in addition to being the company manager and supervising the set up of a set that was sometimes so crude, it was embarrassing.

Of course, Stanley usually did provide him with a workmanlike cast. And that was another thing. If he was going to be the director he should have something to say in the casting. But, oh no, on the first day of rehearsal he's presented with a cast he'd never set eyes on. What kind of a director is that? And then, believe it or not, Stanley lists himself in the program and in all the publicity as the director, not Herb, but himself, not that Herb really wanted the credit, God forbid.

Well, this was it. The last time. He was really going to watch his pennies. He's got to save enough to see him through for, at least, a year. And what with the twenty weeks of unemployment he would be eligible for after the tour, there shouldn't be any problem. And Helen did have those occasional gigs. Of course, that would come to an end when the baby came.

You look very nice, said Helen, trying to cheer him up.

He was wearing his sports jacket, plus a dress shirt and tie, which he wore only when necessary.

Thank you, said Herb, then looking apologetically he said, *I'm sorry.*

About what? said Helen

For being such a grouse

This too shall pass.

I know, I know, said Herb.

You said yourself he usually gives you a decent cast.

It's not the acting I'm concerned about, said Herb. *I'm going to have to spend eight months with these people. I'm more concerned about temperament than I am about talent.*

There's no way you can judge temperament without spending time with someone, said Helen, smiling lovingly at Herb.

Once I get past the first rehearsal, said Herb, *I'll be all right.*

Rehearsals for the American Drama Guild productions took place in a large room which was part of the company's administration office. Stanley actually saved money that way and it was convenient for him to look in on rehearsals whenever he so wished. Herb picked up a container of coffee and a date nut cream cheese sandwich at the nearby Chock Full Of Nuts on the corner, and brought it up to the office.

The rehearsal was scheduled for ten thirty. He made a point of arriving an hour early. Stanley was at his desk on the phone. He was in the process of finalizing bookings for the other two shows he was sending out, "John Love Mary," an old warhorse of a comedy, and "All My Sons," an early Arthur Miller play, which Herb actually would have preferred. It's true he expressed his admiration for Claude Rains' performance in "Darkness At Noon" but the prospect of spending eight months in a Russian prison, on stage or not, was not a cheerful one. When Stanley hung up Herb asked to see the head shots of the actors he was going to be directing very shortly.

So Betsy's going out again, said Stanley as he handed Herb the photographs. There was a tone in Stanley's voice which Herb deeply resented. Well, what could you expect? Stanley was a notorious letch, and married or not, he had no qualms about using the "casting couch." How he managed to fool his wife, Marilyn, was astonishing, since Stanley sure had a reputation. *Oh, no,* said Marilyn, *my Stanley is not like those others. He doesn't do things like that.* And Stanley sat next to his wife beaming unashamedly.

Yeah, she's going out again, said Herb, referring to Betsy. *We work well together.*

Good, good, said Stanley. *She's very talented. Though I really can't afford to give her that raise, after what I'm paying you.*

You're still saving money on what you're paying me, said Herb.

I'm not complaining, said Stanley. *I'm giving her the raise, ain't I?*

Yes, Stanley.

Herb dug into his food and studied the eight by tens. What can you tell from a photograph? Though Betsy's picture was not that bad. At least you got a feeling of her personality. The other five people in the cast were complete strangers. The most appealing picture was that of Ted Lombard, a middle aged, distinguished looking gentleman with a dapper mustache. There was something amiable about the face, someone you'd enjoy talking to, someone who'd have interesting stories to tell. Studying the credits Herb noticed that Ted had actually worked in silent pictures and in vaudeville. Herb held the picture up for Stanley to view.

Ivanov? Herb asked.

Stanley nodded. Ivanov was an old colleague of Rubashov, sympathetic and supportive.

The other four pictures were not that interesting. Two juveniles: one, sturdy looking, Ralph Krumsky; the other rather spoiled looking, Paul Thomas. Then there were two young leading men, Alvin Gorman and Nat Brenner, nice looking, blank faces. Alvin had a Broadway credit and came from the West Coast. That could mean trouble. Nat had some interesting, though minor, credits, but the picture was so posed. The actor probably paid a lot and wasted his money. Herb held up Alvin's and Nat's pictures.

Which one is Gletkin? asked Herb.

Alvin Gorman, said Stanley.

Really?

You'll see, said Stanley.

Gletkin was the vicious, ambitious young Bolshevik, the villain of the piece.

Are you gonna sit in? asked Herb.

Don't I always sit in on the read through? said Stanley. *You've got a good cast,* he added.

That remains to be seen, said Herb. *It would have been helpful to sit in on the casting.*

You were in Paris, said Stanley. *You're a lucky man. Young, healthy, beautiful wife, and now you're going to have a son.*

How do you know it's gonna be a boy?

I know these things, said Stanley. *And now you're gonna have a major role in a very important play. It wasn't easy getting the rights, you know.*

How did you manage it?

That's my secret, said Stanley.

Can't we afford a stage manager? asked Herb. *At least for the rehearsals.*

What do you need a stage manager for?

If nothing else, to hold the book when we're trying to learn our lines.

You can take turns holding book, said Stanley.

What would Equity say about that?

Please, said Stanley. *It's early in the day.*

I'm serious, said Herb.

You've managed before, said Stanley. *All right, if you really need someone, you can have Lillian for one or two run-throughs.*

Thanks a lot.

Stop complaining, said Stanley. *I'm paying you more than I've ever paid anyone.*

Then I must be worth it, said Herb.

Otherwise I wouldn't be paying you, said Stanley. *The table and chairs are all set up for the reading. And don't waste too much time on discussion. Get the play on its feet.*

Herb sighed and shook his head. The two men rose and made their way into the rehearsal room.

They found Betsy and Nat Brenner deep in conversation. Nat looked younger than his picture and more animated, and Betsy seemed intrigued. Was there a romance in the offing? That Betsy might find love during the tour never occurred to Herb. There was always that possibility, of course. On the tour of "The Heiress" the handsome leading man was a womanizing, conceited bore and Betsy was turned off immediately. But this might be different. Herb introduced himself to Nat and shook hands. He was taken aback by the intensity in the young man's light blue eyes. He couldn't tell why but he found the look disturbing. Was this someone he could trust? Or was this a rival? But a rival for what? Herb smiled uneasily at Betsy, as if to ask, what have we got here?

Ted Lombard and Ralph Krumsky came in together. Ted, dressed rather elegantly, was all smiles, gracious and confident, emanating an old world charm. There was a touch of grey in the wavy hair that gave him an added air of distinction. Ralph was a stocky, fair haired young man, with broad cheek bones which gave him a Slavic appearance. He looked straight out of college and eager to please. Herb sensed a rather sweet disposition. As the two newcomers joined Betsy and Nat around the table Alvin Gorman entered. Herb saw immediately what Stanley meant when he said, *You'll see.* The face was all angles and, Alvin had gotten himself a crew cut. The long hair that was featured on his picture was gone. His short dark hair just bristled, and his cold, deep set eyes sent out a warning, I am trouble. Herb introduced himself, shook a rather clammy hand, and Alvin sat down at the table.

Herb joined the cast at the table and had them call out their names and the role they were playing. When they got to Nat, who was second after Betsy, who was first, he said, *I don't know what role I'm playing.* Herb looked at Stanley. *Prisoner 402,* said Stanley. Though he did run through the entire play Prisoner 402 had no big scenes. Of course, he did have a number of scenes with Rubashov, but nothing big. Nat said nothing and tried to conceal his disappointment. After the roll call Herb looked at his watch. It was ten after ten. He was about to start the reading without Paul Thomas when the young man strolled in, took his seat at the table and smiled at Stanley.

Paul? said Herb, addressing the young man.
Yes?
The rehearsal was scheduled for ten o'clock.

Yes, I know, said Paul. *The subway, you know.* He then opened his script and seemed ready to begin. Herb looked quizzically at Stanley who just shrugged.

Sitting around the table they read through the entire play, taking a brief respite at the end of each act. The cast was then given a half hour break before they went on to stage the play. Stanley had installed a coffee urn. The minor expense was compensated by the time saved. Nobody could run out and dawdle looking for a container of coffee.

Herb and Stanley retired to Stanley's office to discuss the reading. The crucial questions were: Ted as Ivanov, Alvin as Gletkin and Nat as Prisoner 402, an old Tsarist, who, as an example of the effects of life in a Bolshevik prison, was actually a rather key role. It was agreed that Ted, as Ivanov, was serviceable, not very dynamic, but adequate. Alvin, as Gletkin, on the other hand was so intense that he bordered on the comic.

You've got to tone him down, said Stanley.

And then there was Nat.

Maybe I made a mistake, said Stanley.

Herb expressed surprise, because he thought that Nat, of all the men, gave the most interesting reading.

He's too young, said Stanley.

You knew that, didn't you?

I like him, said Stanley, *and I wanted to use him.*

He read very well, said Herb.

Let's wait and see, said Stanley.

When Herb returned to the rehearsal room he found Betsy, Ted and Ralph Krumsky talking amiably. Paul was talking to Nat, who seemed to be listening politely. And Alvin was sitting by himself staring into space.

The cast gathered around the table and Herb explained that they had ten days before they opened in Rochester. Actually Stanley wanted seven days, but Herb insisted on an extra three days. Herb described the set. It was a backdrop which represented the prison wall. There were two openings in the backdrop for two prison cells which, behind a scrim, held Prisoner 402 and Prisoner

403. Prisoner 403, a young prisoner, was played by Paul who doubled as a young revolutionary. All the action took place in front of the backdrop with just different pieces of furniture, moved on and off, to depict the various locations. These consisted of Rubashov's prison cell and places around the world visited by Rubashov in his mind. Except for one brief scene, Rubashov never left the stage.

Alan wanted to discuss the role of Gletkin before he got on his feet.

Let's wait till we get accustomed to the lines and to each other before we get into any discussion, said Herb, hoping fervently to avoid all discussions. He was not a director, he was an actor, God help him, and he cursed Stanley silently.

Herb rose and started to move the chairs to the side of the room. Nat rose quickly to help, followed by Betsy and Ralph. The actors, according to Equity, were not supposed to perform these menial tasks. Ted positioned himself at one end of the table. Nat took the other end and they moved the table out of the way. It was interesting to note that neither Alvin or Paul Thomas participated in the set up. They were perfectly right, thought Herb, and tried not to hold it against them.

When the space, now a stage, was cleared,Ralph Krumsky as the Prison Guard, took his place Stage Right beside Herb as Rubashov. It was March 1937. The Prison Guard led Rubashov, the former comrade of Stalin, now a political prisoner, into the dank dark cell of a Russian prison. As the guard starts to leave Rubashov calls out, *They've taken away my cigarettes.* Herb heaved a sigh, sent up a prayer and began to stage the play, wondering what the hell was life like under Stalin.

STALIN

In the summer of 1903, after fourteen months in prison, young Koba, now an experienced, streetwise revolutionary, was about to receive his first taste of exile. Dressed in his threadbare overcoat he was transported through the freezing cold to what seemed like the end of the world, the village of Nizhnyanya Urda in Siberia. In this flat, barren land, surrounded by snow, snow, snow...snow everywhere, he was sentenced to spend four long years. In this dreary isolation he was warmed by a letter from Lenin, signed personally by his idol. All right, so it was a form letter sent to all Lenin's provincial supporters, but it was sent to him, to him personally. He had finally come to the attention of his god.

News traveled fast, even to the end of the earth. and Koba was electrified by an historic event which went completely unnoticed by the world at large. In a small barn in Brussels in July of 1903 forty revolutionaries called to order the first meeting of the Congress Of The Russian Social Democratic Workers Party. The prevailing note at the beginning of the meeting was similar to that of a European social democracy. Lenin, however, soon put an end to all that nonsense. There was no room for an amorphous, wishy-washy policy. He forged through a more zealous and rigid central idea, an unbending fire from which it was forbidden to stray. The result was a party split in two: the more reasonable "minority men" or Mensheviks as opposed to the fiery "majority men," known as the Bolsheviks.

After four long months of Siberian winter with its blizzards and bone-chilling frost Koba was eager to return to the fray, to take part in all the exciting events that were taking place. In November of 1903 he made his first abortive attempt at an escape. Frostbitten and stiff with cold, he gave up and was barely able to make his way back. Biding his time, he harbored his strength and in January of 1904, he tried again, this time successfully. Dressed as a peasant, with a forged passport, he managed to make his way all the way across Russia back to Tiflis.

There he lived underground, sometimes hiding in the apartment of Sergei Alliluyev and his wife. Sergei was a founding member of the party and one of the railway workers to whom Koba had preached Marxism. Fourteen when she eloped with him, Sergei's wife was a wildly passionate woman who took advantage of the free lifestyle of the revolutionary to indulge in many love affairs, always returning to her good natured husband.

Usually a fugitive enjoyed four or five months of freedom before being apprehended by the police and sent back to finish out his term. Strangely enough, a fact that Stalin later concealed, during this period he was arrested twice and twice, supposedly, succeeded in escaping, remaining free in Tiflis, under the eagle eye of the police, to carry on his work. Revolutionaries were often compelled to be *provocateurs,* to play both sides in order to survive. And why not? Doesn't the end justify the means? If one has to compromise, so be it. If one has to pay a price, if one has to bargain for ones freedom, wasn't that freedom, after all, dedicated to the cause? It was simple enough. Give the police information that they already possessed.

At this time, without the aid of the Party, the Russian revolution erupted. There were mass demonstrations throughout the land. The police were attacked. There were mutinies within the army. Koba, however, had other fish to fry. He'd been writing articles for the Caucasian Workers News Sheet, as well as working on a paper outlining the theories of Lenin, when he was summoned by the great man himself to join him in Finland where the first Bolshevik Conference was about to take place. Armed with a passport carrying a Russian name, the young Georgian boarded a train and, despite the myriad secret agents on the lookout for revolutionaries, he somehow managed to cross the border. At the first Bolshevik conference in Tammerfors, he finally met his idol. He was surprised to find that this genius, this giant of a man was not much taller than he was. The great man would arrive early for meetings and would actually sit and chat amiably with the hoi poloi. Koba was habitually late, crude and direct. But apparently a rapport was established between these two very different temperaments. Lenin summoned the young Georgian to join him at a conference in Stockholm and another one in London.

It was in London that Koba first came face to face with Trotsky, who arrived there as a conquering hero. Not only a brilliant theorist and an eloquent orator, this multi-talented man actually took part in the revolution, plunging into the very thick of it and urging on the crowds. Even before that this Jewish firebrand had become a legend. Having been arrested, he spoke boldly and eloquently in his defense. What better platform than a courtroom? Sentenced to Siberia for life he escaped and crossed the four hundred miles back to freedom on a dog sled.

Envious, perhaps, the young Georgian spoke derisively of this glamorous figure's Jewish identity. As a matter of fact, the Jews came under Koba's scorn, not only in reference to Trotsky. He spoke disparagingly of the Mensheviks as circumcised Yids, treacherous shopkeepers useless in battle. "It would not be a bad idea if us Bolsheviks were to organize a pogrom in the Party," he wrote.

Yet, oddly enough, though Lenin had Jewish blood in him, and the Party itself was heavily populated with Jews, the intelligent, well born Lenin chose to ignore the bigotry and the earthy vulgarity of his young compatriot. After the London conference he summoned the no-nonsense-Koba to Berlin.

Up until the revolution of 1905 the Socialist Party was a popular movement among the intelligentsia. Money poured in to support the cause, and Lenin lived quite comfortably in exile in the various capitols of Europe. But the violence and the bloodshed put an end to all that. Theories were fine, but things became a little too uncomfortable when this violence and bloodshed became a reality. The Party was now badly in need of funds.

Unknown to the Party at large, unknown even to the Central Committee, Lenin had his own little committee, more accurately his own little gang of thugs, chief among them our young Georgian. Since Lenin could not be tainted by outright acts of violence or bloodshed he would call upon his favorite Koba for assistance. Koba had access to bombs. Koba had a childhood friend, a hulk of a man eager to do his comrade's bidding. At the moment it was money that was needed.

TOURING WITH STALIN

On June 26, 1907 a large shipment of money was scheduled to be delivered to the state bank in Tiflis. It was a hot summer day when two carriages, escorted by a team of Cossacks, rode into Erevan Square. As usual the square was populated by a large cheerful crowd. As the two carriages entered the square, as if from nowhere, two light, horse-drawn carriages appeared. One carriage held two ladies; the other a large man dressed as an officer. The "officer" called out a command and suddenly fifty people appeared. The newly arrived carriages blocked the carriages that were carrying the money. Bombs exploded. During the chaos and the smoke the thieves seized the sacks of gold and, firing at the Cossacks or at anyone in their way, they made their escape. Cossacks, policemen and scores of innocent bystanders lay dead, dismembered by the bomb or wounded by the gunfire. The square had become a bloody tomb. Several arrests were made. Koba was not among the criminals that were apprehended.

The robbery, however, was just another notch in Koba's belt. The military dictator of Georgia was slated for assassination by the Mensheviks. Koba came to the rescue. As a matter of fact, the young Georgian was becoming a little too active, a little too well known. He was shipped off to Baku, a region known for its oil fields. There he worked assiduously with the oil workers. He organized strikes. He exacted protection money from the oil companies. Sometimes it was necessary to set fire to an oil well or two. Money came pouring in, all of it going straight to Lenin. Koba lived the life of a hermit. Well, not a hermit exactly. The revolutionary was human after all. Koba had fallen in love. He had a family now.

She was called Katerina the same as his mother. Kato, as she was called, in contrast to the free, easygoing female revolutionaries, who hopped from bed from bed, was a pure, sweet, gentle creature, and pretty, too. She had a handsome suitor but, strangely enough, she fell in love with this comparatively ugly, puny little man with the pockmarked face. She was swept away by this Robin Hood, who robbed the rich to feed the poor. Kato was religious, too, like his mother. Since religion was frowned upon by members of the Party, the fact that the wedding took place in a church, was kept a deep, dark secret.

The couple lived in a rented room on the oil field. Kato worked as a seamstress and kept the room spotless. But married life wasn't easy for someone whose husband was a revolutionary. Her husband's life was that of a fugitive. It was impossible for him to spend much time with her. He was able to come home only in the dead of night. They had a child. The boy was named Yakov. The poor woman had a difficult time making ends meet. Money meant nothing to Koba. Everything went to the Cause. Sergei Alliluyev needed money to attend a conference. He was told to contact Koba. When he saw how poor the couple was he refused to take the money. Koba forced it on him.

Toiling alone most of the time with a crying infant, Kato fell ill with tuberculosis. Koba was unable to spend much time to take care of her and there was no money to spend for doctors. He took her to Tiflis to stay with her family, but it was too late. His young wife died in his arms. Koba was broken-hearted. *Whatever feeling I had for humanity has been buried with her,* he muttered. Leaving the boy with Kato's sister the revolutionary threw himself even more intensely into his work.

He became involved in a series of assassinations...priests, aristocrats, bourgeoisie. His miraculous escapes gave rise to the suspicion that he might actually be a provocateur. The rumor was soon squelched by his arrest. At the time of his arrest he had papers on him, proving that he was a member of the banned Baku Committee of the RSDRP, which left him open to imprisonment with hard labor. Instead it was decided to exile him for three years. Then, strangely enough, the term was reduced to two years. So began Koba's second exile in the small town of Solvychegodsk.

JULY 1951

Mystery writer, Dashell Hammet, author of *The Maltese Falcon,* is sentenced to six months in prison for refusing to name individuals who contributed to a bail bond fund for four communist leaders who subsequently jumped bail.

THE OPENING

On the sixth day of rehearsal, except for Herb and Betsy, who knew they would never be fired, the cast of "Darkness At Noon" heaved a sigh of relief. Up until that time, according to the union contract, one could be given two weeks rehearsal pay, and let go. Thankfully, no one was fired.

Herb dreaded the rehearsal period since he had to direct and play the lead as well. Actually the staging was relatively simple. Herb, as Rubashov, had scenes involving only one other character at a time, and Prisoner 402, played by Nat Brenner, and Prisoner 403, played by Paul Thomas, played their scenes confined to their prison cells, which was revealed through a scrim when the lights came up on them.

Herb's scene with Ted Lombard as Ivanov, an old comrade of Rubashov, was particularly easy and they quickly established a very comfortable rapport. Alvin Gorman, as the villainous Gletkin, sometimes became a little too violent, but pulled back when Herb admonished him very gently. The frightening thing was that in real life, this inhuman Bolshevik would probably have behaved as viciously as Alan portrayed him. And Alvin kept changing the blocking. Finally Herb sighed and just played along until Alvin finally settled on where he was going to be and when.

It was the scenes with Betsy, however, that gave the most trouble...for both of them. In the tour of "The Heiress" Herb and Betsy played father and daughter, and the relationship between the two characters was a dysfunctional one. Though the personal relationship between the two actors was fraught with danger, the work on stage in that production did nothing to acerbate the situation. Now they were playing lovers. Betsy was playing Luba, Rubashov's secretary and mistress and there were lines of dialogue like:

Rubashov: *You know there can be nothing more between us.*
Luba: *Yes, I know.*

And there was a bedroom scene with kissing and touching, and this situation was scheduled to go on for eight long months. Herb began to have regrets about having approached Betsy.

As the rehearsals progressed the grouping of the actors offstage seemed to fall into a general pattern. Ralph Krumsky, the youngest in the cast and the least experienced, tended to gravitate toward Herb as a father figure. Ted Lombard, the veteran of the group was drawn to Herb whom he looked upon as his only equal. Paul Thomas, who turned out to be a rather smart-alecky young man, and Nat Brenner seemed to be drawn to each other because of their opposing viewpoints. They developed an amicable banter based on a fundamental agreement to disagree. Nat, slightly older, was more idealistic. Paul, for one as young as he was, was quite cynical. They were discussing careers and success in the "business."

If you're talented, said Nat, *I think it'll pay off in the long run, if you stick it out that is.*

Wanna bet? said Paul

You don't think so, said Nat.

It's who you know...and luck, said Paul.

And you don't think that talent is important?

Not really, said Paul.

Well, said Nat, *that remains to be seen, does it not?* hoping, prayerfully, that he was right.

Alvin Gorman was the loner. Offstage he was either buried in a book, or scribbling away at something, probably writing letters though he certainly seemed to be secretive about it.

The opening in Rochester, New York was scheduled for a Friday evening. The venue was a high school auditorium, one that Herb was familiar with. "The Heiress" and "Born Yesterday," a popular comedy Herb had toured in two years before, both opened there. There had been hope to have the dress rehearsal in the theatre on Thursday evening, but the auditorium was booked that night, so the dress rehearsal was held in New York in the rehearsal room.

Marilyn, Stanley's wife was in charge of costumes. She took great pride in her responsibility and the costumes turned out to be quite respectable. Alvin was in his glory, strutting about in his uniform, turning on his heels and snapping to attention. As a matter of fact the dress rehearsal went quite smoothly, which left Herb a little uneasy. It was usually a bad dress rehearsal that meant a good opening night. And the only opportunity for a tech rehearsal was two hours before the opening, which did not help to put ones mind at ease.

The cast met at 9:00 AM Friday morning in front of the office building at Fifty Seventh Street and Broadway, where the van was parked. The actors deposited their bags in the small trailer attached to the van, which also carried the backdrop. As they started to pile into the van Ralph asked Herb if it was all right for him to sit up front with him. Herb assured him that it was. Behind them sat Ted and Betsy. Alan, Nat and Paul sat in the back seat, the roomiest of the three. Herb shifted the gear, started up the van and moved up Broadway then headed East toward the highway. "Well, here goes," he said to himself. "What is this one going to be like?" The first little problem was not long in coming.

Alvin, sitting on Nat's left, lit up a cigarette.

You're really going to smoke? asked Nat.

Alan didn't reply. He just continued puffing away. He didn't even inhale. He just puffed away.

That's very inconsiderate, you know, Nat continued.

Alan, without a word, opened the window next to him and blew the smoke in the direction of the open window. The wind, of course, blew the smoke right back into the van. Nat waved the smoke away and faced the other direction. Paul, sitting on Nat's right, and impervious to what was going on, opened his window and lit up as well. Nat, sitting between the two smokers, sighed and shook his head in dismay. He didn't want to make a scene, especially with two strikes against him, but it was difficult for him to contain himself. An hour later, when they stopped for a bathroom break. Nat cornered Herb.

You know it's very inconsiderate of both Alvin and Paul to smoke inside that closed in space, said Nat.

I'll see what I can do, said Herb.

It's unhealthy, and not very good for the throat.

As they started up again Herb announced that only one cigarette at a time could be smoked in the van.

Very sensible, said Ted, and pulled out a cigar from inside his jacket pocket.

Betsy looked at him.

Ted smiled. *Don't worry,* said Ted, *I'm not going to light it.*

The hotel was a modest one, and right across the street from the theatre. Nat and Paul shared a room, as did Ted and Ralph. Alvin, Betsy and Herb had private rooms. By time the cast settled into their respective rooms it was after four, too late for lunch and too early for dinner. The woman in charge of the restaurant in the hotel, which Herb recommended, offered to accommodate the cast and serve whatever they wanted.

One by one the cast drifted down to the restaurant. The woman had the waitress put together two tables and the entire cast sat down for their first meal together.

Opening night hung in the air; opening night with its dangers and its hopes, and no one seemed very talkative. Of course, their jobs were secure. The bookings had been made and they knew they'd be working for eight long months which, had advantages and disadvantages.

They'd be working at their craft, of course, and making money. On the other hand, they'd be wandering around in the wilderness, far from the streets of Broadway, far from the producers' offices, the agents' offices, the television casting people, the soaps, the commercials, far from the opportunities to climb farther up the ladder. And now, except for each other, they'd be exposed, primarily, to civilians, alien aborigines who knew nothing about their world; people who had absolutely no idea of what it was like to be an actor, who had no idea of the insecurity, of the glory, of what it was like to be one of the chosen.

They eyed each other guardedly, seven unknown quantities who were now, or at least for the next eight months, a family. Whether they liked each other or not; whatever their individual dreams happened to be, they spoke the same language; they were in the same boat. They could turn to one another, exchange confidences, which they might not have done under different circumstances. It was as if they were to be stranded with each other on a desert island.

What was this special world they belonged to, you might ask. Was it some sort of a religion? Was it some sort of primitive cult? Whatever it was, and whether they were actually aware of it or not, somewhere deep in their subconscious was this instinctive knowledge that they were part of an ancient ritual; that they had special powers to create something magical. They could enthrall an entire crowd of strangers seated in a darkened theatre or crowded into an open air cockpit or seated in an amphitheater in the middle of the day; they could make them listen intently as one. They could make them laugh in unison. They could make them cry. They could shock them.

Herb Volpe left the table without even waiting for his coffee. He walked quickly across the street to the high school. Two of the local crew were old hands, former students of the school, and Herb greeted them warmly. The backdrop representing a prison wall lay spread out on the floor of the stage. Herb left the charge of raising the backdrop to one of the veterans. He consulted with the young man in charge of the lighting, which was simple enough. There were only a few areas to be lit; the center of the stage where Rubashov's prison cell and the corridor outside of it was located, an area stage right where the prison office was located, and the two prison cells stage left. After the lights were focused he went through the setting up of the furniture for the different scenes, and made sure the props were on hand; there was just a few of them.

The cast began to wander in for the tech rehearsal, which was scheduled for six. Starting at the top of the play they ran through the light cues, entering at the beginning of the scene, then jumping to the end. Herb expected to be finished before seven, but time was taken up deciding which light cues should be fadeouts and which should be blackouts. It was almost a quarter after seven when the cast was dismissed to prepare for their opening night performance.

All the men were assigned to one classroom as their dressing room. Betsy, as the only woman in the cast had her own room. While the men were getting into their costumes Stanley entered. *I just came to wish you all good luck,* he called out. There were a couple of muted thank yous in response. Stanley motioned with his head for Herb to join him and they went into the hall.

Everything okay? asked Stanley.

Yeah. Fine, said Herb. *Is my wife out there?*

She's sitting next to me and Marilyn. You're a lucky son-of-a-gun. Stanley patted Herb on the shoulder. *Break a leg,* he said and left.

At a quarter after eight word came back from the front of the house that the audience had settled into their seats. Ralph, who was doubling as the stage manager called, *Places.* Nat and Paul stationed themselves in their prison cells. Ralph, as the Guard, then took his place next to Herb. The young man on the lights darkened the theatre. Herb nodded to the young man on the curtain. The young man, hand over hand, pulled on the ropes. The curtain opened slowly. The stage lights came up. Ralph, as the Guard, and Herb as Rubashov, the veteran Bolshevik, took a deep breath and made their entrance into the bowels of a Soviet prison, into life in the Soviet Union under Stalin.

STALIN

If you're going to be a revolutionary you've got to be prepared for a harsh existence. You've go to be prepared to spend a great deal of time either in prison or in exile in Siberia. The destination of Koba's (as Stalin now called himself) second banishment was a little godforsaken town called Solvychegodsk. On the way to the frozen north the twenty eight year old veteran, dressed in his customary threadbare black coat and black felt hat, came down with typhus. He spent several weeks in the hospital before he finally reached his destination.

At this time life in exile was not quite as grim as it later became. Supported by the government, the exiled activists spent their days arguing the fine points of the Party line and dreaming of the coming revolution. By time summer came around Koba was fully recovered and ready for his next escape. He made his way back to Baku. Nine months later he was arrested again. He spent three months in prison under interrogation. The Deputy Director of the Baku Gendarme Administration recommended five years in the farthest regions of Siberia. Once more, for some strange reason, the sentence was mitigated. Koba was sentenced to spend his third exile back in Solvychegodsk.

This time his banishment had even more perks. A young widow, Maria Kuzakov, answered the door to find "a middle aged man" who came looking for a room. His friend had recommended her establishment. The man in a "thin black overcoat and felt hat" turned out to be only twenty nine years old. This was a lively household with a number of rambunctious children, each with a different father. Apparently Koba made himself very much at home there for, at the end of his third exile Koba's son, Yasha, was blessed with a baby brother.

Denied the right to return to the capitol he spent the final days of his exile in the half way town of Vologda. In Vologda Koba received a request from his mentor, Lenin, to journey to St. Petersburg. This would be a violation of his sentence. Armed with a professionally doctored passport, and under the watchful eye of the police and, against his better judgement, Koba made his way to St. Petersburg. The uneasy venture was short-lived. Three days after his arrival in the capitol he found himself in jail. This time he was exiled for three years. He was, however given permission to choose his destination. He chose Vologda.

In Vologda he was visited by Sergo, a good friend of his, who bore some very exciting news. Sergo was a bit younger than Koba. He had a quick temper, made lots of noise at meetings and Lenin found him very useful. It appeared that Lenin had engineered a coup. Out of the blue, he'd called a meeting of the Bolsheviks in Prague, claiming that they were the sole representatives of the Party. As such they elected a Central Committee of only Bolsheviks, leaving the Mensheviks with very little power. Elected to this committee was Lenin, Sergo and Zinoviev, a brilliant young orator...and a Jew. Shortly thereafter, Koba, to his delight, was also elected, in absentia, to the Central Committee. He was ordered to escape from Vologda, which he promptly did.

On the way to St Petersburg he exercised his position as member of the Central Committee and checked on local party committees. The police noted in their report that he now sported a black mustache. In St. Petersburg Koba took charge of the electoral campaign. For several weeks he managed to escape arrest sleeping in taverns, in out of the way places, working himself to exhaustion. When he was finally arrested he was sent further north to a much harsher region.

But that didn't stop him. In spite of police surveillance, in spite of the fact that he didn't even have a passport he traveled back and forth between St. Petersburg and Cracow. There he consulted with Lenin. The two agreed that the true revolutionary did not advocate reform. The true revolutionary advocated change, a change that would inescapably entail bloodshed.

With Lenin he moved from Cracow to Vienna. There, with Lenin as his editor, he wrote articles condemning the Jewish Socialists. There could be no "national cultural autonomy." There must be only one world, a world without nations, a world without barriers. Now, for the first time, Koba began to sign himself as Koba-Stalin; Stalin being Russian for "Man Of Steel."

He returned to St. Petersburg where he continued his work, keeping one eye out for the police. Unfortunately one eye was not enough. At a charity concert, given to collect money for the Party, the place was surrounded by the police. Koba-Stalin was hauled off to jail. This time the banishment was the worst of all, and had a very deep effect on him.

Across the frozen plains, across icy rivers he was driven beyond the Arctic Circle. to what seemed like the edge of the earth. There he was deposited at a desolate settlement called Kureika. He was sentenced to spend four years in this sparsely inhabited, icebound, barren land, a land where a comrade of Lenin committed suicide, and another died of tuberculosis.

Now he was completely alone. The police, apparently, had no further use for him and, since he was no longer a double agent, his value to the Party was severely diminished. Deserted and poverty stricken, he wrote pathetic letters to the Central Committee complaining of his dire circumstances. In addition to having no money, he was in poor health. He wrote to the editor of the paper he'd written articles for. He needed money, badly. He was starving. Anything would help. He complained to his old friend, Sergei Alliluyev. When Sergei sent him some money, however, he wrote back apologizing for burdening him when he knew how little he had.

"Don't send me anymore. Just send me your good wishes to keep me warm, to keep my spirits up."

Amid the blizzards and the icy winds Stalin learned a bitter lesson. It was an addendum to his first disillusionment. Long ago he decided that the Christian God did not exist. Now he discovered that Lenin, his human God, was actually a man with feet of clay, a man not deserving of his adulation, not deserving of his unwavering faith. And perhaps it was all to the good. Never trust anyone. Not only does one die alone, one must live alone as well.

Three years went by. World War I was now in progress. Stalin was relieved from serving his fourth miserable year in that frozen hell hole. He was drafted.

Tracing his steps back over the ice and the snow he appeared before the army doctor. Luckily, because of his withered left arm, he was rejected. His exile now had seven more months to go. The authorities were lenient. He was freed five months early.

The year was 1917. In Petrograd a revolution erupted. The jails were opened. The prisoners freed. Police Headquarters was burned down. The list of secret agents went up in flames. The tsar abdicated. A provisional government was set up. Stalin, together with his good friend, Kamenev, the editor of Pravda, traveled to Petrograd in the company of a group of Siberian exiles. The group was given a royal welcome as "victims of the accursed Tsarist regime."

In Petrograd his first stop was the home of his good friend Sergei Alliluyev. His friend found him looking much older, wearing the same old suit, the same old Russian blouse and felt boots. Despite the harshness of the existence he'd been leading, it was a jubilant Koba-Stalin who greeted Sergei. He performed for the family, imitating the speakers at the railway station who welcomed the exiles.

The city was also jubilant. The soldiers who had carried out the revolution, soldiers who remained in Petrograd, finding ways to avoid fighting the Germans, sat and drank in cafes free of charge. Female stars stepped in front of the curtain and sang an inspiring "Marseillaise." Red flags few everywhere.

Soon, however the celebrations got out of hand. There was violence. The violence escalated. Military officers were shot by their men. The police were abused. Crowds joined in to help the assassins beat them up. It was not only the police who fared badly; government officials were being murdered.

While all this was happening Lenin was still in exile. There was no way for him to get back, since he wasn't able to pass through a Germany still at war with Russia. He was completely cut off and missed this revolution just as he had the one in 1905. The Bolsheviks in Petrograd were now controlled by a young Molotov.

This group took over the former house of one of the Tsar's mistresses and, amid luxurious surroundings, began to print the official Bolshevik newspaper. Molotov and his cohorts were not in charge for very long, however. Koba-Stalin and his comrade Kamenev, moved in and took over. Like his mentor, Lenin, Koba-Stalin took no active part in this second revolution. He was busy writing and printing articles for "Pravda." His writings, however, now took a different turn. He took an active stand against Lenin. Contrary to Lenin's policy, he advocated taking part in the war against Germany. He praised the Russian Social Democratic Party. He actually advocated uniting with the despised Mensheviks.

A new power had emerged in Petrograd, the Soviets of Workers' and Soldiers' Deputies. This organization united with the Mensheviks and, with the aid of the Soldier's Deputies, took control of the army. This new faction simply added to the chaos and the violence. Kerensky's Provisional Government had a difficult time holding on to its power. The Tsar, in spite of his abdication and despite the Provisional Government's stand, was arrested along with his ministers.

Koba-Stalin, who had many friends in the Soviet, became a member of the Executive Committee of the Soviets and soon was the most powerful figure on the scene. Going further against Lenin's policy he advocated nationalism rather than a Communist world without barriers of nationality. This move succeeded in ingratiating him with Kerensky and the Provisional Government. Koba-Stalin was now his own man. He was playing every angle, with alliance to no one but himself and his own vision of the Revolution.

AUGUST 1951

The U. S. ends tariff privileges for all communist-dominated countries.

THE OPENING: PART TWO

DARKNESS AT NOON, a play in three acts by Sidney Kingsley, based on the novel by Arthur Koestler, AS ADAPTED BY THE AMERICAN DRAMA GUILD, for a national tour, 1952-1953.

ACT ONE

March 1937. The scene is a Soviet prison. The lighting is dim and foreboding. Rubashov, a veteran Bolshevik, enters escorted by the guard. He's led into his prison cell. The old Bolshevik surveys his grim surroundings. He reaches into his pocket then calls out to the Guard. He has no cigarettes. They've been taken from him. The Guard ignores the request. Rubashov complains that he's been dragged out of a sickbed. He's in pain with an infected tooth. The Guard curses him and leaves.

Rubashov takes off his jacket, uses it as a pillow and lies down on the cot. He contemplates his future. What is the fate of the Old Timers? Are they doomed to be discarded? Is that what it's come to? Their usefulness is over? His thoughts are interrupted by the sound of tapping. He sits up, looks about and listens. He goes to the wall, puts his ear close to it and listens intently. He returns the taps with his spectacles. He begins to recognize a code and communicates with the tapper.

The lights come up on Prisoner 402. 402 is an old Tsarist delighted to find that the enemy has begun to turn on one another. He gloats and passes the information along to Prisoner 403. We hear the news being passed from cell to cell.

Rubashov returns to his thoughts. We hear his inspired speech as one of the leaders of the Revolution. The Monarchy and the Provisional Government have been overthrown. We've been victorious. A glorious future stands before us.

He is roused from his reverie by Prisoner 402 who asks for news. The two men taunt one another. Rubashov asks for some tobacco. Prisoner 402 scoffs at him and they exchange insults. Rubashov returns to memories of the past. He's in his office as Commissar of the Iron Works. He's dictating a letter to his secretary, Luba Loshenko. He notices her earrings and criticizes her frivolity. It's obvious that they find each other attractive. It's a charming and humorous encounter. The memory arouses in Rubashov a feeling of guilt. Was he responsible for the tragic fate of this woman?

He hears the old Tsarist tapping. Rubashov returns to the past and vents his anger on the aristocracy. He may have been responsible for many deaths in that quarter, but the monarchy met a fate it richly deserved. The reverie is interrupted by Prisoner 402 who offers to send him some tobacco. Rubashov thanks him. He begins to wonder about his responsibility in the of case of the aristocracy as well.

Prisoner 402 calls for the Guard and asks him to take some tobacco to Rubashov. The Guard refuses. Rubashov demands to see the officer in charge. The Guard mocks him. Rubashov pulls his rank. The Guard laughs and tells him that he's just another prisoner who's probably going to be shot. Rubashov insists on seeing the Commandant. The Guard threatens to report him. Rubashov urges him to do so. The Guard leaves in a huff.

Prisoner 403, who's recently been tortured, asks Prisoner 402 to send Rubashov his greetings, but he doesn't give his name. The Guard returns with Gletkin, a gaunt, forbidding looking officer. He reprimands Rubashov for making a rumpus. Rubashov demands to see the Commandant. Gletkin taunts the old veteran and tells him that his days are over. He's part of the past. He asks Rubashov if he wants to see a doctor about his tooth. Rubashov doesn't trust prison doctors. It's just an abscess. It'll burst by itself. Gletkin tosses the prisoner a rag, tells him to clean his cell and leaves.

Prisoner 402 gets Rubashov's attention. The poor man has been in prison for fifteen years and hasn't seen a woman for all that time. He wants to talk about them, their bodies, their breasts. He's eager for a description of a sexual encounter. He asks Rubashov if he's ever been in love. Rubashov says no.

He begins to remember his affair with his secretary, Luba. They are in her bedroom. Romantic music is playing on the phonograph. They have just made love, but there is sadness. He must leave. The Party is sending him on a mission. He can't tell her where. He tells her not to wait for him. He encourages her to marry and have a family. But Luba loves him and wants no one else. Rubashov's revery is interrupted by the Guard.

Rubashov has been summoned. The Guard won't tell him by whom. Rubashov enters the office of the prison and meets the Commandant who turns out to be Invanov, an old comrade and friend. They reminisce about old times. Ivanov remembers Rubashov's glory days, when he served under him. Ivanov survived many wounds and lost a leg in an encounter. The meeting grows somber.

Rubashov demands to know what he's being accused of. It now appears that Rubashov is disillusioned with the way things have turned out. The glorious ideals they started out with have deteriorated. The revolution has lost touch with the masses, whom it was supposed to have served. Their pockmarked leader is conducting a blood bath. Ivanov accuses Rubashov of joining the opposition, of instigating the assassination of their leader. Rubashov denies it. Ivanov says there is a witness. He won't tell him who the witness is. Ivanov tries to persuade his old comrade to confess to deviation and then, seeing the error of his ways recanting. If Rubashov stands up in court and is contrite he can escape being shot in secret. The phone rings. Ivanov picks up the phone. He receives some information. He hangs up, looks at Rubashov, shakes his head, smiles and accuses his friend of being an old fox.

Ivanov picks up the phone and summons Gletkin. When Gletkin arrives he reprimands the young officer for the way he handled Rubashov's arrest. Gletkin defends himself. Rubashov resisted, locked himself in, and they had to shoot off the lock. They had to carry him off shouting and making a big fuss. Ivanov tells Gletkin he should have known better. He has to handle matters more discreetly. He has much to learn. He tells the young officer to wait outside.

Ivanov asks Rubashov to think things over. Rubashov stands firm. He will not compromise his integrity and confess to a crime he didn't commit. Ivanov tells him he will have time to reflect, and will eventually come to his senses.

After Rubashov leaves, Ivanov summons Gletkin and tells him that he's to treat Rubashov with respect. Rubashov is to be the key witness in the upcoming trial. Gletkin says that he knows how to get a confession. Ivanov says yes, by breaking him into little pieces. He's to keep his hand off Rubashov. Gletkin expresses his contempt for the old Guard. Ivanov says that Rubashov will come around of his own accord. He points out that Rubashov survived torture by the Nazis without giving in. Gletkin says that he knows how to find the weaknesses in the Old Guard. Ivanov warns him to keep hands off. Gletkin clicks his heels and marches out of the room. Ivanov takes a drink.

Back in his cell Rubashov receives a request from Prisoner 402. All the prisoners ask him to keep silent, not to let them put him on trial. Rubashov asks how the prisoners were tortured. Steam, is the answer. Rubashov holds out his hand and places the lighted end of his cigarette on it and holds it there. Will he die in silence, asks Prisoner 402. Rubashov answers yes, he will die in silence. The word is passed from cell to cell. Rubashov will die in silence. Rubashov will die in silence. Rubashov sits lost in thought as the lights come down on Act One.

There is a ten minute intermission.

ACT TWO

As the lights come up we find Rubashov asleep on his cot. He's feverish. The abscessed tooth he'd complained about before is bothering him. He's haunted by voices from the past. In the corridor outside the cell Ivanov encounters Gletkin. The older man warns the fanatical young man to keep away from Rubashov. We become aware of the fact that Gletkin has plans to ignore the order surreptitiously.

Prisoner 402 alerts Rubashov that something is about to happen. Does he know someone named Bogrov? Rubashov says that he did. What about him? Prisoner 402 doesn't know. Rubashov reminisces about Bogrov, a young protege whose entrance into the Party he sponsored. Rubashov remembers celebrating the end of the civil war with the young man. He sings a patriotic song glorifying the victory. The reminiscence is interrupted by Prisoner 402. He wants to talk. He's half mad, being isolated for all those years. He's obsessed with the thought of women and sex. For the second time he asks Rubashov if he's ever been in love. The response again is no.

Rubashov remembers his last encounter with Luba. He's returned to the Iron Works where she still works as a secretary. The reunion is a poignant one. She still carries the torch for him. He cautions her that the factory is in trouble. They're behind in production which is a fatal flaw. The people in charge, as well as Luba, have been summoned to Moscow for interrogation. This probably means certain death. She asks him if he could help her. He says that he can't. He assures her that she'll be all right, knowing all the while that she won't be. He's ridden with guilt.

The nightmare deepens when Prisoner 402 informs Rubashov that a tortured prisoner is soon to be led to his execution. The man's identity is unknown. Battered and bloody the young prisoner appears in the corridor outside the cell. Gletkin is standing beside him. He whispers into the prisoner's ear. The condemned man turns out to be Bogrov, Rubashov's former protege. As Bogrov is dragged to his death he calls out Rubashov's name. Rubashov, overcome, calls out to his young comrade and falls to the floor in a faint.

When he comes to he finds Ivanov standing over him. Ivanov explains that Bogrov was used by Gletkin as a weapon to break him, to capitalize on his humanity, a fatal flaw in a Bolshevik. He finally persuades Rubashov that he has no choice but to cooperate. He will not only save his own life, but help the Party as well. There is no alternative. Rubashov agrees to think it over. As Ivanov leaves the cell he encounters Gletkin and expresses contempt for the young hothead. He tells Gletkin that he's had success with Rubashov in spite of the young fanatic's harsh efforts.

Gletkin stands lost in thought. The lights of the second act come down.

There is a ten minute intermission.

ACT THREE

As the lights come up Rubashov is deeply absorbed in something he's writing. He looks much healthier, calm and collected. He's interrupted by Prisoner 402 who asks him what he's doing. Rubashov informs Prisoner 402 that he is confessing. He agrees that a dictatorship is necessary. Prisoner 402 expresses his contempt. Rubashov's convinced he's doing the right thing. The Guard enters and rudely informs Rubashov he's to be interrogated.

The lights come up on the prison office. Expecting to find his old comrade, Ivanov, Rubashov is surprised to find Gletkin. Gletkin insists that Rubashov confess. Rubashov is willing to confess his deviation from the Party line, which he admits was a mistake. Gletkin accuses him of planning the assassination of our leader. Rubashov denies it. Gletkin insists that Rubashov persuaded someone else to do his dirty work for him. Rubashov denies it. Gletkin has a witness.

He brings in Prisoner 403 who, we learn, is the son of a good friend of Rubashov. The young man claims that he was persuaded to get rid of Stalin by Rubashov. Rubashov points out that the time this was to have happened Prisoner 403 was on a plane to Moscow. Prisoner 403, obviously brainwashed, denies it. Rubashov learns that his old friend, Ivanov, has been executed. He refuses to cooperate with Gletkin. He speaks eloquently of his devotion to the cause. Infuriated, Gletkin derides Rubashov. He brings up Luba, and taunts the old Bolshevik with deserting her. Rubashov admits it, but he had no choice. He is devastated, defeated. His Communist dreams of a great future have failed. Assaulted by guilt he collapses, a broken man.

Back in his cell Rubashov and Prisoner 402 have a touching farewell. We learn that Prisoner 403 has been executed. Prisoner 402 envies Rubashov facing the release of death. His future is much worse, eternal imprisonment, his senses deteriorating little by little.

In court Rubashov demeans himself and the entire Communist movement, *"We were dead long before the Public Prosecutor demanded our heads."* Rubashov goes to his death with the realization that the Communist dream was flawed from the outset. When Gletkin asks if he has a last wish, he responds, *"Yes. To die."* Gletkin draws his pistol and leads Rubashov off to be shot as the lights slowly dim.

THE OPENING: PART THREE

The audience for the first performance of the American Drama Guild production of Darkness At Noon was not a large one. This was customary for Rochester, and Herb Volpe, in the leading role of Rubashov, and the reluctant director, was grateful that they made the decision to open there.

All things considered Herb thought the first performance went as well as could be expected. Everyone was certainly up. Betsy Landers, in the role of Luba, Rubashov's mistress, came through as beautifully as Herb expected her to. Ted Lombard, veteran of vaudeville, tent shows, carnivals "et al", was okay, in the role of Ivanov, a member of the old guard, but not as impressive as he'd been in rehearsal. Nat Brenner, enjoying his first big job as an Equity member, came through nicely in the role of the sex-starved aristocrat, Prisoner 402, though Herb thought he still looked a little too clean cut. Alvin Gorman, the mystery man, was even more intense and over the top in the role of Gletkin, the young fanatic, than he'd been in rehearsal, but Herb had a feeling that his performance would probably find favor with Stanley Warren, the producer, who was in attendance. Ralph Krumsky, fresh from college and delighted to be part of a professional production was a bit nervous as the Guard, but calmed down eventually and was serviceable, while Paul Thomas, the young Broadway veteran, as Prisoner 403, merely went through the motions, neither adding or detracting from the show, but irritating the hell out of Herb by his nonchalance.

The applause at the curtain call was extremely polite. With Stanley in attendance, this made Herb a little apprehensive. Sometimes Stanley could be rather quixotic. The response of the cast to the less than enthusiastic reception varied considerably. Betsy was apprehensive because her old colleague, Herb, was apprehensive. Nat Brenner was simply relieved that the ordeal of opening in his first Equity show was now history. Applause was applause. Now he could concentrate on refining his performance. Ralph Krumsky was just happy to be part of this professional production. Ted Lombard was grateful for the familiar sound of applause and wished that Edie, his wife, was with him, instead of in Chicago. Young Paul Thomas was indifferent to the reception. This wasn't Broadway. This was Rochester, God help us. What could you expect? And Alvin Gorman, still in the throes of his very intense performance as the villain, Gletkin, was barely aware of the fact that there was applause.

Stanley, leaving his wife, Marilyn, in the auditorium and telling her that he wouldn't be long, went backstage. He cornered Herb before Herb reached the classroom which served as the men's dressing room.

I'm going right back to New York, said Stanley. *Let's talk.*

Ralph Krumsky, on the way to the men's dressing room, smiled nervously at Stanley as he passed the producer and Herb. The other members of the cast watched uneasily as Herb, accompanied by Stanley, entered an empty classroom nearby, closing the door behind them.

The producer hadn't even acknowledged any of them, and he didn't look too happy. The bookings, of course, had been made, but they could be cancelled, couldn't they? Stanley did produce slapdash, cut down versions of popular plays in the Catskills during the summer, but he did take pride in the quality of the full productions he sent across the country during the rest of the year. There were only two or three of them a year and, though the production values were meager, the quality of the cast and the performances were always respectable.

Stanley didn't look too happy, said Nat as he wiped off the dark circles under his eyes, and sat studying his face. Actually he was a little too young for the leading role of Rubashov, he mused, but he certainly could play it; not that Herb was inadequate. Herb was fine, but maybe just a little too stolid. Yes, that was the word stolid. There could be just a smidgen more passion in the performance.

I thought it went pretty well, said Ralph Krumsky.

There was silence.

Didn't you? he continued, looking at Nat.

Nat shrugged.

For our first performance, I think it went quite well, said Ted Lombard, adding, *Of course, there's always room for improvement.*

Isn't there some sort of an opening night party? asked Nat.

There certainly ought to be, said Ted. *If nothing else, we could get together at the bar in the hotel.*

If they're open this late, said Nat.

Well, I could certainly use a drink, said Ralph Krumsky. *What do you say, Paul?*

Every show I've been in we've always had an opening might party, said Paul. *In "Life With Mother" we had an opening night party in Sardi's.*

Well, this isn't Broadway, said Alvin, *and I, for one, am exhausted.*

You did work pretty hard, said Paul.

What is that supposed to mean?

It was a compliment, said Paul.

Some people take their work seriously, said Alvin.

Oh, I know, I know, said Paul.

You certainly have a lot of growing up to do, said Alvin.

Don't we all, said Nat.

Alvin started to gather up his things. *If Herb has any notes for me, he can give them to me in the morning. I'm going back to the hotel.*

Sleep tight, said Paul.

Alvin gave Paul a dirty look and left.

What is his problem? asked Nat.

No one volunteered an answer.

There was a knock at the door. Paul, nearest to the door opened it, to discover a well proportioned, attractive brunette.

Can I help you? asked Paul.

I'm looking for Herb, said Helen. *I'm his wife.*

He's with the producer, said Peter.

Thank you, said Helen. *Tell Herb I'll wait for him in the auditorium.* Addressing the entire room, she added, *I thought you all did very well. Congratulations.*

Thank you, said Ted, Nat and Ralph, almost in unison.

Good luck, said Helen as she left.

Lucky Herb! said Nat, after Paul closed the door.

She's lovely, isn't she? said Ted.

Nat grew strangely silent, as he was reminded of a part of his life it was painful to remember. The presence of Helen brought into the room an aura of another world. There was the business world, the theatre...work and money and success, maybe even glory...but there was also love, such as it is.

Ted decided he was going to call Edie as soon as he got back to the hotel, instead of waiting until tomorrow morning, as had been arranged. Ralph thought about the girl on which he'd had his latest crush. He just didn't seem to have any luck with women. He felt awkward in that heavy set body of his. He was shy. He may not have been handsome, but he certainly wasn't ugly. His Slavic features were quite respectable. Maybe it was just a matter of luck; finding the right one at the right time. Paul was reminded of the fact that he often had trouble relating to women. They didn't seem to appreciate his finer qualities. They didn't show him the respect he felt he deserved.

Herb entered the dressing room and proceeded to get out of his costume. The men waited for some comment, at least some sort of a report. Finally Nat spoke up.

Stanley looked sort of grim, said Nat.

He always looks that way on opening night, said Herb.

Your wife said she'll wait for you in the auditorium, said Ted.

Thank you.

She's very attractive, said Nat.

Thank you, said Herb. He glanced apprehensively at Nat out of the corner of his eye.

We thought we might gather in the bar at the hotel for an opening night drink, said Ted.

After a moment, Herb said, *I'd like to join you, but under the circumstances... It's going to be our last night together for quite some time.*

That's quite all right, said Ralph, *and I certainly don't blame you.*

I think it went well for a first performance, said Herb, *especially since we had so little rehearsal.*

That's what I thought, said Ted.

Paul tried to hide his contempt for their so-called director. Well, what do you expect? And he wondered how long he could stick it out. He could use the money, but where was this getting him? What a bunch of has-beens!

There was a knock at the door. Paul opened the door. It was Betsy.

Is everyone decent? she asked.

Come in, come in, said Herb.

Is anyone going for a drink?

Some of us are, said Ted. *We're going to the bar at the hotel. Would you care to join us?*

I'd love to, said Betsy.

Why don't you all go on ahead, said Herb. *I'll see you in the morning.*

Aren't you joining us? asked Betsy.

Helen's spending the night, said Herb.

Oh, said Betsy. *I didn't even know she was here.*

It's our last night together, said Herb.

Yes, of course, said Betsy. She felt guilty and resented herself for it. Actually, she had no reason to feel guilty.

You're my date for tonight, said Ted, as he put his arm around Betsy and led her off. Paul and Ralph followed them off. *See you tomorrow,* said Nat as he left the room, closing the door behind him.

Herb joined Helen in the auditorium and they walked across the street to the hotel. When they stopped at the desk for Herb to pick up his key the clerk, a rather prim, middle aged man looked askance at the two of them.

This is my wife, said Herb. *I mentioned that she might be staying over.*

The clerk handed Herb the key rather reluctantly. When they were out of earshot Helen started to laugh.

What's so funny? asked Herb.

The two of us, being taken for naughty children, said Helen. *You don't think that's funny?* As they waited for the elevator she ran her fingers across his forehead. *You're tired,* she said. As they got into the elevator Helen asked, *What did Stanley have to say?* Since Herb didn't respond Helen dropped the subject. Obviously Herb had a lot on his mind. When he was ready, he would speak.

I spoke to Lillian before I left, said Herb. *I made sure she'd be sending you the checks on time.*

This room is really depressing, said Helen as Herb closed the door behind them.

They sat down on the edge of the large double bed with its lumpy mattress, and held hands.

And it's cold, said Helen. *I didn't even bring anything with me. Oh, Honey, you look so sad.*

I'm just thinking of all those weeks and months.

I know, I know, said Helen, and she sighed.

This is the last, said Herb, *the very last.*

And it'll be over before you know it.

And Stanley gave me a hard time. He wants to fire Nat Brenner.

Why?

He doesn't think he's good in the part.

I thought Stanley was the one that vouched for him.

I know, I know.

Have you told him yet?

What?

Nat Brenner? Have you told him yet? Since Herb didn't respond Helen waited a moment and then said, *You said you thought he was talented.*

He is, said Herb. *I did. Stanley said he'd come to the performance in Lewisburg and take another look. But I've got to give him his two weeks notice.*

Oh, God!

It'll kill him, said Herb.

What's wrong with his performance, except that he's a little too young for the role.

He's not lecherous enough. He doesn't slobber; and he doesn't look like he's a man that's been in prison for all those years.

That's true, said Helen. *It's just a matter of makeup.*

I told him that. Stanley, I mean. And he's very independent, Herb added. *Nat, I mean. I told him to age more. He said he didn't want to overdo it.*

Well, that's all you can do, said Helen. *If he wants the job, he'll listen to you...and Stanley.*

I'd hate to lose him.

Herb!

What?

I'm here. Helen. Your wife. Remember? I want you to forget about Rubashov, and Darkness At Noon and Stanley and Nat and everyone else. I want your undivided attention.

Herb sighed and looked at the lovely woman beside him. *What would I do without you?*

What you do with me is what I'm concerned with at the moment.

They both laughed. Herb blushed. Helen kissed him. He responded. They undressed, made love, and Herb, for the moment, forgot all about Russia, and Stalin, and death and persecution.

STALIN

On April 3, 1917 the train, which carried the notorious emigre, Lenin, crossed the border into Russia, having passed untouched through Germany, Russia's wartime enemy. It passed through Germany, not only unharmed, but carrying Germany's approval and financial support. Germany, it appears, benefited from the arrangement since Lenin advocated Russian nonresistance to Germany. The Communists benefited since Germany offered them money, much needed money to support their revolution. "The end justifies the means."

Now that the Leader was back, it was time for Koba-Stalin to switch gears. There was no more opposition to Lenin's principles, no more compromise with the despised Mensheviks, no more Social Democracy. Koba-Stalin retreated quietly from the limelight and let Kamenev, his co-editor on Pravda take the reins. It was Kamenev who greeted the Leader on the advent of his triumphant return. It was Kamenev who was the one appointed to shoulder the great man's wrath.

Lenin's fury, however, was soon appeased. To his great relief. instead of being hauled off to confinement in the Peter and Paul fortress, as he feared he might be, he was greeted with a tumultuous welcome. He was overwhelmed with staunch support from the Soviets. He soon learned that this support was engineered by his old tried and true comrade, Koba-Stalin.

Yes, Koba-Stalin was now ready to resume his role as faithful henchman. The Bolsheviks held a conference after Lenin's arrival. When Kamenev was bold enough to oppose some of Lenin's views, Koba-Stalin lashed out in defense of his Leader. He cheered when his Leader called for the downfall of Kerensky. He cheered when Lenin deserted Marx's sacrosanct theory of a triumphant bourgeoisie. No, no. The Revolution belonged to the proletariat. A new revolution was now in the offing. Blood must be shed!

When elections were held, Lenin saw to it that Koba-Stalin was elected to the Central Committee. Within the Central Committee a further election was held. Supreme power was given to a group of four. This all powerful group, which ultimately came to be known as the Politburo, consisted of Lenin, Zinoviev (a brilliant young orator and, incidentally, a Jew, Kamenev (who was obviously forgiven for daring to oppose the Leader) and Koba-Stalin, a Koba-Stalin who was now moving higher and higher up the political stepladder.

As plans for the new Revolution was getting underway an old familiar figure reappeared on the scene. Trotsky, the brilliant orator and charismatic actor, made his entrance at the Petrograd train station. He mesmerized his audience with his fiery words. Lenin had no choice but to make peace with his former enemy. He sent Zinoviev and Kamenev to pave the way for a meeting, and the forming of a coalition.

An uneasy alliance was formed, Trotsky behaving as though he was in charge; Lenin now advocating Trotsky's cry for a "permanent revolution." Together they called for the downfall of Kerensky and, instead of war with Germany, a civil war in Russia. Koba-Stalin, aware of Lenin's fear and distrust of Trotsky, aware of the fact that both Zinoviev and Kamenev disapproved of the Trotsky alliance, made no bones about his hatred for the upstart, another Jew.

When the first All-Russian Congress of Soviets met on June 3, 1917 the Bolsheviks represented a mere nine percent of its members. When it was stated that no one party had the strongest sway, Lenin moved secretly to organize a demonstration...a "peaceful demonstration" to proclaim the power of the Bolsheviks. If the demonstration led to violence, well, so be it. Secretary Koba-Stalin was in charge of covertly recruiting demonstrators and organizing the proceedings.

When the plans were discovered Lenin, Zinoviev, Kamenev, all involved in the venture expressed amazement. All voted unanimously against the demonstration, all, that is, except Koba-Stalin. Koba-Stalin boldly voted against calling off the demonstration thereby revealing his covert role in the scheme. He volunteered to resign from the Central Committee, knowing full well his resignation would not be accepted.

A stormy debate ensued. Koba-Stalin's bold maneuver resulted in a move for a full fledged peaceful demonstration to display the power of the entire Congress of Soviets. This, of course, played into the hands of the Bolsheviks, giving them the opportunity to demonstrate with the full approval of the Congress. A magnificent demonstration took place with the Bolsheviks on glorious display. Both Lenin and Koba-Stalin wrote articles for Pravda describing the triumphant display of Bolshevik power.

At this time the Provisional Government was facing all sorts of troubles. The Bolsheviks took advantage of the situation and encouraged an army regiment, unhappy at the prospect of being sent to the German front, to rebel. Sailors soon followed suit. As the uprising began to get underway Lenin disappeared from sight. Outwardly calling for restraint, Koba-Stalin surreptitiously continued to encourage the revolt.

The sailors, now armed, arrived in Petrograd and, in unison with the rebellious soldiers, marched through the city streets. The mob made its way to the headquarters of the Congress and called for their leader, Lenin. At first they were told that Lenin wasn't in the building. Then they were told that he was ill. Finally the great man had to make an appearance. He made a rather tame speech and the armed mob moved on. They arrested the leader of the Socialist Revolutionary Party and would have executed him if Trotsky hadn't arrived on the scene. The charismatic performer charmed the mob and prevented the assassination.

The uprising continued throughout the day. Finally the army of the Provisional Government arrived on the scene and clashed with the rebels. They prepared to storm the Soviet headquarters. The rebels were prepared to make what was certain to be a futile stand. Koba-Stalin succeeded in persuading them to surrender and avoid certain death. At the Peter and Paul Fortress the armed sailors were prepared to defend themselves. Koba-Stalin persuaded them to drop their weapons and return home peacefully, avoiding more bloodshed. Koba-Stalin turned out to be the hero of the day.

Previous to the uprising Kerensky had been conducting an investigation of the Bolsheviks' ties to Germany. Proof had been found of German gold reaching Lenin and other Bolshevik leaders. Koba-Stalin was the only one with clean hands. He was able to use his influence in preventing the use of this information to brand the Bolsheviks as German spies.

He was not entirely successful however. One newspaper slipped through the cracks and published the defamatory information. The Provisional Government issued a warrant for the arrest of the Bolshevik leaders, namely Lenin, Trotsky, Zinoviev and Kamenev. Trotsky was taken from his bed and imprisoned. Koba-Stalin, whose name was not on the list, helped hide Lenin and Zinoviev, first in the Alliluyev's apartment, then in various other places. Finally he escorted them to the train station where they took a train out of the city to a place where they could remain comfortably in hiding. Kerensky dropped the espionage charges fearing it might give power to the far right.

The Bolsheviks, undeterred, continued to operate. Their Sixth Congress was attended by three hundred delegates. Koba-Stalin presided. Lenin, however, still exercised control by sending Koba-Stalin speeches from the shack in which he was ensconced. Koba-Stalin read these speeches, in addition to making the closing speech. He met with Lenin a number of times. He was informed of Lenin's next step. The Leader planned, not only to pursue the overthrow of the Kerensky Government, but to break ties with the Soviets as well.

After Lenin's departure Koba-Stalin, who'd been living in a dreary bachelor apartment, moved in with the Alliluyevs, taking over the room which had sheltered Lenin and Zinoviev. He was the ideal guest. So unobtrusive that he never even took a meal in the apartment. He was seen eating bread and sausage at a stall opposite the apartment building.

This change of abode coincided with the Sixth Congress over which he presided. At the time he owned one cotton shirt and a worn out jacket. The Alliluyevs decided he was not properly dressed for this important position. They went out and bought him a suit. Since he refused to wear a tie Zhenya, Sergei's wife, sewed up the collar of the shirt so that it looked like a military tunic. This dress was later adopted by Lenin and became the official Bolshevik uniform.

Koba-Stalin was a fiery rebel. At the age of forty, however, he was still a vigorous man, without a wife or feminine companionship. The Alliluyev apartment contained two charming, innocent teenage girls, brown-eyed Nadya and her sister Anna. Nadya, in particular, was fascinated by this heroic figure. She was entranced by his tales of derring-do. The lonely warrior, in turn, was enchanted by the adoring child-woman. This encounter planted the seeds for a love affair and a second marriage, a marriage which was to add another melodramatic chapter to the history of the man who became Stalin.

SEPTEMBER 1951

In response to their concern about Russian and Chinese expansion, and the revival of Japan as a sovereign nation, Australia and New Zealand sign a mutual defense pact with the U.S.

NAT BRENNER

Nat Brenner couldn't keep it to himself. For one thing, he couldn't believe it. It wasn't happening. It couldn't be happening. To say that he was overcome by despair would be putting it mildly. Maybe if he let it out, it would go away. *I've been fired,* he said to Paul Thomas, with whom he shared the hotel room.

Paul wasn't quite sure how to respond. Nat was a bit of a silly, idealistic fool. You couldn't not like him and, I guess, feel sorry for him. But anyone who let's himself wide open like that deserved it. *You're well out of it,* said Paul. *I don't know how long I'm going to stick it out.*

Nat just sat there in a daze. Suicide flashed through his mind. That's ridiculous. The idea, however, was rather persistent. He'd lay himself down on the street and let Herb drive the van over him. Then there was the roof of the hotel. He'd jump off. Ridiculous. It's not that high. He'd only cripple himself. At least it would end his career as an actor. What a stupid decision that was! He couldn't go back! He just couldn't go back to New York and all that despair! Someone was speaking to him.

I said there's no use brooding about it.

That idiot, Paul. That arrogant little snit. Maybe he was right. The world is shit. He really should go back to school, get a degree and teach like his mother wanted him to. She was right. It would be the sensible thing to do. The walls of ivy. No, it's the halls of ivy. Whatever it was, he didn't want it. Those who can, do. Those who can't, teach. He wanted to do.

They're blowing the horn. We'd better get going, said Paul.

Fuck the horn, he thought to himself, as he picked up his suitcase and his typewriter and followed Paul out of the room, down the elevator and out of the hotel, that shitty hotel. Well, he didn't have to worry about hotels anymore. He'd kill himself. That's what he'd do, he'd kill himself. He was now on the verge of tears.

Herb Volpe took one look at Nat and turned away. Oh, God! What an awful profession! For what? He thought of Helen back home in New York, all alone in that apartment...he hoped. And then he chided himself for even contemplating such a thought... What a way to start a tour!

TOURING WITH STALIN

Nat climbed into the back of the van and sat there glumly. I'll kill myself. That's all there is to it. I can't go on. Isn't that a line from Beckett? That godawful, boring Waiting For Godot! And that's what they call a play! Pretentious, pretentious, pretentious! The world is pretentious!

Paul Thomas stood outside the van. He was not going to sit next to that silly fool. Nat glowered at him through the window of the van. That arrogant snit is right after all. Talent doesn't mean a thing. It's who you know.

Betsy Landers came out of the hotel with her suitcase. She placed it in the trunk and climbed into the van. Debating which row to sit in she ended up sitting next to Nat. He turned a woeful face to her.

I've been fired.

What?!

Was the woman deaf? *I said, I've been fired.*

I'm so sorry. Then she looked quizzically at him *Are you sure?*

I've been given two weeks notice.

Well, you're still here, said Betsy.

Nat sat thoughtfully for a moment. *Stanley's coming to the performance at Lewisburg to take another look at me.*

Well, there you are.

I'm not lascivious enough.

Betsy made a manful effort to keep from laughing, but she couldn't keep from smiling.

Herb said to make my makeup heavier.

That should help.

Nat laughed...weakly. Almost in tears, he said, *Isn't this a ridiculous profession, pretending to be someone else? What do we really know about other people?*

Ralph Krumsky climbed into the van and took the seat in the back row next to Nat and Betsy. *It's a beautiful day,* said Ralph.

Beautiful? said Nat. *What are you talking about?*

*I mean...*Ralph was about to defend himself when Nat broke in. *It looks like it's going to rain any minute,* said Nat.

Well, said Ralph, *the sun was shining a few minutes ago.*

Well, it sure as hell isn't shining now!

Nat's been given his notice, said Betsy.

I've been fired, snapped Nat.

You haven't been fired, said Herb as he climbed onto the front seat.

What then?

You've been put on notice, said Herb. *I told you. Stanley is going...*

I know all that, Nat insisted, *but he's made up his mind.*

And he has been known to change it, said Herb. *So just calm down.*

What's been happening? asked Ted Lombard as he took a seat.

Nat's been fired, said Paul as he sat down next to Ted.

He hasn't been fired, Herb insisted. *He's been given his two weeks notice, but Stanley's coming to Lewisburg to see the performance again, and everything's going to be fine. Paul, will you please see what's keeping Alvin?*

Yes, sir, said Paul. He climbed out of the van and went back into the hotel.

Were you able to reach your wife? Herb asked Ted Lombard.

Oh, yes, said Ted. *We had a nice long talk. It's freezing in Chicago.*

It's always freezing in Chicago, said Herb.

There was silence in the van as everyone sat waiting for Alvin Gorman.

Ted turned to Nat and said, *I'm sorry about your problem.*

Thank you, said Nat.

Everything's going to be fine, said Herb.

Privately Ted wondered why Nat had been cast in the first place. He was too young for the role, though he was not without talent. A little too full of himself, perhaps. These young people.

Well, it'll be good for him. That's the only way to learn. If you haven't been through the ringer, you come out wet, wet behind the ears.

And his thoughts turned to his little grandson in Colorado, the one month old infant he hadn't even seen yet. Well, at least he had that picture, and at least Edie was there. And here he was missing out on his first grandchild. Edie warned him. He should have listened to her. Did he really need this job? He turned to Herb. *Have I shown you the picture of my grandson?*

No, said Herb.

It came in the mail the day before yesterday, said Ted as he pulled out his wallet.

Let's see it, said Herb. *My wife is pregnant, you know.* Herb studied the snapshot of the sleeping infant. *That's a beautiful baby,* said Herb.

They say it looks like me, said Ted, *though I don't think a baby looks like anything but a baby.*

Let me see, said Betsy. *That's a darling baby,* she said as she gazed at the snapshot.

It looks just like a baby, said Nat, and then could have kicked himself for being so snide. Why did he do that? *I'm just kidding,* he continued. *It is a beautiful baby.*

Thank you, said Ted as he placed the picture back in his wallet.

He overslept, said Paul Thomas as he climbed into his seat.

And the amazing thing is, thought Herb about Alvin Gorman, Stanley thinks his performance is fine. That overwrought caricature of a performance.

I'm sorry, said Alvin as he climbed into the seat next to Herb. *I forgot to set my alarm.* He turned to address the rest of the company. *I'm sorry, if I've kept you waiting,* he said stiffly. How he wished he could have someone to talk to, someone he had something in common with. Not a soul, not one soul. He hated them all, all of them, part of a world that hated him. Eight long months, eight long months of isolation. Well, at least he had a role he could sink his teeth into. And who knows? Who knows what lies ahead on the path of life? There are other people in this world, other people aside from this dreary little company.

Herb started the motor, shifted gears and the van took off. It was a cool October morning. The sun was in, the sun was out. But the breeze was consistent as it flowed through the open windows of the van.

Nat's hysteria was now under control. He was aware of the fact that Herb was on his side, and Stanley certainly had great respect for Herb. He should have listened to Herb when he told him his makeup could be heavier. Herb should have insisted on it. Nat remembered the review he received when he played the old native in O'Neill's "Emperor Jones" at the Playhouse on the Cape. "Typical of the weakness of the production was Nat Brenner, who played the character of Lem with his usual rather poetic features." Vanity, vanity, vanity! It was the makeup. That was it. He'd go whole hog on the makeup. He just couldn't let it happen. This was the setup he'd been dreaming about; to earn a living as an actor while he learned how to write a play. He couldn't let it happen. And the part, after all, a sex-strarved prisoner in the bowels of a Russian prison? What's not to like?

STALIN

What with increasing civil unrest and the war with Germany going badly, the Kerensky Government grew weaker and weaker. Taking advantage of the chaos, Lenin emerged from his Finnish hiding place, where Koba-Stalin had helped install him, and made a surprise appearance on October 10, 1917 at a Central Committee session. He called for an uprising. Kamenev and Zinoviev objected. Trotsky labeled their stand as traitorous and demanded their expulsion. Koba-Stalin came to their defense and saved their skins. If the revolution failed, he reasoned, it would appear that he had been against it. In addition to that he again gained the support of two important figures in the party. He then withdrew from the picture and let Trotsky conduct the uprising. On October 24, the day of the start of the uprising Koba-Stalin published an article urging its support.

In the event that the revolution might fail, Lenin was hidden in an apartment. Choosing anonymity with regard to the revolution, faithful Koba-Stalin now devoted himself to the welfare of the Leader. He arranged an escape route just in case it might be needed. The revolution seemed to be in full swing when Lenin, growing impatient and heavily disguised, put in an appearance at the Bolshevik headquarters.

During the night he called a meeting of the Central Committee in order to form a new Bolshevik Government. The new ministers were to be called the People's Commissars. Trotsky was proposed by Lenin as president. He refused the position, citing the fact that he was a Jew as one of the obstacles. Lenin, feigning reluctance, and embarrassed at the open acknowledgement of anti-Semitism within the idealistic party, accepted the position himself. Koba-Stalin was appointed Head of the Commissariat for Nationalities.

During the early morning hours on October 26 the remnants of the Provisional Government were ousted from the Winter Palace. There was more violence. Drunken sailors and soldiers raped and murdered. The revolution, however, had actually succeeded.

The dream of Socialism was about to be realized. Ownership was to be abolished. Money was to be abolished.

Government was to be abolished. The people themselves would take turns governing. Koba-Stalin left the Alliluyev apartment and moved into the Smolny Palace which served as the headquarters for the Bolshevik led revolution. He was ensconced in Lenin's office and worked with him, side by side.

Conflict arose between the Lenin/Trotsky alliance, which insisted on one party, and those who wanted a multi-party government. Lenin and Trotsky forged ahead, squelching all opposition. They established the CHEKA, The Extraordinary Commission for Combating Counterrevolution and Sabotage by Officials. The torture chambers of the Peter and Paul Fortress welcomed those government officials who opposed the one party system. These revolutionaries found themselves right alongside the fallen aristocrats whom they'd ousted. The women's cells were filled with wives and daughters of the opposing government officials together with criminals and prostitutes. Only two newspapers now existed, Pravda and New Life, edited by the writer, Maxim Gorgky, a supporter of Lenin. The Soviets were shoved aside. The Bolsheviks reigned supreme.

Lenin officially described the new government as a provisional one and, as promised, undertook to conduct elections. Perfectly aware of the fact that the Bolsheviks would be defeated he invited the Left Socialist Revolutionaries to be their ally. It was the military, however, that he was counting on; the soldiers and sailors who, under the Bolsheviks, were free to do as they pleased, to shoot officers, to break into apartments and rob and rape, to hold drunken public meetings.

As expected, the Bolsheviks and the Left Socialist Revolutionaries were defeated. The first Constituent Assembly was held. It was, however, the soldiers and sailors who demonstrated in the streets, who made up the audience and it was the out of control military who were actually in charge of the meeting. Shouts disrupted the meeting continually. When the unruly audience had enough, the sailor in charge of the guards tapped the chairman on the shoulder and informed him that the guards were tired and wanted to go home. The meeting came to an abrupt end. The

TOURING WITH STALIN

Constituent Assembly became history, labelled by Pravda as "lackeys of the imperialists" and "stabbers in the back."

The next step was peace with Germany. Trotsky was sent to meet the Germans. Words flew back and forth...between the Russians and the Germans and between the Russians back home who opposed the treaty. Koba-Stalin, at first, lent his support to the opposition. He was quickly reined in by Lenin, but he'd made his point. As usual he'd played both sides. The shameful treaty was signed. The Bolshevik Party now became known as the Communist Party.

The capital was moved from Petrograd to Moscow, which was more central. The government was installed in the magnificent Kremlin. The chimes now rang out with the Internationale instead of God Save The Tsar. Koba-Stalin was installed in an elegant apartment. Looking around, the first thing he did was to smash the antique mirror and dispose of the ornate furnishings.

Though Lenin easily succeeded in getting rid of "his allies," the Socialist Revolutionaries, he was faced with a much more serious problem, a country torn apart by all sorts of wars. The Germans and the Turks helped themselves to a good part of the Russian Empire. Petrograd and Moscow still belonged to the Bolsheviks but the section of the country that belonged to them became torn by a civil war. Several bands of Tsarist cossacks organized and, labelled as the White Guard, took on the Bolsheviks who became known as the Red Guard. The country became divided. It was brother against brother, father against son. Trotsky was put in charge of the army and succeeded in exercising some discipline in the unruly military.

In addition to the wars the Bolsheviks were faced with famine. The wealthier peasants, known as Kulaks, refused to provide the grain without payment. The poorer peasants were organized to seize the grain but they soon turned into marauding, drunken gangs. Koba-Stalin was given the assignment.

At the end of May 1918, accompanied by the son and daughter of his friend, Sergei Alliluyev, as his staff, Koba-Stalin set out for Tsaritsyn to increase the flow of grain to Moscow.

TOURING WITH STALIN

Young Fyodor served as his assistant while the nubile, brown-eyed Nadya was his secretary. In spite of his position it took some doing to commandeer a train. They traveled through treacherous territory. The train stations were dark and dirty; drunken soldiers playing accordions or shooting off their rifles. There were the Germans and Cossacks on the loose, in addition to all sorts of gangs and mountain tribes. They did, however, have a guard of four hundred strong to protect them, Latvian riflemen and veteran execution squads, which Koba-Stalin intended to make good use of.

In Tsaritsyn they found an abundance of food and a plethora of grain supplies. In order to galvanize the shipment of the grain to Moscow Koba-Stalin executed everyone involved in black marketing, even those who might become involved. The local CHEKA was busy night and day with executions. The bodies were buried at night. During the day families would dig up dead relatives, carry them off from the communal grave to bury them decently. Koba-Stalin was soon able to wire Lenin that eighteen thousand tons of grain was on its way to Moscow.

During this time Koba-Stalin slept in the lounge car while Fyodor and Nadya slept in a separate compartment. But it was close quarters for the three of them during that hot and dangerous spring and early summer. Not only did Koba-Stalin succeed in fulfilling his assignment, he was also successful in acquiring a wife. In those close, overheated quarters the veteran and the neophyte found romance. In those revolutionary times a formal ceremony wasn't necessary. Koba-Stalin and Nadya now considered themselves husband and wife.

On the other hand the assignment seemed to have had a disastrous effect on young Fyodor. Shortly afterwards, for some unknown reason, the young man lost his mind. He seems to have suffered some sort of shock. From that time on, through the rest of his life, he experienced bouts of madness.

OCTOBER 1951

The White House announces that the Soviets have tested a second atomic bomb.

NAT BRENNER

Herb was rather peeved with Nat Brenner for broadcasting his dilemma. It made everyone in the cast uneasy. There was now that feeling of Could I Be Next?. And he was still trying to figure out Stanley's reasoning. Stanley seldom fired anyone. He was behaving like some disappointed lover. He'd been so gung-ho about Nat's talent and, apparently, he expected... God knows what Stanley expected. The young man was talented, but he was not a genius. He was young for the role, but he was certainly doing a respectable job. The more Herb thought about it the more upset he became...angry at Stanley, angry at Nat and angry at the fact that he'd signed up for another long eight months.

Honey, said Helen on the phone, *if you're that unhappy, quit. Give in your notice. You've got a good excuse. You're expecting your first child and you're needed at home.*

Helen did have the gift for bringing him down to earth.

The company had been together for less than three weeks, including rehearsals, and already they were a family. It was them against the world of strangers, which was good, thought Herb. His apprehension, however, was certainly justified. The tension engendered by opening night was replaced by concern about the loss of a family member.

Ralph Krumsky expressed his sympathy openly. He'd pat Nat on the back or he'd look at him with pity; the same pity he would have shown to a whipped dog, thought Nat. Betsy said nothing but she grieved inwardly. She liked Nat. As a matter of fact she found him attractive. Paul Thomas said nothing, but grudgingly admitted to himself that he'd miss Nat. The man was a bit of a fool, but Paul did have to admit that he did have a sense of humor, which he found lacking in the rest of the cast. The silly banter between the two of them did make this dreary experience more bearable. Ted Lombard felt sorry for the lad, but then again, that was show business. The only one who was entirely indifferent to the situation was Alvin Gorman. Alvin had problems of his own. When you take on all of Society, losing one's job is pretty small potatoes.

Nat was uneasy about the sympathy he aroused. He kept

wishing that Ralph wasn't that sympathetic. I mean, after all, as Herb insisted, he hadn't been fired. He'd been put on notice, and Herb was in charge of the company and he was decisively on his side. And Betsy looked so sad whenever she looked at him. Paul's banter was a little too cheerful, and Ted Lombard smiled kindly at him instead of almost ignoring him. He was actually grateful for Alvin's indifference.

Nat began to apply more make-up. Darker circles under the eyes were accompanied by more stubble on his chin (he neglected to shave) which he darkened, and he blacked out two of his teeth. Try as he might he could not act more lascivious. He knew he'd get a laugh if he did. Even so he heard a titter or two on the lines about a woman's breast, and some gasps. But that was it! He could not overact. He just couldn't. It was just not in him.

The only benefit gained from this agonizing situation was the fact that no one smoked in the van during the trip to Nyack, New York. Alvin, however, lit up on the trip to Poughkeepsie, where they performed in the auditorium at Vassar College. On the way to Lewisburg, Pennsylvania, the dreaded sink or swim date, Paul finally lit up followed by Alvin. Paul, at least, had the good grace to feel a little self conscious.

All through the drive from Poughkeepsie Nat was so on edge that he felt he was really too nervous to give any sort of a decent performance. He still couldn't accept the fact that, in a matter of days, he might be out of a job, that this dream opportunity would no longer exist, that he'd be cast from the heights to the lower depths. Suicide, by this time, was looked upon merely as melodramatic nonsense, and he wished that he could weep.

The hotel in Lewisburg was surprisingly elegant, and even more surprising relatively cheap. Just my luck, thought Nat. Why couldn't it have been a hotel I'd be glad to be rid of, typical of the hotel about which I could say to myself, "Look at what you won't be missing." And, to top it all off, it was a chilly, damp, dreary day, a day fit for an execution.

They arrived in Lewisburg later than expected. Herb barely

had time to see to the setup. Stanley phoned that he was behind schedule, but not to hold the curtain if he was late. The venue in Lewisburg was a high school auditorium. Thankfully it wasn't enormous, like the one in Nyack. After Nat made up he reported to Herb for inspection.

Is my makeup okay, do you think?

It's all right, said Herb, *but overdo the sex lines. I know, I know. But that's Stanley for you. Just for tonight overact, just a little.*

Nat sighed and said, *I'll try.* But in his heart he knew he couldn't try very hard, and so did Herb.

Is Stanley here? asked Nat.

I don't know, said Herb, *but he said not to wait.*

Places, called Ralph, and then to Nat he whispered, *Good luck.*

Thank you, said Nat, wishing that Ralph hadn't emphasized the importance of the performance. His heart sank as he took his place in his prison cell behind the scrim. He wished he was religious. He wished he could pray to someone, and maybe subconsciously he was praying, but to whom? To himself, maybe? The fact that he didn't know if Stanley was in the audience or not had a twofold effect on him. On the one hand he felt freer at the possibility that he wasn't there. There was less pressure. On the other hand, if he wasn't there, it meant that his fate might be delayed or, God forbid, he might be executed without a trial.

The curtain parted, rather noisily, thought Nat. The lights came up on Rubashov's prison cell. Herb, as Rubashov, entered, escorted by Ralph as the guard. They had this argument about a cigarette and Rubashov was left to ponder his fate. Nat heard his cue and, as Prisoner 402, began to tap out the code. Rubashov became aware of the tapping. He eventually responded. The lights came up on Prisoner 402. He tapped and spoke his first line loud and clear, *Who are you?* He waited for a response. Receiving none, he continued. *Is it day or night outside?*

As the performance progressed. Herb seemed to be up. So did the rest of the cast. Stanley must be out there, thought Nat.

TOURING WITH STALIN

Everyone's giving their all. Nat couldn't tell, however, how his own performance was going. He was sort of numb.

Then came those fateful lines. *When did you last sleep with a woman,* Prisoner 402 spoke and tapped. Nat tried to give the lines as much eagerness as he could possibly muster. Herb had told to him salivate as he spoke the lines, but he just couldn't, God help him, he just couldn't. Dogs are the ones who salivate, not human beings. And besides, the actor was not the one who should be undergoing those feelings, it was the audience, and if he delivered the lines clearly, so that they could be heard in the back of the auditorium and, if he spoke the lines as if he meant them, the playwright's lines would do the rest. *When did you last sleep with a woman,* said Prisoner 402, as loudly and clearly as he possibly could. There was a titter in the audience. *Tell me, tell me. What were her breasts like?,* Prisoner 402 persisted, eager for the response. He heard a gasp and more titters. The hell with it, thought Nat. That was it. He'd done his best. His fate rested in the lap of the gods, or to be more specific in Stanley's lascivious mind, that goddamned womanizer.

The curtain came down on Act One. As they left the stage Nat asked Herb, *Do you think Stanley's out there?*

Probably, said Herb.

But you don't know for sure?

No, said Herb.

The men retired to their dressing room. As they settled in their seats there was a knock at the door. The men exchanged glances, and looked questioningly in the direction of the door.

Come in, said Herb.

The door opened. It was Betsy.

Do you mind if I join you? asked Betsy.

We would consider it an honor, said Ted Lombard, always the gentleman.

Is Stanley out there? asked Betsy.

I don't know, said Herb.

If he were here, he would certainly come back, wouldn't he? Betsy asked.

If he's here, said Herb, *he'll be back. He may be waiting until the end of the show.*

That makes sense, I suppose, said Betsy.

It"s time, said Ralph.

Already? asked Nat.

It's been twelve minutes, said Ralph.

The cast trooped out of the dressing room and took their places for the second act.

There was a universal feeling that the second act went very well. There seemed to be a team spirit prevalent in the performance that had never been there before. The only one who didn't seem caught up in this invigorating atmosphere was Alvin Gorman, as the maniacal Gletkin. But even Alvin seemed to be a more integral part of the cast. There was not that over the top edge to his readings which made his characterization more believable.

When the curtain came down on the final scene the applause seemed stronger than it had ever been. Instead of the one perfunctory bow, Herb led the cast in three bows. As the cast left the stage there were smiles and pats on the back.

I think it went very well, said Ted Lombard. *Didn't you?* he asked Herb, his arm around Herb's shoulder.

I think so, yes.

The cast headed to their dressing rooms. There was still no sign of Stanley. As the men changed into their own clothes there was a knock at the door. This must be Stanley.

Come in, said Herb.

It was one of the young students who helped with the lights. *Mr. Volpe,* said the young man, *Mr. Warren would like to speak to you.*

Where is he?

He's on stage.

I'll be right out, said Herb. *Thank you.* He finished dressing and left the room.

You'd think he'd have the courtesy to come backstage, said Nat.

It went very well, said Ralph.

Well, said Nat, *just in case, it's been nice working with you all.*

Now, now, now, said Ted, *let's not jump to conclusions. I was fired from my first job...*

What was that?, Nat asked.

It was on a tour of "Diamond Lil."

With Mae West?, asked Nat.

That's right, said Ted. *And two weeks later she called me up and hired me back.*

Why did she fire you?, asked Ralph.

I was late for an entrance, said Ted. *She was a tough lady. You had to toe the line. But she could be very generous, too. Holiday presents for everyone, and expensive ones, too.*

Did you work with her in the movies?, asked Nat.

I could have, said Ted, *but Edie and I quit the business then. We had a farm in Iowa, raising corn and raising three kids.*

Do you regret missing all that?, asked Nat.

We didn't miss a thing, said Ted. *Who watches those movies nowadays? And I've got three smart kids that I'm proud of.*

I guess there are priorities, aren't there?, said Nat.

That's right, son.

Nat sat and wondered what his priorities were. He'd thought his career was paramount, and now he began to wonder. Maybe he ought to rethink his life.

Alvin Gorman left without a word.

I don't understand that man, said Ralph.

He has problems, said Ted.

Don't we all?, said Ralph.

He can be very charming, said Paul

All eyes focused on Paul.

I saw him at a bar in Nyack, chatting away with some young man.

I'm glad to learn he's human, said Ted.

Oh, he was human all right, said Paul.

After a moment Nat said, *I wonder what happened to Herb.*

I guess he and Stanley have a lot to talk about, said Ralph.

TOURING WITH STALIN

It's amazing, said Nat.

What?, asked Ralph.

Last summer I was the white haired boy. Stanley really liked me. I mean he went out of his way to keep me on, and then, all of a sudden, he just changes his mind. All right, I am a little young for the part, but he knew that, and I am doing a decent job, I think. He paused for someone to agree with him. No one did, so he remained silent and pondered his fate.

The door opened. Herb entered, followed by Stanley. Nat looked up eagerly. Stanley avoided his eyes.

The show's much better, said Stanley. *Have a good trip.* And he left.

That was it?

Herb put his arm around Nat's shoulder and led him aside.

What did Stanley say? asked Nat.

He said it's much better, but it's still not what it should be.

Does that mean I'm not fired?

He said, "Okay, let him stay on for now. Let's see what happens."

That means I'm not fired.

I'm telling you what he said.

Nat stood bewildered, angry and frustrated. The hell with it, he finally concluded. I'm not fired. I've got the job, and that is that.

Betsy entered through the open doorway. *What's happening?*

I'm buying everyone a drink, said Herb. *One drink! Come on.*

Herb threw one arm around Nat, another around Betsy and led them out of the room, He was followed by Ted, Ralph and Paul. It looked like Nat's confinement in a Russian prison might go on for quite some time.

STALIN

Koba-Stalin, having succeeded in freeing the supply of grain being shipped to Moscow, realized that it was with the military that the power lay. In that area he was far outshone by his rival, Trotsky. His next step was clear enough. With a new found ally, Klim Voroshilov, who was fresh off a military victory, he complained to Lenin that the Tsarist officers appointed by Trotsky were guilty of treason. Lenin reprimanded Koba-Stalin for the fuss he was making about Trotsky, though Koba-Stalin knew that Lenin secretly welcomed it since he, too, looked upon Trotsky as a rival.

Lenin ordered Koba-Stalin to crush the left wing which was causing him a great deal of trouble. Koba-Stalin, stepping up his complaints about Trotsky, obediently delivered the goods, eliminating the annoying opposition within the party. In addition to that he succeeded in supplying Lenin with much needed oil from Baku. Next he joined with Voroshilov in taking an active part in the battle against the insurgents, fighting from an armored train. Unfortunately his military effort was defeated. But it did result in Trotsky's appointee being recalled to Moscow for interrogation. This left Koba-Stalin in charge.

Lenin was informed of a "conspiracy" on the part of some of Trotsky's people. These so-called "conspirators" were loaded onto a barge which sailed down the Volga. There they were summarily shot.

In August of 1918, after Lenin had just finished addressing a group of factory workers, an attempt was made on his life. Trotsky rushed to Moscow, since he did consider himself Lenin's heir. Koba-Stalin decided to remain in Tsaritsyn. He was still not as powerful as his rival, Trotsky, and without Lenin's patronage he felt he didn't have that much power. Lenin, fortunately for Koba-Stalin, was not seriously wounded. The assassin, a woman, was executed.

At this time a student killed the chairman of the CHEKA, a close ally of Trotsky. Trotsky made an impassioned speech calling for retribution. There was a violent debate in the Central Committee. As a result the Bolsheviks launched the Red Terror. Not that the terror hadn't already been in effect since the beginning of the year. It started with the slaughter of the royal family. And then there was Koba-Stalin's elimination of the officers on the barge in Tsaritsyn; there were the dead Jews littering the streets in the towns of the Ukraine in addition to the murder of kulaks, priests and white guardists. The prime motive of the terror was to strike fear in the hearts of everyone, in addition to the fact that nothing works better to unite people than the sharing of guilt.

The flow of blood, however, was beginning to raise some criticism within the party itself. Koba-Stalin added his voice to the complaints. He continued to play both sides of the field. It was recommended that less torture take place. As a result, there was less publicity about the CHEKA's executions, which continued unabated.

Meanwhile the rivalry between Koba-Stalin and Trotsky became more virulent, each calling for the others' dismissal. Trotsky triumphed with several military victories. Koba-Stalin, for the time being, beat a hasty retreat. He sent a congratulatory telegram to his rival.

The first anniversary of the October Revolution was marked with a great celebration. There was no bread in Moscow; there was no firewood, but red banners waved bravely in the air. Basements and doorways gave shelter to homeless children, but a platform was built for Lenin to give a speech. Trotsky, as the heir apparent, stood nearby.

While the anniversary celebration was going on, Alexander Kolchak, a very able Tsarist general was leading a successful uprising across Siberia. Lenin sent Koba-Stalin, who was able to whip the dissolute Red army in the area into shape by a series of executions. Kolchak received a setback, but still remained a threat.

Koba-Stalin's career, however, was on an upswing. Constantly at odds with Trotsky, which secretly pleased Lenin, he was given one title after another, one more responsibility after another. He was sent to Petrograd to prevent it being captured by the White army. Arriving in the city he executed aristocrats, priests, officers...anyone sympathetic, or even suspected of sympathy for the enemy and saved the day. When Moscow was threatened, however, it was Trotsky who saved the day. The rivalry continued unabated.

By 1920 it looked like the Bolsheviks had eliminated the enemy. Kolchak retreated, was captured and shot. His body was pushed through a hole in the ice on the river.

Having engaged in one battle after another, Koba-Stalin was now growing weary of the war. He kept sending letters to Moscow pleading to be recalled. Not only was it a matter of battle fatigue; victory was at hand. The place to be was the capitol. That's where the important activity would now be taking place. In addition to that, Koba-Stalin had reached the age of forty. Nadja, his young wife, was pregnant. He wanted a home where he could also raise his first son, Yasha, with whom he had had little contact.

Back in Moscow there was a great celebration to commemorate the third anniversary of the October Revolution. Here Trotsky shone. Since he hadn't taken part in that momentous event, Koba-Stalin was left to celebrate on the sidelines as an observer.

The man, however, was human, after all. Koba-Stalin fell deathly ill. It was a very serious attack of septic appendicitis. The operation was a complicated and dangerous one. He had a fifty/fifty chance of survival. He was so weak that they decided to use a local anaesthetic. He was in so much pain, however, that they had to sedate him. He barely survived the operation. He lay there pale and corpselike. Lenin inquired about his protege's health twice a day, insisting on learning every single detail.

It was now apparent that Koba-Stalin was Lenin's true heir. Unlike the highly intellectual Trotsky, Lenin and Koba-Stalin were true, bloodthirsty revolutionists, merciless in their dedication to the cause. Anything was permissible if it brought one closer to the goal.

Lenin sent Koba-Stalin to a sanatorium located in his favorite's homeland, the Caucasus. After a month amid the pure mountain air Koba-Stalin recovered. He journeyed to Tiflis, his home town, to attend a party meeting and support a comrade. While in Tiflis he paid a visit to his mother, whom he hadn't seen in quite a while. Lenin, meanwhile, sent an angry telegram to the sanatorium demanding a full report on the health of his protege.

Fully recovered, Koba-Stalin returned to Moscow. In addition to his wife he now had a newborn son named Vasily, as well as Yasha, his firstborn. He requested a convenient apartment. The Kremlin was overcrowded as it was. Lenin, however, insisted on installing Koba-Stalin even if it meant taking over one of the historic state rooms. Trotsky's wife, who was in charge of the Kremlin, protested. Lenin suggested storing the valuable furniture in one of the state rooms in a safe place somewhere. The crisis was solved when a close friend of Lenin gave up his apartment.

Lenin also had the Politburo pass a resolution stating that Koba-Stalin was to spend three days a week in his country cottage, with which he'd been presented. Half in jest, half in earnest he offered Koba-Stalin his sister, Maria, in marriage. He expressed surprise when he learned that his favorite was already married.

Lenin's solicitous treatment of his aide wasn't purely out of sentiment. The Leader would need all the help he could get when he introduced his new plan, a new plan which he feared would arouse a storm of protest.

The New Economic Policy would have made Marx turn over in his grave. The Communist Policy of a state run country, which had been enforced during the Civil war was abandoned. Russia was in dire financial straits and something had to be done. The free market was resurrected. The Bolsheviks began to trade with capitalist countries. Russia, itself, began to resemble a capitalist country. This changeover, which he let people think was a permanent one, actually gave Lenin some breathing space. The terror was still in the offing, and well prepared for.

Confusion, however, ran rampant. Around the world the changeover, was greeted as a pleasant surprise. At home, the right, though suspicious, welcomed the change. The left, however, was appalled. Trotsky, in particular was shocked and perplexed at the sight of women in mink coats driving up to casinos in smart hansom cabs.

First, in order to stem the protest, Lenin forced through a

resolution that opposition within the party was punishable by expulsion. Then in the spring of the following year, 1922, Lenin created the post of General Secretary of the Party. On the face of it, it was a rather routine position. Lenin, however was getting weary. He was also troubled by unexplained headaches. He needed someone to help him control the party. That was one of the tasks of the General Secretary...who turned out to be his ever faithful Koba-Stalin.

It was arranged that Koba-Stalin had the power to decide matters of the greatest importance. Koba-Stalin had his old buddy, Molotov (nicknamed by Lenin "stone arse" because of his endurance) named Second Secretary. Between the two of them they now controlled all appointments within the party.

November 1951

November 8: The Soviets reject a U. S. plan for UN control of atomic power.

The American Drama Guild's touring production of Sidney Kingsley's dramatization of Arthur Koestler's novel Darkness At Noon had been out for two weeks and given nine performances. Wending their way West from the East Coast they played three dates in Pennsylvania, then headed north, played two dates in Ohio, three dates in Illinois and played their ninth date in Eau Claire, Wisconsin.

The show had settled in and was beginning to be well received. As far as the company's personal relationships were concerned, the members of this newly formed family were still trying to assess one another, still trying to be patient with one another. After all, what choice did one have?

Herb Volpe, as leading man, company manager and director, naturally fell into the role of the father figure. Ted Lombard, the oldest member of the cast (he was fifty three) and a veteran of practically all aspects of Show Business from tent shows, to vaudeville, to Broadway (briefly) and a couple of early films, was a rather aloof grandfather figure. Alvin Gorman, a refugee from the West Coast, where he'd made a brief stab at getting into the movies, was engaged with a bitter inner battle with Society. He was the loner, a member of the company, but not really a part of it. Ralph Krumsky, a recent graduate from Syracuse University, where he majored in English literature and minored in Communications, was the eager neophyte, fascinated with the world of the theatre. He looked to Herb for guidance. Paul Thomas, in his early twenties, was the company cynic, with one very youthful Broadway credit and a mistrustful attitude toward the theatre as a career. He was the sort of rebel...without a cause. Nat Brenner was the ambitious young writer, who sought to survive as an actor while he honed his skill as a playwright. When he tore himself away from the umpteenth draft of the play he was working on, he did give some thought to his fellow actors and, subconsciously, he tried to analyze them. Where were they coming from? Where were they going?

And then there was Betsy Landers, about whom just about everyone in the company felt protective. When Betsy accepted the role of Luba, Rubashov's mistress in Stanley Warren's production of Darkness At Noon, she couldn't help but notice that she was the only woman in the company. She hated herself for it, but she couldn't help scanning the cast at the first rehearsal and wondering if there was one member of the company who might turn out to be a likely prospect. "Easy, girl," she said to herself, "You have been through the mill. Then again, if you fall off a horse, the best thing to do is mount it again," which did sound rather lewd. "But let's face it," she told herself. She was a woman as well as an actor. To put it bluntly, she was a female, among a company of males, a hen among a company of roosters.

Betsy didn't particularly enjoy playing Luba. Luba was a submissive woman. In addition to that there were those love scenes with Herb, which was painful enough. With great difficulty, they had somehow sublimated their mutual attraction, which was pointless since Herb was happily married, and established a platonic relationship. Actually it was more like a father/daughter relationship, and then there was Ted Lombard, who was also like a father. If only she were content with that. But no, there was that damned libido!

Well, Alvin Gorman was out of the question. She'd been married to one of those. Paul Thomas was a smartalecky kid, and Ralph Krumsky, sweet as he was, and eager as he was, was really just a boy. Which left Nat Brenner, and she couldn't figure him out. He was certainly attractive enough to be of interest. She wasn't exactly a beauty, she knew that. But she certainly wasn't...ugly. Actually what Betsy had to offer was sweetness, purity and honesty.

In Eau Claire, Wisconsin they played to a full house and the performance had been up. The following morning Betsy and Herb found themselves alone in the coffee shop next to the hotel, which turned out to be a rather seedy one, but was conveniently located.

What do you think of Nat? asked Betsy as she started on her second cup of coffee.

In what way? replied Herb.

Betsy didn't answer.

You find him attractive? Herb continued.

Betsy still didn't answer.

Is it that serious?

No, it isn't serious, said Betsy, rather annoyed. *I was just wondering.*

What do you think of Nat? Herb asked Ralph Krumsky who had just joined them in the booth.

Betsy kicked Herb under the table.

What? asked Herb as he looked innocently at Betsy.

He's okay, said Ralph. *Why?*

I was just wondering, said Herb.

He got a good mention in the review this morning, said Ralph.

Oh? said Herb. *Is the review out?*

Yeah, said Ralph, *and it's not bad.*

Well, that ought to satisfy Stanley, said Herb.

Nat's very good in the role, said Ralph. *Don't you think?*

Yes, he is, said Herb. But Herb was, after all, human, and though he had fought to keep Nat in the company, there was that sense of competition. Nat kept growing in the role of Prisoner 402, and Herb had to work to keep up with the young man, in what was really a supporting role. He looked roguishly at Betsy and said, *I think Betsy may have a crush on Nat.*

Betsy gave Herb a withering glance.

I don't know what gave you that idea, said Betsy, with as much calm as she could muster. There were times when she wondered what she ever saw in Herb. He really was a boor.

You don't have a crush on Nat? Herb continued.

No, I don't, said Betsy, a little too emphatically.

That's good, said Herb, *because I wouldn't want you to make the same mistake twice.*

You think...?

I don't have any proof, said Herb, *if that's what you want to know. However, I am a good judge of character...*
And you think...?
I think Nat Brenner and Alvin are sisters under the skin.
You think so? asked Ralph.

Having made his point, and feeling slightly guilty, Herb rose and picked up his check. *I've got some letters to write. We'll be taking off at two.* After all he did feel responsible for Betsy, and he didn't want to see her hurt, and even if Nat wasn't homosexual, and he probably was, he still wasn't right for a fine woman like Betsy Landers. He approached the cashier, paid his bill and left the coffee shop.

I don't think so, said Ralph.
What's that? asked Betsy.
What he said about Nat, said Ralph. *But, I guess he is sort of wrapped up in himself.*
Oh?

Between the two assessments of Nat, Betsy was beginning to think that maybe she ought to write Nat Brenner off. Even if he wasn't homosexual, he didn't seem to express any interest in her, romantically that is. Though he was certainly pleasant enough, and charismatic...

Though Ralph did not agree with Herb's assessment of Nat, nor did he approve of his voicing an unfounded opinion like that, he was grateful for it. It did much to better his chances with Betsy. After all, who else was there? Paul was the only other young man, and Paul was a spoiled, snooty kid. Of course, Betsy was a little older than he was, and more experienced. But he was intelligent, and he was a man, and he really had great respect for her, and he found her very attractive. What more could she ask for?

I guess I better get packing, said Betsy, and started to reach for her check.
We've got plenty of time, said Ralph.
A woman has more packing to do than a man, said Betsy.

As Betsy reached for her check, Ralph put his hands on hers. *Let me treat you to breakfast,* said Ralph. It was a stupid, clumsy way of going about it, but he had to make his move, and it just came to him, spontaneously.

Thank you, said Betsy. She wasn't quite sure how to respond. The move came so suddenly and it caught her by surprise. Not that she wasn't aware of the fact that Ralph was interested. His eyes lit up every time he saw her. She sat back down and decided to take the bull by the horns. There was no point in leading the poor boy on. *I'm very fond of you,* said Betsy.

Oh, oh, thought Ralph. He waited for the axe to fall.

I'm divorced, you know, said Betsy.

No. No, I didn't, said Ralph. He did, of course and he couldn't understand why he found himself denying it.

And, well, I'm guess I'm just not ready for anymore personal involvements.

How long has it been? asked Ralph.

Almost three years, said Betsy.

That's a long time, said Ralph.

I guess I've just closed the door on that part of my life, said Betsy.

I find that hard to believe, said Ralph. *Aren't you ever lonely?*

Isn't everyone, from time to time, married or single? Involved or not?

I think you have so much more to offer, said Ralph. *It seems to me that just acting, for someone like you, just couldn't be enough.*

Between classes, making rounds, studying and visiting my family every once in a while, by time I get to bed, I am exhausted. Can we be friends? said Betsy, hating herself as she said it. It was so...cliché.

We are that, I think, said Ralph.

Yes, we are, said Betsy.

Well, if you change your mind...

Betsy wasn't quite sure how to end it. A kiss was out of the question, and a handshake was just too corny. She picked up her check, rose, smiled that sweet smile of hers and made her way to the cash register. She waved at Ralph as she went out the door.

Ralph waved back and smiled at her. He was not quite ready to give up hope. They had seven long months ahead of them, and lots of things can happen during seven long months.

STALIN

Koba-Stalin's appointment as Secretary General gave him unprecedented powers. Instructed by Lenin to make way for a younger generation, Koba-Stalin saw to it that the leadership throughout the country was placed in the proper hands, that is to say, men faithful to Lenin. In other words, faithful to Koba-Stalin as well. Trotsky watched with dismay as his rival began to eclipse him.

To bolster the Lenin/Koba-Stalin leadership the bloodthirsty CHEKA was supposedly replaced by an organization known as the GPU, dedicated, ostensibly, to dealing with serious crime. Actually the GPU was still dedicated to eliminating the opposition. In addition to that, they kept tabs on the private lives and private affairs of everyone, including the faithful. The decadent behavior of a number of the Bolsheviks was duly noted.

One of Koba-Stalin's jobs was to oversee the Comintern (Communist International) whose task it was to spread Communism throughout the world. People in Russia were starving, but huge sums of money were sent to Germany, to Italy, to France to bolster the Communist parties in those countries. Koba-Stalin saw to it that these expenditures were kept within reasonable bounds.

To solidify the power of the Bolsheviks Lenin also began a purge, exiling one hundred and sixty eminent intellectuals, professors, writers, philosophers who did not toe the party line. It was at this time that Lenin's career hit a snag from which it would never recover. The Leader suffered a stroke.

Throughout 1921 he'd been the victim of excruciating headaches and attacks of nerves. Koba-Stalin suggested a trip, a vacation to get away from it all. Lenin insisted he was too weak to travel. He spent less and less time in the Kremlin. Since they were considered the best, German doctors were summoned. They removed the bullet which had been left in Lenin's head since the attempted assassination. The operation brought no relief, and it was shortly afterwards that he suffered the stroke. His right side was partly paralyzed and his speech was affected. He had to learn to speak and to write all over again.

Koba-Stalin visited Lenin regularly. They joked about the fact that the doctors forbade him to talk politics. What else was there to talk about? Koba-Stalin wrote an article for Pravda describing his visits with the Leader. There were pictures of the two of them sitting side by side. The so-called purpose of the article was to demonstrate that Lenin was on the road to recovery.

What was not known were certain particulars of their conversations. During his first visit after the stroke Koba-Stalin spent just a few minutes with the stricken man. When he came out of the room he took Lenin's sister aside. He told her that Lenin was convinced he was paralyzed for life and asked Koba-Stalin to give him some poison. Even though the prognosis was not that good, that a second stroke was probable, the sister and Koba-Stalin agreed to try and change Lenin's mind. Koba-Stalin returned to the room. He informed the sick man that he'd just spoken to the doctors and that Lenin's chances of a full recovery were very good. Lenin looked relieved and became hopeful.

During his illness, however, Lenin realized how much power he'd given his protege. He began to have second thoughts. Koba-Stalin was ruthless and, as such, could be useful from time to time, but the thought of this cold blooded man in full charge of the country was alarming. Lenin, fully recovered...for the moment, formed an alliance with Trotsky and began to look for ways to oppose Koba-Stalin and take him down. He found it in the question of the various republics...Ukraine, Belorussia and The Transcaucasian Federation.

Lenin was planing unification. He opposed Koba-Stalin in the manner these satellites were to be handled. Combined with Trotsky he could easily over power his former favorite and unseat him. The formal attack was planned for the upcoming Party Congress.

Koba-Stalin now realized that his former patron was now his enemy. Luckily the struggle proved too much for Lenin. The doctors ordered complete rest for the Leader, hoping to avoid the next imminent stroke. Koba-Stalin saw to it that a resolution was passed that all political information was to be withheld from Lenin. The great man was much too fragile to handle important matters. The Leader was no longer the Leader. Koba-Stalin emerged as Stalin, the most powerful man in Russia.

The struggle for supremacy, however, was not yet won. Lenin contacted Trotsky about taking on another offensive against Stalin. Stalin was well aware of what was transpiring in the Lenin household. He phoned Krupskaya, Lenin's wife, and scolded her soundly for disobeying the doctors' orders and allowing political information to reach Lenin. Krupskaya grew hysterical, sobbing uncontrollably at being so insulted. She complained to Lenin. She wrote a letter to Stalin breaking off relations with him. She soon realized, however, that Stalin was no longer her husband's pet, but a power to be reckoned with. She persuaded Lenin not to send the letter to Stalin which he'd prepared. Stalin realized that he'd gone too far. He decided that humility, at this point, was called for.

Meanwhile Lenin became well enough to start writing a letter to be read after his death. In this letter he warned of the danger the country would be in if Stalin, with his rude, crude, erratic behavior were to be left in charge. He went on to deprecate Trotsky as well. Trotsky was able enough, he wrote, but too vain and by-the-book. A copy of Lenin's letter fell into Stalin's hands. Stalin promptly passed it on to Trotsky, knowing full well that his rival, too, would try to prevent its exposure.

Lenin then added a postscript to this letter advising that Stalin's power be limited. The report of his new attack reached Stalin. Suddenly the doctors forbade Lenin from receiving newspapers and political information. Lenin was fully aware of the real source of this ban. He wrote a letter to Stalin chastising him for insulting his wife. Stalin replied that he was only concerned about the Leader's welfare and, if he'd been overzealous, he would certainly apologize. He then asked the Politburo to be relieved of his duties as caretaker of Lenin. His request was turned down, as he knew it would be. He was left in sole charge of the Leader's welfare.

TOURING WITH STALIN

Word came back that Lenin had suffered a setback. He could neither read, write or speak. Stalin received a letter from Krupskaya, informing him that Lenin had asked for some potassium cyanide. Actually she had decided to poison him herself, but stopped short. She lacked the courage. She needed Stalin's support. Stalin presented her letter to members of the Politburo, to make sure that, when Lenin died, he would be held blameless.

The battle for Lenin's successor heated up. At the next Party Congress Trotsky's supporters spread a rumor that Lenin had named Trotsky as his heir. Trotsky rose and made a brilliant, impassioned speech. Stalin saw to it that the Leader's health would no longer be publicly reported. Lenin, ostensibly, was on the road to recovery. Removed from the Kremlin on a stretcher, Lenin took up residence in his country home. Unflattering photographs were taken of Lenin, giving evidence of his immobile state. Stalin then commissioned a final portrait of Lenin. Krupskaya forbade the painting.

Back in his country home Lenin began to improve. With Krupskaya's help, Lenin slowly regained limited use of his speech. All the while Stalin kept close watch on the Leader's progress. Pamphlets began to appear in the streets, and in the provinces as well, with information that Lenin had always been opposed to Trotsky. Lenin became well enough to make a very brief visit to Moscow. During his visit he made a frantic search in his office for his final letter, the one to be read after his death. It could not be found. Greatly upset, he returned to his country home. It was obvious that his recovery had been short lived. The Leader was now on his last legs.

On this last visit to Moscow Lenin had been accompanied by his wife, as well as his sister, Maria Ulyanova. It was his sister who recorded Lenin's desperate search. This search continued when he reached home. It was the strain of this physical and mental effort which led to his final convulsions. No word was ever mentioned of this frantic search. Maria Ulyanova, who recorded the incident, died soon afterwards.

While Lenin was busy dying, chaos ensued. Trotsky,

supported by a number of followers led a fight for democratization. Stalin counter-attacked by revealing, for the first time, Lenin's secret resolution: "expulsion from the party for factional activity."

The Tsar was gone, but Stalin understood the need for the people of his country for a figure they could look up to in awe, a figure he could lead in worship. Lenin was to be deified. The two men were, actually of one mind and this would go a long way to solidify his position. All sorts of ceremonies were organized in honor of the dying man. The Leader was not yet dead when Stalin brought up the matter of the funeral with the Politburo. Lenin was not to be buried underground like an ordinary mortal. He was to remain with us above ground. Krupskaya objected. She was overpowered by the Central Committee.

Stalin saw to it that the dying man had no visitors. He took no chances in someone upsetting his plans. Trotsky wasn't feeling well and was ordered by his doctors to take a cure at a spa some distance from Moscow. On January 31, 1924 Lenin was felled by a fatal stroke. The body received a temporary embalming so that it could lie in state. It was announced that Lenin would be preserved in his coffin and housed in a specially built mausoleum on Red Square near the Kremlin wall. The city of Petrograd was to be renamed Leningrad.

Stalin sent a telegram to Trotsky informing him that the funeral would be held on Saturday and it would be impossible for him to make it on time. Actually the funeral had been postponed until Sunday. Trotsky was not present at the ceremony. The elaborate funeral began with the arrival of the body on a train. With great solemnity it was borne from the station through the streets of Moscow to the Hall of Columns of The House of Unions. There Lenin lay in state, clad in his khaki tunic. Stalin, also wearing a tunic, stood by. The public was admitted at 7:00 PM. They filed by all night long. It was bitter cold and bonfires were lit, the smoke and the frosty mist created an eerie picture. Following the funeral, expert biochemists, who had been sought out, stepped in to embalm the body in such a unique way that, not only would it be well preserved, but it would look as if it was still alive. The effect was very impressive.

On the eve of the next Party Congress when Lenin's letter was to be read, Krupskaya presented the Central Committee with the important papers. There was great embarrassment. The version of Lenin's letter that was finally read publicly seemed incomplete. Lenin repudiated Stalin, but he was certainly wise enough not to have left a vacuum. He would certainly have recommended a replacement. What were Lenin's last wishes?

Lenin's criticism of his protege without any further suggestions was finally put down to the Leader's illness, and with his irritation that his wife had been offended. After all, the Leader, himself, was the one that had placed Stalin in the position of power. In order to preserve Lenin's reputation, instead of reading the letter publicly, it was given to each delegate to be read in private.

Stalin offered to resign in order to comply with the Leader's wishes. His resignation, of course, was rejected out of hand. Trotsky thought it wise to remain silent. Stalin was now officially elected General Secretary.

Trotsky later spoke of "Stalin's poison." The scientific analysis of Lenin's death rejected arsenic poison. His death was attributed to atherosclerosis. Nevertheless the rumor that Lenin was poisoned persisted.

DECEMBER 1951

After meeting with FBI director, J. Edgar Hoover, Truman announces he will make new efforts to purge the government of disloyal workers.

RALPH KRUMSKY

When Herb Volpe told Betsy Landers, in no uncertain terms, that Nat Brenner was gay Ralph Krumsky was very upset. For one thing Herb had no proof; he admitted that. Here Ralph looked up to Herb as a role model. If only he could turn out the way Herb had, in charge of his life with integrity and know-how. And here was Herb actually defaming a member of the cast, a group which Ralph really took to heart.

Ralph was very disappointed in Herb. He was fond of everyone in the cast. They were his family. He even tried ways to find some line of communication with Alvin Gorman, who defied anyone to like him. And the fact that one member of the cast was casting aspersions on another left him deeply disturbed.

The unpleasant incident took place at a coffee shop in Eau Claire, Wisconsin. When Betsy left the coffee shop Ralph was joined by Nat. Ralph was surprised to see the aspiring playwright, since he routinely got up at the crack of dawn, had his breakfast before most of the cast was out of bed, and returned to his room to work on his play.

I need a break, said Nat. *I'm on the seventh draft and it keeps on growing and growing like Topsy.*

Ralph really liked Nat. He admired the man's dedication, and he did not think Nat was gay.

What's wrong with Betsy? Nat was saying.

What's that? asked Ralph.

I just ran into Betsy, said Nat. *She's always been so friendly. I started to chat with her, and she just cut me short, acted sort of embarrassed, and left. Is she upset about something?*

Without a moment's hesitation Ralph blurted out, *I think you ought to know. Herb told Betsy that you were gay.*

Nat was silent for a moment. Then he chuckled and said, *That's interesting.*

I just thought you ought to know, said Ralph.

Thank you, said Nat. He chuckled again and smiled.

Ralph was puzzled by Nat's reaction. Was Herb right? Nat actually seemed relieved, as if a burden had been lifted. Life gets to be more and more complicated, thought Ralph. It was still hard to believe that Nat was gay. If it had been him he would have been furious.

As a result of this incident his opinion of two people in the company had been altered. Herb was not the saint he thought he was and Nat...well he wasn't quite sure what to make of Nat. He's not denying the allegation, which means... He still couldn't believe it.

At any rate that left Betsy still up for grabs and, despite the fact that she had discouraged him, there were still many months ahead of them. At any rate he had made his interest in her clear and the door was always open.

Little by little, the companionship he had hoped to find seemed less likely to appear. Herb had a lot on his mind, managing the company, performing, driving the van, on the phone with his pregnant wife. Nat always seemed to be in communion with the play he was writing. Alvin Gorman...well, there was no common ground there to speak of. Paul Thomas was just too cynical and too snotty. That left Ted Lombard.

Ralph never tired hearing about all the exciting things Ted had been a part of; working in a carnival as part of a magic act; working in vaudeville as a straight man as part of a comedy team. And then there were all those stories about the fabulous Mae West. Ted had actually been on Broadway in her play, "Diamond Lil." And to top it all he had been in a movie with Gloria Swanson, and he'd actually met Charlie Chaplin at a party.

That was all fine and good, but Ralph finally had to admit to himself that what he was really looking for was romance or, to put it bluntly, sex. He could never discuss this with anyone in the cast, but he was twenty two years old and he was still a virgin. Things finally came to a head in Columbus, Ohio. They were playing the Hartman Theatre, which was really a big one, and the show was run by experienced union stage hands. He became friendly with the stage hands, especially Marty, an old timer who was extremely kind. The company had an extra day in Columbus and Ralph asked Marty what there was to do in Columbus.

And if you wanna get laid, said Marty, *I know of a nice*

lady that doesn't charge too much. I can give you the phone number if you like.

Thank you, said Ralph.

Ralph didn't really want the phone number, but Marty was so amiable, and so eager to be helpful that Ralph, out of politeness, wrote the number down. The young man was still hoping that his first time would be a romantic experience. It did come pretty close during his senior high school year, just before he left for college. The girl he was dating almost gave in, but she changed her mind at the very last minute, which was a very frustrating experience, to say the least. And when he came home for the Christmas holidays the traitor was dating someone else.

At Syracuse University he just didn't seem to be able to make out either. He wasn't exactly a very glamorous figure, he was perfectly aware of that, but guys he knew, who he thought were not so hot, seemed to be making out. He could have gone to the campus whore, but he resented paying for it and, besides, he was on a very tight budget; not that he couldn't have managed it, but he had indulged himself with a season pass to the football games.

After the performance in Columbus that night he had a few beers with Ted Lombard and Herb and Betsy and left them to write a letter home. He had promised to write his young sister regularly. He knew she looked forward to his letters, and he had been neglecting her. He sat down at the desk in his room, took out the hotel stationary and wrote about his recent experiences, the funny things that happened backstage and running into the touring company of "Mister Roberts" in Ashland, Wisconsin where he met a classmate of his who was in the cast.

As he signed his name, with love, he noticed a pinpoint of light on the wall he was facing. He folded the letter, placed it in the envelope and sealed it. He took out his wallet, removed a stamp from the little book of stamps he carried with him and placed the stamp on the envelope, all the while curiously eyeing the pinpoint of light.

He placed the letter on the dresser where he would be sure

to remember to mail it, then walked over to the wall to examine the curious light.

When he put his eye to the wall he found himself looking into the adjacent hotel room. He'd discovered a peephole some enterprising guest had carved out. He was about to walk away when he saw a woman enter the room from the bathroom and begin to undress. This was getting rather interesting. The young lady was really stacked. Not an ounce of fat, and breasts to die for. The naked woman turned to greet a healthy looking, rather well endowed nude man who appeared to be ready for action. With eyes bulging out of their sockets Ralph watched the couple move onto the bed and go into action. Ralph, his heart pounding, unzipped his trousers and joined the party in the only way he could. He got so carried away that he let out a moan. The man, who was pumping away, looked around, then went back to the business at hand.

Having relieved himself of a burden he'd been carrying around for a few weeks, he went to bed hoping for a good night's sleep. In the middle of the night, however, he awoke with an erection which, of course, had to be dealt with. And in the morning, while taking his shower the problem arose again and had to be disposed of.

In the afternoon he joined Betsy, Herb, Ted and Nat for a trip to the Ohio State Campus and then the art museum. As they walked around the campus he remembered that the woman Marty, the stage hand recommended, lived nearby. He decided to take the bull by the horns, so to speak. This was getting ridiculous, a twenty two year old virgin!

The group stopped at a restaurant near the campus for lunch. Ralph excused himself, saying he was going to the men's room. He found a pay phone and searched into his jacket pocket for the phone number. It wasn't there. He looked into the other pocket. It wasn't there. He remembered he'd put the slip of paper with the phone number and address in his wallet. He found the number and dialed.

Hello, said a voice so sexy he envisioned Marilyn Monroe.

Hi, said Ralph. *My name is Ralph. Ralph Krumsky.*

TOURING WITH STALIN

Yes? murmured the sexy voice.

Marty gave me your phone number.

Marty who?

He's the stage hand at the Hartman theatre, said Ralph. *And I was wondering...would you have any time this evening?*

What time?

I don't know, said Ralph. *Say nine o'clock?*

Make it eight, said Doris Sanford. That was her name. Doris Sanford.

How much do you charge? asked Ralph. He remembered that Marty had said fifty dollars, but he wanted to make sure.

Fifty dollars, said Doris. *Have you got fifty dollars?*

Yes, said Ralph.

Have you got the address? asked Doris.

Ralph checked the address, and said he'd see her at eight.

Use the side door, said Doris, and she hung up.

Ralph's got a date, said Herb as Ralph rejoined the group at the table.

What makes you think that? asked Ralph.

I saw you on the phone, said Herb. *Who is she?*

She is my sister, said Ralph. *It's her birthday, and I forgot all about it.*

A likely story, said Ted Lombard.

It's the truth, lied Ralph.

Thankfully the teasing was abandoned and they ordered lunch. The group planned to see a movie after dinner. They were going to see "Monkey Business" with Cary Grant and Marilyn Monroe. Ralph was dying to tell someone that he was going to have some monkey business of his own, with someone who sounded exactly like Marilyn Monroe. After dinner at the restaurant in the hotel, which was quite good and not too expensive, Ralph rose and said he was going to write some letters.

You like Marilyn Monroe, said Nat. *Why don't you come along?*

I'm sort of pooped, said Ralph.

Are you all right? asked Betsy.

TOURING WITH STALIN

Yes. Yes, I'm fine, said Ralph.

We're leaving at eight thirty sharp, said Herb. *We've got a long trip ahead of us.*

Right, said Ralph, and he left the restaurant.

He kept watch from the his window to make sure the group had left for the movie. It was a couple of minutes after seven when he saw them emerge from the hotel and head down the street. He waited five minutes and then raced down the stairs, too impatient to wait for the elevator. He caught the streetcar to the Ohio State Campus, at which stop the woman told him to get off. After asking several times, he located the house.

It was a couple minutes after eight by time he found it. The house was a grey, wooden two story affair with a porch that ran all around it. It had gotten very chilly and he wished he'd worn a sweater under his jacket. As he climbed the three steps onto the porch it began to snow. The door was next to a large, picture window. The venetian blinds were drawn, which added a mystery to the tension. He began to wonder if this was such a good idea. He hesitated, plucked up courage and pushed the bell. When there was no response he pushed it again. Someone moved the venetian blinds aside and peeked out. He couldn't see the face. A few moments later the door opened a crack.

Yes? asked the Marilyn Monroe voice.

It's Ralph. Ralph Krumsky.

You were supposed to use the side door, said Doris. Her voice didn't sound very sexy now.

I'm sorry, said Ralph.

Go around the side, said Doris. *I'll let you in. I don't want all the neighbors to know my business.*

I'm sorry, Ralph repeated.

The door slammed shut. Ralph shivered slightly as he walked around to the side of the house. It was really chilly. He was about to knock on the door when it opened.

Come on in, said Doris.

Ralph entered what looked like the kitchen. He was led through a hallway into a bedroom, a rather seductive, feminine looking room with pink sheets on the bed and frilly little lamps on the small side tables next to the bed. He finally got a look at Doris Sanford. She had a full, round face, with a nice complexion, soft brown eyes, pink lipstick and lustrous brown hair which was not too short and not too long. She was dressed in a quilted orange housecoat. which encased what promised to be a full figure. A chill ran through his body. He hoped he wasn't catching cold.

Can I have the fifty dollars? said Doris. The voice was melodious, but not as sexy as it was on the phone.

Ralph handed her the money which she placed in the pocket of her housecoat.

Why don't you get undressed, said Doris, *and get into bed.*

This was rather a little too businesslike for the young man's taste. He hesitated. Doris walked into another room which looked to be a bathroom. Ralph sighed and proceeded to do as he was told. He removed all his clothes, except for his socks. His feet were really cold. He slipped under the cold silk sheets and lay there shivering. Doris came into the room and took off the housecoat. It was certainly a body to be proud of.

As he gazed at her breasts Prisoner 402's speech echoed in his mind:

What were her breasts like?

Snowy, fitting into champagne glasses, replied Rubashov.

Well her breasts would not have fitted into champagne glasses. They were too large for that, but they were well shaped. But why, for God's sake wasn't he turned on?

Doris lay down beside him and reached under the sheet. She said nothing when she found him unprepared. As he gazed at the expressionless face the woman reminded him of someone. Oh, God! She looked like his mother. The same brown eyes. His teeth started to chatter from the cold. Right then and there he knew the situation was hopeless.

A sound was heard in another room. As Doris manipulated his privates in a rather businesslike manner, she called out, *Marjorie?*

It's me, Marjorie responded.

I'm busy right now, said Doris. *Make yourself comfortable.*
I'm in no rush, said Marjorie. *Take your time.*
She turned to Ralph. *Is this your first time?* she asked.
No, said Ralph.

Doris continued her very businesslike effort, getting just a little too rough. *Have you had sex recently?* asked Doris.

No, said Ralph.

Well, said Doris, *I don't know.*

He felt like saying, let's just give up. She continued her rather disinterested maneuvering, which was really getting to be annoying. Finally she stopped and said, *Look, why don't you come back some other time. I'll give you a rain check.*

Okay, said Ralph. He was glad she stopped before she did any damage.

Doris got out of bed and put on her housecoat. Ralph put his clothes back on. Doris led him through the kitchen to the back door. *You call me any time,* said Doris.

Thank you, said Ralph. His teeth were still chattering.

As he stepped out onto the porch all he could think of was the fifty dollars down the drain. Fifty dollars was a lot of money to throw out, just like that. He found his way back to the main thoroughfare and waited patiently for the streetcar. Luckily the wait wasn't too long. He sat looking reflectively out the window as he traveled through the streets of the alien city. Ah well, he thought, there's still Betsy. Just being in her company was, somehow, gratifying, a promise of someone, some day.

STALIN

After Lenin's death Stalin found himself in the catbird seat. For the moment his only threat was Trotsky. Trotsky's first maneuver was an article praising Lenin for reviving his, Trotsky's, theory for a permanent revolution.

In a political battle the truth is of little or no importance. Stalin asserted that Trotsky "had not or could not have played any part in the party or the October Revolution," which, of course, was a lie. Emphasis was placed on the past disagreements between Trotsky and the dead Messiah. Trotsky insisted that he had converted and was in total alliance with all of Lenin's theories. With the help of the literate, intelligent Bukharin, Stalin continued his attack, revealing the long lasting gap between Lenin and Trotsky. A move was generated to expel Trotsky from the party. To everyone's amazement Stalin opposed the move. Apparently Trotsky's presence might still be of use.

Trotsky's power, however, was severely diminished. The man responsible for the creation of the Red army was no longer chairman of the Revolutionary Military Council. Trotsky's replacement, however, fell ill and died during an operation. The man's wife claimed that he was murdered, and she committed suicide. Stalin's loyal follower, Lim Voroshilov, was then placed in charge of the army. Voroshilov saw to it that all Trotskyists were purged.

Oddly enough, Bukharin, who was now one of Stalin's aides, was head of a right wing, which advocated continuation of the Lenin's NEP, a capitalistic system. Old, staunch members of the Party were appalled. Stalin smoked his pipe and was silent.

Attempts were soon made to unseat Stalin and create a more democratic party. Trotsky decided to sit this one out. He showed his indifference by sitting through the meetings reading French novels. The attempts were easily defeated. Stalin simply got rid of his opponents by appointing them to posts abroad...Prague, Paris, Vienna, Sweden, Persia.

When a subdued Trotsky finally did get up to speak at a Central Committee meeting he was shouted down. Opposing demonstrations were squelched. When Krupskaya, Lenin's widow, spoke in favor of the opposition Stalin jokingly told her that he was thinking of providing Lenin with another widow. Krupskaya became a loyal Stalinist.

While demonstrations by the opposition were being crushed preparations were being made for the tenth anniversary of the October Revolution. The great film director, Eisenstein, was supposed to show his new film "October," but it hadn't been finished in time. Stalin asked if Trotsky was included in the film. The reply was that he was in several scenes. The order came that those scenes had to be eliminated. The film was shown without the Trotsky scenes.

In December, at the fifteenth Congress, Stalin, knowing full well there would be no response, asked that the opposition declare themselves openly, or be dismissed from the party. Of course, no one stepped forward. This was used as an excuse to expel Trotsky and seventy of his followers from the Party. Stalin finally put into action the move he'd been planning for years. Trotsky was dealt the "coup de grace." He was banished. Kicked out of his Kremlin apartment he had to find shelter with a friend.

As a final gesture, Trotsky planned a demonstration on the day of his banishment. Bukharin informed Trotsky that his banishment was postponed for two days. Then immediately an escort arrived to take Trotsky to the train station. When he locked himself in, the door was battered down and he was carried out of the building. Trotsky's son ran through the building ringing doorbells and shouting *They're carrying Trotsky out.* No one opened their door.

At the train station Trotsky's son continued his protest and appealed to the railroad employees to no avail. The station was empty and his pleas fell on deaf ears. Trotsky sailed away on a steamship named "Ilyich," which, ironically, was Lenin's first name. Someone joked, *Moses led the Jews out of Egypt, Stalin led them out of the Politburo.*

Several distinguished emigres had been disgruntled with what had been happening in their country. Gorky, for example, left "to seek medical attention" intending never to return. In an attempt to add luster to his reign, Stalin welcomed the distinguished writer back and persuaded him to stay. The composer, Prokofiev, was also lured back. He was treated royally, and he, too, decided to remain.

It was at this time that the country suffered from a shortage of bread. It was the same old story, the peasants refused to sell the bread to the state at a lower price. Stalin realized that if the NEP continued to be enforced the country would eventually revert to capitalism. The time was now ripe to return to the Marxist policy; a huge industrial economy with one bank, a country with collective farms, controlled by one leader and supported by a huge army; a state ready to realize Lenin's dream of World Revolution.

It was now necessary to crush the bourgeoisie and the wealthy peasants. Agents were sent from village to village, from farm to farm confiscating the grain. Stalin, himself, journeyed to Siberia to confront the peasants. Some of them were bold enough to taunt him. Infuriated, he returned to Moscow and issued a decree declaring harsh punishments for withholding grain.

Bukharin was appalled by the Boss's tactics and opposed him openly. Stalin argued with him in public and privately tried to win him over. Bukharin stood fast. Stalin, unfazed by Bukharin's open and organized opposition forcibly advocated a return to the elimination of the existence of a class society. This elimination, of course, entailed a reign of terror.

The weapon Stalin had and would continually put to use was irrefutable. The Party, like the church, was always right. One had to renounce everything for the good of the party. The country suffered terribly during this reversion to Socialism. There was famine, fear, neighbor betraying neighbor. Living conditions unbearable. The people needed someone to blame for all their afflictions. Thus began the infamous show trials.

The fault of all the agony one had to endure lay at the feet of the abominable traitors. With the help of the GPU these miscreants were publicly unmasked. Once the country was rid of this vermin things would be fine. Members of the GPU became the country's heroes, and there was no greater contribution to the welfare of the land than to inform on ones neighbors. The government was doing what it had to do and you had to do your bit.. It was just a matter of time before everything would be fine. One just had to be patient.

The first spectacle staged for public consumption was the trial of twenty two engineers employed by the Dunbass mines. All during 1927 and 1928 these men were grilled in regard to sabotage. Bewildered, they were informed that if they confessed to their crimes, not only would they be serving their country, their lives would be spared. In court they fell all over themselves professing their guilt and promising to reform. Only five of the twenty two innocent men were executed.

All through 1929 the battle with Bukharin continued. The GPU reported that a group of young Marxists calling themselves the "Bukharin school" met regularly to hear reports from their leader. Little by little the Rightists capitulated and were made to crawl. They were continually denounced in all the media. One trial was followed by another. A group of people belonging to the old Aristocrats were denied work and evicted from their homes. When they sought shelter in a monastery they were arrested and accused of sabotage. And, finally, Bukharin was ousted from the Politburo.

Religion was tossed onto the dust heap. Following in Lenin's footsteps Stalin pulled down church after church. People cheered as these houses of worship were demolished: the famous seventeenth century church of Paraskevi, the Monastery of St. Simon, and the church of the Christ of the Savior, the largest of them all.

In place of the latter Stalin erected the Palace of the Soviets crowned with a statue of the new God, Lenin. Children were told to bring icons to school to feed a huge bonfire. They were given posters of Lenin to replace the icons. Letters to the editor told of former priests breaking from religion forever. The byword of the day was, "Religion is the opiate of the people."

1929 saw the celebration of Stalin's fiftieth birthday. The country broadcast his ascension, and he had much to celebrate. Lenin's followers had all been replaced by loyal Stalinists. The leaders of the Right sang his praises. Bukharin arrived at the Boss's apartment on the night of January 1, 1930 with a bottle of wine to welcome in the new year.

Shortly before his birthday Stalin published an article entitled "The Year of the Great Turn." In this article he explained that the ordinary peasants would not be much of a hindrance in enforcing the collectivization of the farms. It was the kulaks, the wealthy peasants, that were the problem. They had to go.

Cattle trains were commandeered and filled with kulaks, hundreds of thousands of them, destined for the Urals, Kazakhstan and Siberia. The counterrevolutionary activists were either held in camps or shot. Their families were sent far away. It was not always easy to distinguish a kulak from an ordinary peasant and people could vent revenge by pointing a finger at an enemy or a rival.

Fifty thousand families were sent up north to an area prepared to accommodate half that number. People were dropped unceremoniously onto an open steppe surrounded by barbed wire. Rebellions were quashed by the Red Army. The bloodshed was blamed on overzealous inspectors, an excellent motive for a new series of show trials.

When Pope Pius XI called for a day of prayer for the ousted priests and the lost churches, Stalin again blamed overzealous inspectors and went about restoring a few of the churches, an easy way for glossing over what amounted to a pogrom.

The intelligentsia were next. Scholars, scientists and technologists were arrested, tortured and, after they publicly confessed, were executed. This was followed by a wave of show trials involving "The Industrialist Party." Workers clamored for the execution of these traitorous leaders of industry. The Boss himself personally masterminded these show trials. As far as the people were concerned, however, Stalin was the good leader who was served by evil ministers. And the good leader held the country in the palm of his hand by the use of terror.

JANUARY 1952

In his State Of The Union address President Truman states that until the Soviet Union accepts a sound disarmament proposal, and joins in peaceful settlements, we have no choice except to build up our defenses.

ALVIN GORMAN

When Ralph Krumsky tried to befriend Alvin Gorman he met with a blank wall. He did his best to strike up a conversation with this strange man, and was rewarded by a look of surprise, as if to say, What in the world have we got to talk about? Ralph decided that the man had a chip on his shoulder, and that he was determined to be a loner. Actually Alvin was not unappreciative of Ralph's interest, but he really had nothing in common with this naive, innocent young man.

As far as the company was concerned, Alvin was grateful for Herb's paternal interest and his almost infinite patience. Now why hadn't he had a father like that? Not that he wanted to have anything to do with Herb outside of the production. He would have liked to establish some line of communication with Betsy Landers, but Betsy was rather cool, for some strange reason. He didn't like Nat Brenner. Nat smiled benevolently at him, and seemed to find him somehow amusing, and Alvin resented it. He was fascinated by Ted Lombard's colorful showbiz background, but Ted didn't seem very congenial. Which left Paul Thomas. Actually Alvin liked the cold, arrogant young man. The fact of the matter was the two had something in common. They shared a mutual contempt for the entire company.

Alvin was lonely, it's true. But he did have a wonderful role to play each night and he gloried in it. It was a magnificent vessel with which to launch all his frustration, all the bitterness he felt. Why was he chosen to be an outcast, a pariah? Why were people so brutal, so cruel, so insensitive? How could it be a sin to love someone, to see beauty in another man? He poured all his unhappiness in the role of Gletkin, the malevolent, ambitious young Bolshevik. He vented all his anger each night in the role he felt was created for him, personally.

And then there was city after city to look forward to, and who knows who one might meet along the way? One did have to be careful though. There was that unpleasant incident in L.A. where he just escaped being beaten up.

Away from the hustle and bustle of the city, with nothing much to think about, except the performance in the evening, there was plenty of time for reflection. He often thought about Daryl, sweet, silly, irresponsible Daryl. He could never take him back. No, Daryl, for the most part, was a memory, at times extremely pleasant, at times...otherwise. And, during the day, when he sat in the van, looking at the passing scenery which, for the most part, was not very interesting, or in bed at night, just before he fell asleep, he would review his life with Daryl.

There was Daryl in the cottage they rented on Fire Island one summer. He did have a beautiful body, and he knew it, flirting shamelessly. Daryl asleep on the pillow next to him, looking like a little boy. Daryl standing naked in front of the window in the apartment, with that sheepish grin of his.

Good morning, said Daryl. He managed to be bright and cheerful every morning. It would light up one's day.

For God sakes, said Alvin, chuckling fondly, *people will see you.*

So what? said Daryl. *I'm not ashamed of what I've got.*

And the next morning there was a knock at the door. It was a policeman.

May I come in? said the policeman.

Is there anything wrong, asked Alvin.

I'd like to come in, if you don't mind, insisted the policeman.

Alvin stepped aside and the policeman stepped into the apartment. *Do you mind?* said the policeman as he headed for the living room. The policeman stood by the window and looked out. *Do you know that you're in full view of that house across the street?*

I hadn't thought about it, said Alvin.

Yes, well, the woman in that apartment complained that there were strange things going on in here.

What strange things? asked Alvin.

She saw a naked man standing in front of the window.

Well, it certainly wasn't me, said Alvin.

Okay, okay, said the policeman. *I'm just letting you know.*

Thank you, officer, said Alvin.

TOURING WITH STALIN

You might pull down the shades, said the policeman, and he left.

A few minutes later, Daryl finally emerged from the bathroom. This was the morning for his hair treatment, which took half an hour. Daryl was very concerned about making his beautiful curly hair look its most lustrous.

There was a policeman here, said Alvin. *The woman across the street complained about seeing a naked man in front of the window.*

What was she doing, looking into our window? asked Daryl.

You're really too much, said Alvin.

Was he cute? asked Daryl. *The policeman? Was he cute?*

Not really, said Alvin. *And I hope he doesn't visit us again. And I hope you didn't leave a mess in the bathroom.*

You're going to scold me, pouted Daryl.

You are impossible, said Alvin.

Improbable, maybe, said Daryl, *but not impossible.*

Alvin did miss him, but the memory was better than the reality. For one thing, Daryl drank. And when he drank, sweet, charming Daryl turned into a nasty bitch.

You're a lousy actor, you know.

Why are you so bitter? asked Alvin.

Arnold could act circles around you, sneered Daryl. (Arnold was his former lover, who also kicked him out.)

Why don't you go back to Arnold? said Alvin.

Daryl came to see him in summer stock once and, of course, headed straight for the bar. The first words out of his mouth were, *I could play that part better than you, and I'm not an actor.*

You shouldn't run yourself down like that, said Alvin. But it didn't matter what one said to Daryl when he was drunk, since he was in a world of his own.

Oh, yes, Daryl could be very destructive. He should have broken off with him a long time ago. There was the perfect opportunity two years ago, when Alvin, disgusted with his continual drinking, poured the bottle of Scotch down the kitchen sink. They got into a knock down drag out fight. They fell onto the floor, Daryl on top of him. Alvin cried out in pain. *Let me up. I think something's broken.* It turned out he'd sprained his shoulder. He went about in a cast for three weeks and wasn't able to work. If Daryl felt any guilt at all he certainly didn't show it. That's when he should have called it quits. Of course, Daryl did stop drinking when the doctor told him he had to or else.

He was so phony, and he had to be the center of attention. *Oh, Judy was a camp,* he chattered on and on. *She kept us in stitches with her stories about Marlene.*

Afterwards Alvin asked him, *You knew Judy Garland?*

When I was in L.A., said Daryl. *I met her through Arnold.*

Arnold knew Judy Garland?

I introduced him to her, said Daryl.

I thought you said you met her through Arnold, said Alvin. *And that story about Marlene. Judy told that story on the Jack Paar show the other night.*

She's always telling the same stories, said Daryl. *It's part of her repertoire.*

Oh? She has a repertoire, too?

He was simply impervious to sarcasm or downright insults. *You are a liar, Daryl. How can you sit there and lie like that?*

I tell people what they want to hear, he'd say. *I bring a little entertainment into their dreary lives. I'm the tinsel on the tree.*

Alvin would look to the heavens. How can you dislike someone so ingenuous?

But then he started being unfaithful. Once, okay. It won't happen again. But the second time, when Alvin was away, he came home to find a cigarette case on the floor.

Oh, that's mine, said Daryl. *I treated myself.*

For one thing, Daryl, you stopped smoking, said Alvin. *And for another, the initials on this case are WW. You had someone up here, didn't you?*

Nothing happened, said Daryl.

Why is this case in the bedroom? Alvin parried.

TOURING WITH STALIN

Poor dear Daryl, ran out of lies and that was the end. When one starts to soil the nest, that was the end.

Of course, he could be lovable. And surprisingly intelligent. He read quite a bit and had good taste when it came to literature. He loved "The Catcher In The Rye" and he loved "Herzog" by Saul Bellow, and certain actors who were really first class. And he would sit for hours doing crossword puzzles. He was very persistent and often got through the Sunday Times crossword, which was really impossible.

Yes, he did miss Daryl. He used to think he couldn't possibly live with anyone. But, after a while, he wondered how he ever managed by himself. That was until the relationship began to get shaky. There was no reason on earth, however, why he shouldn't meet someone else.

We've got to stop here for gas, said Herb.

They were riding through Oklahoma on a dreary, uninteresting highway. As they turned into the gas station Alvin became aware of the fact that Nat Brenner, who was sitting next to him, had been staring at him, studying him apparently. He looked Nat in the eye and Nat smiled, that irritating, self satisfied smile of his. And then it occurred to Alvin. He's studying me. He's going to put me into that play of his.

Alvin wasn't sure how he felt about that. It all depended, of course, on the role. And, of course, if it were produced... Alvin decided he'd better be a little more cordial in his relationship with Nat.

STALIN

Having rid the country of the kulaks and weeded out the majority of the scientists and intellectuals, the artists were next on Stalin's list. Writers like Isaac Babel and Osip Mandelstam were called in for interrogation by the GPU. In the next room they could hear people being browbeaten into submission. The artists would leave the premises shaken and ready to cooperate.

Maxim Gorky, who, after having left the country and been persuaded to return, was pampered and feted, thus happy to be back. Many well known writers were summoned to Gorky's residence, not knowing what was afoot. The surprise guest at the gathering was the Boss himself. After lecturing the assembly about their duty to nourish the human soul, the writers then became members of a new organization, the Union of Writers, which, of course, would see to it that they followed the party line. Gorky was put in charge of the union and the organization was supervised by Bukharin, who, at that time, was still in favor.

Of course, it wasn't easy to know when one was in favor. The playwright, Mikhail Bulgakov, was in and out of favor many times, but he was one of the lucky ones. He survived.

After uniformity was created among the writers, the Unions of Artists and Composer was established. All the artists now, like the Party, had to adhere to a single creative voice which was in tune with the Party line. Deviation from "socialist realism," as this new form of art was called, was punished by or was threatened with expulsion. As a reward for following the Party line artists were well rewarded; luxurious, rent free studios, extra rations, dachas in the country.

Soon it was those close to him, who differed in any way, who had to go. This would take place by degrees. After a committee meeting, Bukharin returned to the committee room to retrieve something he'd forgotten. Bending down to pick up a pencil he came upon a slip of paper. On it, in Stalin's handwriting, were the words "Bukharin's pupils must be destroyed."

Bukharin was forced to denounce his beliefs as well as his pupils, who were then banished from Moscow. The GPU informed Stalin that the pupils continued to hold meetings and continued to spread "rightist" propaganda. In October of 1932 forty of Bukharin's followers were arrested. Other provocateurs were beginning to be dealt with as well, but on the evening of November 8th Stalin was distracted from this cleanup by a disastrous event in his personal life.

Nadya Alliluyev was the daughter of his close friend. He'd known her since she was a girl. The Alliluyev women were dark and hot tempered. Nadya was also a very merry girl, always laughing and full of fun, and Stalin had always fancied her. She'd been warned that he was a very difficult man, even dangerous. But she was fascinated by this intense, dedicated man with his burning eyes and dark mustache. When he left Moscow for Tsaritsyn she joined him as his secretary and, eventually his mistress. They waited until she was sixteen before she became his wife.

When they returned to Moscow she worked in Lenin's office as a secretary. This position proved of great value to the up and coming Stalin, since she could report to her husband about all the goings on in the office. When she became pregnant she left her job. Too embarrassed to own up to her condition she said that her husband wanted her at home. Lenin just shrugged. His protege sometimes baffled him. There were periodic Party purges and in 1921 she was dropped for inactivity and lack of interest. Lenin had the wife of his favorite reinstated as a probationary member.

Descriptions of her varied. At times she was beautiful. At times she was ugly. It all depended on her mood. There was definitely a sweetness about her. At first she was completely dominated by her husband, the way Stalin's mother had been dominated by his father. But, like her mother-in-law, she soon turned the tables, exhibiting great spirit and defying her husband. As a matter of fact she could sometimes give way to a violent temper.

The initial years of their marriage were happy ones. They lived in a rather luxurious house. She presented him with a son, Vasily, which meant a great deal to him. They were joined by Yakov, also known as Yasha, his son from his previous marriage. He now had a home and a family.

TOURING WITH STALIN

Yasha, however, was reclusive, shy and difficult to relate to. He also had a temper, as did Stalin and Nadya. This sometimes led to some difficult scenes. Though still very young, Yasha decided to marry. Stalin treated the young man with contempt and made fun of him. Yasha made an abortive attempt at suicide. Finally, the young man had enough. He left with his wife for Leningrad and took shelter with the Alliluyevs. Stalin washed his hands of him.

After she gave birth to Vasily, Nadya stopped working and stayed at home. Stalin spent so much time with his male companions that she was left alone and grew bored. She resumed work as a secretary, but quit her job when she became pregnant for a second time. She gave birth to a daughter, Svetlana, a fair haired happy child whom Stalin loved. But life as a housewife, a "baba," was not very satisfactory. A woman was treated as a nonentity if she was not an active Party member.

The marriage continued to be a stormy one. When they were apart they couldn't wait to see each other again, they were so much in love. And whenever they were together, there were constant quarrels. Luckily, when they were in Moscow, they didn't spend much time together. He'd come home in the evening, have his tea and go to bed.

When she was treated rudely, however, Nadya fired back. Once they quarreled so badly that she left him. Just as her mother-in-law took the children and left her husband, Nadya went back home to her family in Leningrad.

When she returned home Nadya decided not to be a "baba" any longer. With the advice of Bukharin, who was a beloved family friend, she decided to take up a profession. She enrolled at the Industrial Academy. Now she would no longer be an embarrassment to her husband who was saddled with an idle housewife. As soon as she entered the Academy she took an interest in Party matters. She came to the defense of the Rightists, swayed no doubt by Bukharin. Stalin mentally made a note of this.

In 1930 Nadya suffered a serious stomach ailment. She was sent to Karlsbad, Germany for treatment. There she spent a great deal of time with her brother, Pavel. He gave her as a gift, for some strange reason, a little Walther revolver. When she returned she joined Stalin in the South, where he was on vacation. She didn't stay long, however. From Moscow she wrote him that she didn't feel wanted. Apparently she was jealous. Now that he was an important figure women flirted with him. The following year the same thing happened. She returned to Moscow early from their summer vacation.

As time went by he gained the reputation as a lady-killer. She thought more and more about leaving him again. There were violent arguments. He became more unfaithful just to spite her. On the evening of November 8th, the anniversary of the October revolution, Nadya took particular care with her appearance. She wore her hair in a new stylish way. She put a tea rose in her hair to go with the rose pattern applique on her new dress.

There are conflicting reports as to what happened at the party that night. According to one witness Stalin flirted with one of the women. Nadya retaliated by flirting with one of the men. Stalin called out to her, *Hey, you!* She answered, *My name isn't Hey."* and left the party. She walked about the Kremlin grounds accompanied by her sister-in-law, Pavel's wife, and complained, *He grumbles all the time. And why did he have to flirt like that?* Nadya then retired to her room and, supposedly, locked her door. Another witness reported that Stalin was drunk and threw cigarette butts and orange rinds at her, and this was what prompted her to leave the party.

One report had it that Stalin was strongly attracted to his sister-in-law, Pavel's beautiful wife, and, while she accompanied Nadya around the Kremlin grounds she may have let slip the fact that Stalin was attracted to her. Nadya then went to her room in a fury and waited for Stalin to return to confront him. He returned drunk. There was a scene. He left. She took out the pistol and, in anger and despair, shot herself. Stalin heard the shot and returned to her room. He found her on the bed in a pool of blood. Realizing that she was dead, and that he might be held responsible for her death, he went back to his room, and pretending ignorance, waited for one of the servants to discover the body.

TOURING WITH STALIN

In the morning the housekeeper, who had brought Nadya's breakfast, found her body with "the pistol in her hand." Shocked and trembling she reported the death. One story has it that Stalin was home at the time of the shot and didn't hear it. Another has him at the dacha, their suburban home. A third version finds him in the Kremlin that morning. Actually it was confirmed that Stalin had been in the house at the time Nadya shot herself. The official version, however, was that he was at the dacha in the company of Molotov.

There are two interesting additional bits of information. For one thing, a doctor's report was discovered stating that Nadya was scheduled for a very serious stomach operation. Could she have been aware of this when she was in Karlsbad and asked for the revolver in case her condition was terminal and she didn't want to endure long suffering? She had been on edge since her return from Karlsbad. Also it was rumored that a note was found near the body, and that it was addressed to Stalin. No one knows for sure what happened to the note, or what it contained, or if there actually was a note.

The means of the woman's death was kept a state secret. The obituary in Pravda read: "A comrade dear to us, a person with a beautiful soul is no more. A young woman, still full of strength, a Bolshevik devoted to the Party and to the Revolution, has departed from us." The official announcement read: "The Central Committee of the All-Union Communist Party with great sadness notifies comrades that on November 9, the death took place of an active and devoted member of the Party."

The funeral was a rushed affair. One story has it that Stalin went up to the coffin and shoved it in anger. According to Molotov, Stalin, who never wept, shed tears and said, *I didn't take enough care of you.* Bukharin's wife reported that Stalin asked them to keep the coffin open. According to her he raised the dead woman's head and "began kissing it."

Horses drew a "magnificent bier draped with a dark red pall, right across the city from the Kremlin to the Novodevichi cemetery. Stalin walked behind the coffin for a short distance.

Since he was an easy target for some possible assassin, he was replaced the rest of the way by a double." Bolsheviks usually cremated their dead. Nadya was buried untouched in her coffin. Afterwards it was announced that she died of acute appendicitis. Then it was said that she died of a heart attack after an operation for appendicitis.

For the rest of that tragic year Stalin made no public appearances. He shut himself up and, with Molotov at his side, he gave himself up to his grief. After the New Year he convened a meeting of the Central Committee where he summed up the success of the industrialization.

After Stalin's death, when the truth came out, the rumor that he was responsible for his wife's death, which had been in existence all along, became even more persistent.

The death of Nadya would have far reaching effects. Stalin would not forget how Bukharin, the beloved family friend, had swayed his wife to side with his enemies, the Rightists.

FEBRUARY 1952

In Lisbon, Portugal NATO convenes its ninth conference, and agrees to raise a 50-division army in Western Europe in order to deter aggression from the Soviet bloc.

TED LOMBARD & HERB VOLPE

December twenty second found the touring company of Darkness At Noon in Galesburg, Illinois. Despite the fact that it was a small town with a population of about thirty thousand and the major source of employment was the railroad yards, Galesburg featured a gem of a theatre. The Orpheum, an ornate building which had served for many years as a vaudeville house, was where the performance took place. The theatre boasted such past luminaries as Jack Benny, George Burns and even Houdini. There were pictures of all three in the lobby.

There was experienced union help available backstage. The evening performance went quite smoothly and, despite a heavy snow storm the day before, it was well attended. The following day was a free one, and there was talk about visiting the Carl Sandburg House. The poet was born in Galesburg and his ashes, together with his wife's, were buried in the garden.

Several members of the company were planning to get together for a drink after the show. Herb excused himself. He was expecting a call from his wife. After the union crew stowed the backdrop in the back of the van, Herb returned to his hotel room.

Herb's wife, Helen, was approaching the fourth month of her pregnancy. During the first week of the tour they spoke every day. It was getting too expensive, however, and they cut it down to three times a week...sometimes four. Helen was upset because she'd gained almost thirty pounds. She was still singing in a choir and, despite being plagued by morning sickness and fatigue, she was planning on making a record, songs and arias.

This evening, for the first time, she complained about constipation and was extremely irritable. It didn't help that her mother was visiting her. They got along fine for the first two days, but after that, as usual, there were little quarrels and disagreements. Helen complained that her mother got too bossy, and treated her like a child. Her mother was scheduled to leave the following day. She would return in a couple of months, when Helen neared the birth of the child. Despite his wife's complaints, Herb was glad his mother-in-law was on hand and would return. He felt so helpless being miles away. Time and again he wondered if he'd done the right thing in accepting the tour. But, of course, there was no alternative. They needed the money, period.

Herb, fully dressed, lay on his bed thinking about Helen in the apartment. He wondered how she looked thirty pounds heavier. She was not exactly thin, to begin with. She was exactly right in every way, and she took great pride in her appearance. And her appearance was important as far as her career was concerned. When she got too ungainly she'd have to put a stop to her little gigs. She did say that the additional weight had no effect on her voice. She said it even helped, and that she was singing better than ever.

There was a knock at the door.

Come in, said Herb.

Ted Lombard entered. *I hope I'm not disturbing you.*

No, no, said Herb. He got off the bed and pointed to a chair. *Have a seat.*

Ted sat down looking rather somber.

You're turning in early? asked Herb.

I've had some bad news, said Ted, his eyes tearing. *My little grandson, less than a year old...he just died.*

I'm so sorry, said Herb.

And here I am, on this stupid tour.

I know, I know, Herb commiserated.

I've been a lousy father, said Ted.

Look, said Herb, *if you wanna take off for the funeral. We've got two free days ahead of us. And if you miss one performance I can have Ralph walk through, holding the book.*

Thanks, said Ted. *It doesn't really pay, does it? I mean, even if I could book a flight, it would cost a fortune. And how much time would I have after all?* After a few moments, he continued. *Edie was really broken up, and bitter. She didn't want me to take this job in the first place. She wanted me to stick it out in L.A. I tried it for a month and I thought I'd go out of my mind, sitting around, waiting for a call. Have you ever tried L.A.?*

No, said Herb. *No, I haven't.*

It's always talk about "the industry, the business." Sure you gotta make a living, but if I wanted to go into business I would have opened a hardware store. We gave it all up for a while, you know. My grandparents had a farm in Kansas, and when they passed away we took it over. The kids were real young and we thought it was a great idea. I got a kick out of it for a while. Back to nature and all of that, and it was really good for the kids. After two and a half years, though, I began to get restless. I missed performing, and so did Edie, though she hated to admit it. We had a magic act for a while. She was my assistant. Edie started out in vaudeville, you know. That's where we met. She was part of a song and dance act with her sister. I'm boring you with all of this. I don't know how I got started.

No, no, no, said Herb.

It's a crazy business, isn't it? I mean, here we are. It's like we're in a world of our own, cut off from everything. Ted remained silent.

I just had a long talk with my wife, said Herb.

How's she doing? asked Ted.

So, so, said Herb. *Her mother's with her now and, after a while, they get on each other's nerves. This is my fourth year out for Stanley, and my last. If it hadn't been for the baby... I don't know how I feel about being a father.*

I'll tell you something, said Ted. *It's the most important role you'll ever play, and the hardest. It's like playing God. Some men take to it like a fish to water, like a cousin of mine. He's like a kid himself, and he really enjoys it. I guess I'm just not the fatherly type. I think I may be a better grandfather.* Ted stopped and started to tear up again. *God damnit!,* he said, and the tears began to flow. *I'm sorry.*

No, no, no, said Herb.

I don't know who I'm crying for, myself or that poor little bugger. Jeff's the one, my son, Jeff. He had a lousy childhood. We dragged him from one place to another; tore him away from his friends and his school. I'm really proud of him though, the way he turned out. I don't think I was much of a help. You don't realize how important family is until you get older.

I don't know what kind of a father I'm going to make, said Herb. *I don't think I'm ready for it.*

One is never ready for it, said Ted. *No, I think you're gonna make a helluva father. It's a matter of type casting. I'm not really right for the role. You are.*

You thinks so?

I can tell by the way you handle this company, said Ted. *I wouldn't have the patience you have. I wouldn't have stood up for Nat, the way you did. And the way you handle Alvin. I would have kicked his ass, that arrogant son-of-a-bitch.*

Where's your son now? asked Herb.

He's in Colorado, said Ted. *He runs a little radio station there. I guess I should call him. I don't know what to say to him. I'm afraid I might just break down and cry, which would embarrass the both of us. I never used to be able to cry. Edie used to say I had a heart of stone. I guess old age has something to do with it.*

You're not old, said Herb.

I'll be fifty four in March, said Ted.

That's not old, said Herb.

It all depends on the kind of life you've led, said Ted. *I can't wait till I start collecting my pension.*

Maybe you oughta call him, your son, I mean, said Herb.

You think so?

The two men were silent then Herb spoke up. *Ted?*

Yes?

Why do you think you were a lousy father?

I don't know, said Ted. *I certainly didn't start out to be. I thought when I had a kid I wouldn't be like my father. Oh, he wasn't abusive, or anything like that. He just didn't pay any attention to me and my brother. It was as if we didn't exist. And I thought to myself, when I have kids I would never be like that. I'd be a real father.*

And?

I don't know, said Ted. *I guess I felt that they were getting too much love, from their mother, from their aunts and all those relatives. I felt that they ought to be aware of the fact that not everyone in the world is gonna love you. I guess I was wrong. Maybe a child can't get too much love. When the kids were grown I tried to reach out to them, but it was too late. Especially with my son. I thought that maybe we could be friends, buddies, but it just didn't work out that way. There's this gap between us. And sometimes I blame my wife. But it wasn't her fault. It was me. It's all very complicated, human relationships.*

The two men sat pondering human relationships. There was a knock at the door.

Come in, said Herb.

Ralph Krumsky followed by Betsy Landers entered the room. They both looked from Herb to Ted.

Is everything all right? asked Ralph.

Ted's little grandson died, said Herb.

Ohhhh, said Betsy. *I'm so sorry.*

Thank you, said Ted. *I think I'm gonna turn in.*

Is there anything we can do? asked Betsy.

I wish there were, my dear, said Ted. *I wish there were.* Ted rose and kissed Betsy on the cheek. He looked at the two men. *Good night,* he said and left the room, closing the door behind him.

How awful!!, said Betsy. She turned to Herb. *Is Helen all right?,* she asked.

Yeah, she's fine, said Herb.

Well, I guess I'm gonna turn it, said Ralph.

Are you going to the Carl Sandburg home tomorrow? asked Betsy.

Yeah, sure, said Herb.

Well, good night, said Ralph.

Good night, said Herb.

Good night, said Betsy, and she followed Ralph out of the room, closing the door behind her.

Herb sat in the chair for the longest time, contemplating fatherhood, and parenthood and marriage and what sort of a role lay in store for him in real life.

STALIN

Just as life changed for Stalin after the death of his wife, life changed for everyone around him. The Boss had no wife to sit beside him. Therefore his associates could not have a wife beside them. All gatherings, political and social, were strictly male. If there were women present at any occasion, they were seated separately.

His mother was told that Nadya died of appendicitis. She sent him jam and fruit. But he never visited her. He wrote charming letters, and sent pictures of the children.

He built a new dacha for himself in a suburb of Moscow, where he slept and spent a great deal of time. The children were left in the old one, which had memories of the dead wife. The daughter, young Svetlana, was the mistress of the house. He adored her, and they played games. She would issue orders and he would have to obey. Order number one: Papa must take Svetlana to the theatre. Papa took Svetlana to the theatre.

For the country the year following his wife's death was a comparatively peaceful one. The show trials came to a halt. The seizing of the grain and the elimination of the kulaks seem to have had its effect. People seemed better off. Government officials began to live like aristocrats. Officially, of course, all the luxuries they enjoyed were owned by the state, a perfect excuse to reside in a magnificent home and drive about in a fancy car. Similarity, however, to life under the tsar could not be denied. Government officials did not, as Lenin had planned, live like everyone else.

The year was marked by celebrations. The opening of a canal or the rescue of sailors in danger were cause for the country to enjoy elaborate ceremonies. A gigantic new airplane, the Maxim Gorky, was built. It was the largest airplane in the world. Stalin seemed to be at the height of his powers and popularity. People fell all over themselves to praise him and all that he'd accomplished.

Behind this glorious picture, however, all was not that rosy. There were some old Bolsheviks who were not happy with Stalin's autocratic power. They approached Sergei Kirov, a political associate, and asked him to run for Secretary General. Kirov, a close friend of Stalin, refused and was foolish enough to report the offer to the Boss.

The conclusion of the Seventeenth Congress was the election of the Central Committee by secret ballot. When the votes were counted there were a surprisingly number of votes cast against Stalin. He was elected Secretary General, and the news of the negative votes was accepted calmly. The repercussions were to be enormous.

A prelude, perhaps, of what was to come was the arrest of the poet, Osip Mandelstam. This came as a great shock and caused quite a stir. All the poet's letters, phone numbers and manuscripts were confiscated. He was confronted with the poem he'd written about Stalin:

"We don't live, we just nervously tiptoe through his life
At ten paces our words are mere silence
And if an occasion for converse occurs
We remember the man from the Highlands
In the Kremlin, with chicken-necked chieftains all around
The rabble he mocks and relies on

....

His whiskers droop, roachlike, from under his nose."

When Mandelstam admitted that he was the author, he was questioned about to whom he'd shown the poem. He was then grilled as to their reactions. A confused and broken man he confessed everything in great detail. When his wife visited him the grief-stricken man told her to warn the people he'd discussed. Mandelstam was banished. In exile he hallucinated and suffered a nervous breakdown. Boris Pasternak came to the man's defense. He approached Bukharin who pleaded with Stalin to bring the poet back. Stalin, pretending he knew nothing about the incident, phoned Pasternak and reprimanded him for not coming to the aid of a fellow artist. Mandelstam was brought back. Stalin was hailed for his magnanimity. And Mandelstam was restored to his former state...for the time being.

Lenin once pointed out that each generation of revolutionaries became a hindrance to those that followed. Progress could only be made when these hindrances have been removed. The negative votes that Stalin received gave him his cue. Actually those who were in power had been so for twenty years and were beginning to show their age. In addition to that most of them were semiliterate. The country needed new blood, equipped to run an industrial nation. Of course, the old generation could be retired. But those in retirement could be a hotbed for counterrevolution. And, after all, according to Lenin, "You can't make a revolution in white gloves."

The bloodbath began with Kirov. On November 28, 1934 Stalin spent two hours with his friend and close associate. He asked him to move to Moscow. The next evening the two men were at the theatre together. Stalin took him to the train station. On the platform he kissed his good friend goodbye. On December 1st Kirov was walking down the corridor of the Smolny Institute, the Bolshevik headquarters in Leningrad. For some strange (or convenient) reason there were no security guards on duty. As Kirov walked through a narrow passageway leading to his private office, a young man emerged from the darkness. A shot rang out. A secretary rushed out of the office to investigate. Kirov lay on the floor. He was dead.

That very evening Stalin issued a decree. Investigation of terrorist acts against officials were to be completed within a period of ten days. No public prosecutor or counsel would be assigned to the trial. Appeals were not to be heard. The mandatory death sentence was to be carried out at once.

Later that evening Stalin, accompanied by Molotov and two high executioners, set out for Leningrad. He was greeted by Medved, the head of Security Police in Leningrad. Without a word Stalin slapped Medved in the face. Stalin conducted the investigation himself. Apparently young Nikolaev, Kirov's killer, was put up to the crime. He claimed he received the revolver from the head of the Leningrad branch of the NKVD, the new name for the GPU. One witness reported that Stalin ordered, *Take him away,* and after the young man was removed Stalin, snapped, *The prick!*

TOURING WITH STALIN

Stalin banished the Leningrad NKVD chiefs to the Far East, where they lived in comfort.

The examination of Nikolaev lasted twenty seven days. He was a member of the Communist Youth Organization. At the age of sixteen he fought at the front. He worked briefly for the GPU. After he left he held minor posts, but never reached the position he dreamed of. He was a bitter, disappointed young man. Someone told him that his ex-wife was having an affair with Kirov. He confessed to the crime. He was shot immediately.

Kirov's body was displayed in the Hall of Commons of The House of Unions. The street was closed to the public. Red Army guards blocked the entrance. The hall was brightly lit and beautifully decorated with plush banners. Kirov lay in a simple open coffin while a small orchestra played appropriate music. The ceremony was attended by a small, intimate group. Stalin stood near the coffin. As the lights dimmed and the music stopped the guards prepared to nail down the lid of the coffin. Before they could do so Stalin bent down and kissed the brow of his dead friend. Everyone wept, even the men. Later Stalin was heard to say that now he was all alone in the world. He'd lost his wife and his best friend.

No concrete evidence has ever been found to prove that Stalin ordered the death of Kirov. What is known is that Stalin called in Yagoda, one of the heads of the NKVD, several times and asked him to watch Kirov as carefully as possible. The hint was enough. Even the public at large believed that Stalin was responsible for the assassination. A popular song ran, "Stalin murdered comrade Kirov/in his office corridor."

Yagoda, Stalin's lord high executioner, unaware of how high the Boss was aiming, proceeded to arrest priests, ex-landowners and the usual culprits. When Stalin tried to point the way he was heading, Yagoda seemed unable, or unwilling, to take the hint. Stalin then turned to Nikolai Yezhov, a man he'd met in Siberia when he visited there to speed up the grain shipments. Yezhov had become chairman of the Central Control Commission and a secretary of the Central Committee. Though he rose to a vital position in the government, the man was not a very impressive figure. He was extremely short and had a weak voice. Eager to please, he kept an eye on Yagoda, whom he'd succeeded and, for a time became Stalin's mouthpiece.

Mandelstam had been a brief prelude. Kirov was the opening number. The bloody symphony was set to begin.

MARCH 1952

The Supreme Court upholds New York's Feinberg law banning communists from teaching in public schools.

PAUL THOMAS & NAT BRENNER

The reason Paul Thomas and Nat Brenner usually shared a hotel room was a purely financial one. They were both trying to save. The relationship between the two, however, was sort of a sadomasochistic one.

Paul enjoyed pricking holes in Nat's balloons. Paul Thomas was a frustrated young man who didn't know what he wanted to do. He'd been involved in show business for as long as he could remember, and didn't particularly enjoy it. Oh, there were moments when it was sort of fun, but the insecurity of it, the phoniness. He'd seen talented people fall by the wayside, and mediocre performers become big stars. But the Business was what he'd known all his life, from work as a model in his childhood, to work on the radio and his one Broadway show, as one of the Clarence Day children in "Life With Mother," the follow up to the record-breaking success, "Life With Father." He'd reached the pinnacle and, looking down from the heights, he saw nothing but disillusion.

Actually the reason for Paul's attacks was twofold. Yes, there was this sense of release from the frustrating indecision he was facing about what to do with his life. But then again, he really wanted to save the damned fool from more heartache. Did the idiot really know what he was in for? The silly ass with stars in his eyes was certainly old enough to know better.

Nat, on the other hand, welcomed the discomfort caused by Paul's jibes. They were a challenge, a practice session. It seemed to him his life, so far, had been a series of rejections, the latest being the desertion by his wife, whom he thought loved and believed in him. Then there was the continual rejection of his plays and, of course, his daily rejection as an actor, as he faithfully made the rounds of agents, producers and some newfangled obstacle known as a casting director. Why one needed someone special just to cast a play seemed beyond ridiculous. There were agents, there were directors and there were producers. Wasn't that enough? At any rate, Nat used Paul's taunts as a way of hardening himself in preparation for further possible rejections.

The tour of Darkness At Noon was like a shot in the arm for Nat Brenner. It reaffirmed his faith in himself as an actor. He'd survived being fired on opening night, and now he was garnering major attention in what was definitely a supporting role. The mentions he received were enough to turn one's head. He'd been around long enough, however, to take it in his stride. But he certainly intended to make the most of it. When he got back to New York these notices would surely impress the powers that be.

In each city after each performance he'd scan the local papers and find the review. If it didn't appear he saw to it that someone at the hotel would forward a copy to him. If he received a good notice he always tried to acquire two copies. One copy he'd save in its entirety. The other he'd just clip out the section that extolled his performance and paste it into his scrapbook, which he bought in Ashland, Wisconsin where he received his first memorable mention.

Periodically he'd sit and read and reread those unbelievably glowing notices:

Ashland, Wisconsin. The Daily Press: "We were 'knocked cold' by the gripping characterization of Herbert Volpe as Rubashov, the first generation Bolshevik, and Nat Brenner, who took the part, or rather lived the part, of Prisoner 402, the czarist."

Ponca City, Oklahoma. The Ponca City News: "Brenner, a newcomer to Ponca City, immediately captured the attention of the audience with his fine voice. His lines were clever and he handled them well.....It was Rubashov and 402 who held the center of attention throughout the play."

Great Bend, Kansas. The Great Bend Daily Tribune: "Much of the impact of the production came from the reflections of the eerie 402, a Tsarist who had been in prison for 20 years and had some 6,000 days to spend without a girl. The role was played by Nat Brenner."

And then there was his favorite so far.

Big Spring, Texas. The Big Spring Daily Herald: Nat Brenner is superb as 402 and is convincing as an example of what long imprisonment and torture can do to the human soul. He has reverted to childhood ways and is truly more a number than a human being." There, Stanley Warren, what do you think of that?!

TOURING WITH STALIN

Paul laughed as he watched Nat paste this last notice into his scrapbook. *You don't really believe all that shit,* said Paul.

It's not important, said Nat, *whether I believe it or not. What's important is that others believe it.*

The fact that Nat seemed impervious to these attacks really began to irritate Paul. All right, the man was a fool, but maybe one had to be a fool in order to weather the storm. Then again, it occurred to him, maybe he was the fool.

He'd been good so far. He'd limited himself to two drinks after the performance, and he made a point of not drinking alone. Drinking with his coworkers, not only kept him from going over the top, it enabled him to study them and predict the dire future of those poor besotted fools.

This was Herb's fourth time out for Stanley Warren. Herb must be pushing forty, and he still didn't have anything to show for it. And now he was going to be a father, and he was married to a performer as well, and Herb was no Laurence Olivier. He had a great role and, as far as Paul was concerned, Herb was just adequate. Future? None.

Betsy was no great shakes either. She was not without talent, but she'd been around long enough, and she certainly should have made her mark by now. Future? A very big "maybe."

Ted Thomas was in his twilight years. Forget Ted Thomas. Ralph Krumsky on the other hand had possibilities. No great shakes as an actor, but he was a good type, and he was young.

Alvin Gorman was a freak. The fact that he was gay certainly didn't stand in his way. There were so many in the business. But he was strange. Future: None.

That left Nat Brenner, who was the most talented of the lot. But that didn't mean a thing. He didn't have the charisma that made one a star. He did have a certain charm, but he was childlike. Future? A very big question mark.

A rumination similar to this took place at the Big Spring Watering Hole, a popular bar a few blocks from the hotel. The rest of his coworkers had returned to the hotel. Ralph Krumsky, Betsy and Ted Thomas to write some letters, Herb to receive a phone call from his wife. Herb seemed to be concerned about her and the problems she was going through during her pregnancy.

The crowd at the bar was a raucous one. Paul welcomed the noise. It helped dim his ability for further thought. He sat in the booth studying the patrons with contempt. The women were just as crude and loud as the men. What ever happened to womanhood? Whatever happened to the cowboys of yore? The John Waynes? The Gary Coopers? The Randolph Scotts? These yahoos...that's what they were, yahoos. Drunk, loud and boorish. And that goddamned music. It was not only deafening, it wasn't even music. God save us from Country Westerns, that irritating nasal twang. That was singing?

Excuse me.

Paul looked up to see a huge man in jeans and western type shirt standing over him.

Are you expecting anyone? the man continued.

Yes. Yes, I am, said Paul.

I was just asking, said the man, and he moved away.

Paul watched the man make his way through the crowd and enter into a conversation with someone in a dark suit, who looked like he was in charge. The man in the dark suit headed for the booth Paul was sitting in.

I beg your pardon, said the man in the dark suit, *but are your friends returning?*

Yes, said Paul. *They are returning. And while you're at it, could you play a song on that goddamned jukebox?*

You don't like the music? asked the man in the dark suit, very politely.

I haven't heard any yet, said Paul. That'll put him in his place, he said to himself, quite pleased with his clever repartee..

In that case, said the man in the dark suit, *I suggest that you leave.*

Are you throwing me out? said Paul defiantly.

Not yet, said the man in the black suit. *I hope we don't have to.*

In that case, said Paul, *I'll have another Scotch.*

We're out of Scotch.
What about bourbon?
We're out of bourbon.
I see, said Paul.
I hope so, said the man in the black suit.

Unaware of the man in the black suit nodding to another man in a black suit, Paul suddenly found himself being hauled out of the booth. Holding firmly to each of his arms the two men in the black suits escorted the inebriated young man through the crowd. When they reached the swinging doors he made the rest of the journey alone.

Out on the street the brisk, cold air cleared his mind somewhat. He turned around, was about to reenter the saloon, then changed his mind. Those men were too big. He shoved one of the swinging doors and watched it sway back and forth then come to a halt. That was fun. He tried it again. He was about to try it a third time when he heard *Excuse me.* Someone was trying to address him.

He whirled about to face a middle-aged couple who were apparently preparing to enter the saloon. Paul stepped back and bowed low. *Be my guest,* said the young man.

Thank you, said the woman and smiled politely.

You're welcome, said Paul.

There are some civilized people here, after all, he said to himself. Proud of his gallantry he started unsteadedly down the street toward the hotel, that shitty hotel, and that smug Nat Brenner. Well, at least he could talk to Nat. Teasing the poor fool was the only thing that kept him from going bananas on this second hand tour. In a couple of months he'd have enough set aside and would be able to give his notice. Back to civilization.

He thought about his mother, working as a sales clerk in Bloomingdales, dressing up each morning as if she were about to give a performance...pretentious ass with her phoney airs. He watched her once from the distance dealing with a customer. What a ham, mincing and posing! And that deprecating look she'd give him when he'd come home for dinner on a Sunday. Why aren't you a star, those eyes looked at him accusingly. After all the trouble I took. You're a failure. I'm not the failure. She is. I never wanted to be a star, she did. I just wanted to make her happy. Well, she has Gary to make her happy, brother Gary and the little grandson he's given her. And he kicked the trash can on the corner, nearly tipping it over. He was nearly hit by a car as he crossed the street. He could hear the driver cursing him as the man looked back at him through the open window of the car. Fuck you, buddy!

He staggered into the lobby of the hotel. At the desk he asked for his key from the boring looking almost bald desk clerk. Why do desk clerks always look so boring? And why are they all so bald? He pushed the button for the elevator. After a few seconds he started banging on the door. The slowest elevator in Big Water. No, Big Spring. What's the difference? He noticed the clerk staring at him.

Slow elevator, he said, smiling cheerfully at the clerk, who looked away and went back to his newspaper. And why are desk clerk's always reading newspapers? Is that all they have to do?

The elevator door opened slowly and he stepped in. He hesitated for a moment. He thought he was on the third floor. Yes, that was it. Third floor. He pushed the button. The elevator jolted as it started. Fucking elevator! He stood staring at the floor, not seeing anything. He was beginning to feel absolutely numb. He did remember the room number. 301. He opened the door very quietly. Mustn't wake the asshole. He turned and looked for the light switch.

He turned on the light and closed the door very softly. He tiptoed past Nat who was fast asleep. He fell onto his bed face first and was about to close his eyes when he realized he'd left the key in the keyhole and he'd forgotten to turn off the light. Fuck it!

By this time Nat was awake. He was facing Paul's bed. He opened one eye and watched Paul sit up on his bed, take off his shoe and hurl it at the ceiling. There was a loud crash and a thud as the shoe hit the chandelier shattering it and raining down a shower of glass. The room was dark. Paul's head touched the pillow and he was out like the light.

Nat made a note to be very careful when he got up during the night or in the morning. He would not be able to paddle barefoot about the room. He also made a note to inform Herb that when Herb made reservations in advance, as he often did, he would not be rooming with Paul anymore.

STALIN

The curtain was about to rise on the famous Show Trials and the bloodbath that followed. The assassination of Kirov, the close friend and colleague of Stalin, heralded its beginning. The assassin confessed to the murder and was shot without a trial. In his confession, however, it was said that he claimed to have been put up to the deed by the followers of Trotsky and Zinoviev, a prominent revolutionary veteran and member of the Central Committee. At a meeting of the Central Committee Zinoviev joined loudly in the condemnation of the assassination. Nevertheless followers of Zinoviev and Kamenev, a prominent politico and close associate of Zinoviev, were rounded up and arrested. One week later the two veteran revolutionaries were visited by the NKVD and found themselves in prison.

From his prison cell, the bewildered Zinoviev wrote a frantic letter to Stalin protesting his innocence and his loyalty to the Boss. The letter was never answered. Stalin had chosen his first victims very carefully. He knew the two men were weak and would easily cave in. Yagoda, head of the NKVD and Stalin's hatchet man, however, had too much respect for the two victims and treated them with kid gloves. As a result a confession could not be squeezed out of the two veterans. At the end of two months Stalin grew impatient. He met secretly with the two men and, apparently, a bargain was struck. The next day the two confessed their guilt. It's true. They'd been conspiring against the Party. On January 16, 1935 Zinoviev was sentenced to ten years in prison, Kamenev to five.

The arrest of Zinoviev and Kamenev was followed by a wave of arrests. One politico who came to the defense of the two men found himself charged with being the center of a conspiracy. The man's protest made it worse for Kamenev, who was found guilty of further conspiracy and had five years added to his sentence. Anyone who expressed dissatisfaction with the arrests was added to the list of conspirators. It would appear that there was a vast network of conspirators planning to assassinate the Boss. Either that or they were planning a counter revolution.

Appended to this scurrilous list were witnesses to the death of Stalin's wife who made the mistake of talking too much. Several members of his household were sent to the camps never to be heard of again. Wives of the suspects were also included. Kamenev's wife, for example who happened to be Trotsky's sister, was a prime choice. One hundred and ten prominent people were sentenced to prison. In April of 1935 a new law was passed. Children twelve years and older were to receive the same punishment as an adult. This included the death penalty.

After the first wave of arrests the country was allowed a brief respite. During this lull, the magnificent Moscow Metro was opened. Svetlana, Stalin's daughter wanted to take a ride through this glorious new underground. The Boss, himself, decided to accompany his daughter. He rejected the proposal that they go at midnight when it would be safer, since the Metro would be closed to the public. He insisted on going at once without waiting for any safety precautions to be put in place. As he strode through this shining proof of the triumph of Communism his appearance, of course, created a sensation. He was showered with adulation and he bathed in the warm enthusiastic reception. He appeared to be touched by the love of the people. *The people need a tsar*, he was quoted as saying.

He installed his mother in the former palace of the Viceroys of Georgia. Ignoring the ornate luxuries, she chose to live in a plain little room, at a distance from the main building. She had two attendants to look after her. She had her own private physician and wanted for nothing. He wrote to her regularly. He sent the children to see her, and he decided it was time to pay her a visit. The visit, of course, was well publicized. Articles appeared in Pravda, making it appear as if Christ was visiting his mother, the virgin Mary. When his mother asked him exactly what it was he did, he replied that he was something like a tsar. It was reported that she replied, *You'd have done better to become a priest.*

He was still haunted by the suicide of his wife. How could she do that, he asked himself, she who had so condemned the attempted suicide of Yasha, his first wife's son? How could she desert her two children, to say nothing of me? She has crippled me for life. He changed radically the running of the household. Agents of the NKVD took charge of its supervision.

His personal bodyguard looked after the children and reported their progress to Stalin. Without a mother the daughter, Svetlana, seemed to be coping. The son, Vasily, however, was a problem. He was terribly spoiled and self indulgent. He did badly in school, often cutting classes. Stalin was not very fond of Yasha, the son by his first wife, but he loved Vasily. Despite his love, however, he was painfully aware of Vasily's shortcomings and complimented one of his teachers who tried conscientiously to deal with the boy.

His plan for the continuation of the show trials was masked by the preparation of a constitution which promised democracy. The world at large was presented with a rosy picture of Communist Russia. He established diplomatic relations with the United States. He joined the League of Nations and promoted collective security.

Whatever the West really thought of Stalin they found it necessary to welcome him into the fold. Hitler had re-armed. The West had not. They looked to Stalin for support, and he was clever enough not to disappoint. He sent Soviet tanks, guns and NKVD agents to Spain to help fight the fascists who were supported by Hitler.

1936 saw a good harvest and, all in all, it was a good year to continue with his purge. At a conference of the NKVD the members were told that a gigantic conspiracy had been discovered. Trotsky, Kamenev and Zinoviev were its most prominent leaders. The Boss, himself, would supervise the investigation, assisted by the zealous Yezhov. Though those present knew there was no conspiracy, they also knew that one had to exist for the sake of the Party. They quickly got the message when a circular was read stating that torture or any form of illegal interrogation would not be tolerated. Hundreds of people were rounded up from prisons, from exiles. These so-called conspirators were all former party leaders, the remnants of Lenin's old guard. They were sent to Moscow to stand trial. The star defendant in these trials was to be Zinoviev, with Kamenev not too far behind.

TOURING WITH STALIN

In his prison cell the former powerful figure continued to write letter after letter pleading pitifully for his freedom. As time wore on he realized his pleas were falling on deaf ears. He begged the Boss to spare his son a "talented Marxist with a scholarly bent." There was no need to torture Zinoviev. He was a broken man and was ready to plead guilty for the sake of the Party. Kamenev, on the other hand, needed what might be called a little "physical pressure" to come to his senses. The two men stood trial, along with a number of other loyal Leninists, fully convinced that by pleading guilty they would be granted a pardon.

There was one thorn on the rose of Communism that was particularly difficult to remove. The writer, Gorky, was adamant in his defense of Kamenev. They were partners in a publishing house which, in the process, came under attack. Gorky was furious. He let it be known that he was leaving the country. Stalin gave orders to prevent his departure. Gorky became a virtual prisoner; his secretary was his prison guard.

Everything seemed to be going wrong for this famous man of letters. Yagoda began a wildly public affair with his daughter-in-law. The largest plane in the world, that was named after him, crashed. He pleaded with the French poet, Aragon, to pay him a visit. When the poet and his wife arrived they were persuaded to delay their meeting with Gorky. They were encouraged to spend some time with relatives in Petrograd. By the time they finally got to Moscow they found Gorky on his death bed. The great writer was given a magnificent funeral. Not all the Bolsheviks who were marked for distinction were shot. Some, very conveniently, just happened to die. Yagoda was in charge of a well stocked toxicological laboratory which was housed in the NKVD building.

The trial, which also served as the opening of the Moscow theatre season, took place in the building where Kirov had recently lain in state. The room, ironically enough, was called the October Room. It was decorated entirely in red, the suitable color for a revolutionary production. The chairs were embossed with the arms of the Soviet Union. Offstage right was a buffet for the defendants to dine on, as well as restrooms. Among the audience were scattered NKVD agents whose job it was to create a racket just in case one of the defendants departed from the rehearsed script. The prosecutor opened the show by demonstrating how, under Trotsky's instruction, these men were planning to assassinate the leaders of the Party. He went on to point out that they murdered Kirov and created a number of terrorists cells for the purpose of killing Stalin and his loyal followers. The prosecutor then demanded that these miscreants be shot.

After the state presented its case, one by one, all the accused stood up and confessed to their heinous crimes. They then repented and asked to be shot. Kamenev did even better. He added an encore to his performance, asking his children not to seek vengeance, but to follow their great leader, Stalin. All the conspirators were given their wish. They were sentenced to be shot.

On August 25 the execution was attended by Yagoda and Yezhov, the two heads of the NKVD as well as Stalin's personal bodyguard, a man name Packer, who started out as a hairdresser at the Budapest Operetta Theatre. He was still a lover of the theatre and quite a mimic. He acted out, for the Boss's entertainment, how Zinoviev went to his death, clinging to his executioner's shoulder, dragging his feet and then falling to his knees wailing, *Please, comrade, please, for God's sake call Joseph Vissarionovich* (Stalin's real name.)" Stalin howled with laughter at this amusing performance. Despite his father's plea Kamenev's younger son, aged seventeen, was also shot.

Yagoda, who was a great collector, preserved and labeled all the bullets. They would, after all, have historic value. He looked forward to adding many more to his collection. Yagoda, however, had a little surprise awaiting him.

APRIL 1952

Elia Kazan testifies before HUAC and identifies several former associates as communists. He then takes out an advertisement in the New York Times defending his testimony. He argues that communism now poses a grave threat to America and urges others to cooperate with the committee.

THE HOLIDAY BREAK

The year end holiday break the company received was met with mixed feelings. Herb was grateful for the opportunity to spend some time with his pregnant wife. Helen was in her fifth month and beginning to show. There were some blotches on her cheek which she didn't even bother to cover up. She'd given up her singing gigs, had taken up knitting and seemed cheerfully absent-minded. All this time he felt guilty about not being at his wife's side during this very crucial time in their lives. But now that he was home Herb felt like a third wheel. He tried to make himself useful around the house, but Helen seemed perfectly capable of managing without him.

They decided not to determine the sex of the child. He did feel it kicking once and decided that it was a boy. It was a vigorous kick...and he wanted a son. It was an exciting thought.

He, too, became strangely preoccupied. Everything seemed different somehow. It was no longer **their** apartment. They were going to be joined by a third party. Granted this individual was made up of their flesh and blood, but it was an individual nevertheless, with a mind and a body of its own. He began to understand his father...and his mother as well. He was his father, and Helen became his mother in his imagination, except, of course, when they were in bed together and he became aroused. The sex was awkward, but, surprisingly, Helen seemed to enjoy it. Afterwards, however, they slipped into their private separate worlds. As a matter of fact, he felt closer to his wife on the phone in a hotel somewhere in the Midwest. He began to look forward to getting back to work. There was a place where he was essential.

★★★★★★★★★★★★★

Ted Lombard, on the other hand, started out dreading his visit to his family. His wife, Edie, was staying with his son and daughter-in-law in Colorado. The couple had just lost their first child and, as expected, Ted found himself in the midst of a very depressing household. The loss of the child had been a devastating

169

blow. The young wife took it particularly hard. Ted's son, Jeff, a very stable and independent young man, for the first time in his life was shaken to the core, and it seemed as if the marriage itself was in danger.

Ted had hoped for some pleasant moments with his wife, some sex, to be exact...certainly after his long absence. Edie was like an iceberg. Ted got the feeling that she was holding him responsible for the baby's death. Edie's only affection seemed to be reserved for her stricken daughter-in-law.

There was no one else to turn to but his son, Jeff, with whom he was not on the best of terms. Not that there was any animosity, on his part at any rate, but he did feel that Jeff had always sided with his mother and felt that any problems that arose were his father's fault. Jeff, on the other hand, couldn't understand why his father had never really taken much of an interest in him. There was always this distance between them, never an affectionate hug or even a kind word.

Ted found himself in a small town with nothing much of interest there. Why the couple had chosen this town to settle in was a puzzlement. Of course, Jeff was offered this little radio station to run, and the job meant a great deal to him. He was the host and disc jockey on a show which broadcast Monday through Friday from ten in the morning to four in the afternoon, and then again from six to nine in the evening. He chose the music and the topics to be discussed, and it was a most rewarding job.

At a loss for something better to do, Ted accompanied Jeff to his little studio on Main Street, on which most of the town was situated. For the first time the father was able to view his son objectively, and he liked what he saw. This was an intelligent young man, bright and personable. Actually he saw a little of his younger self in this young man.

Jeff introduced his father to Mona, his affable, middle-aged assistant. Ted sat across the table as Jeff began his broadcast. It was a most informal, off the cuff show. Jeff told his audience that his father was visiting him and, to Ted's surprise, he introduced his father to the audience. Jeff spoke frankly about the loss of his child, which was one of the reasons for his father's visit. Eventually father and son found themselves talking about other things, including Jeff's childhood and their relationship. Ted explained the vagaries of a career in show business. He began to tell amusing anecdotes and had Jeff and Mona chuckling. As a matter of fact, they got so carried away that Jeff neglected to play most of the records he'd lined up. Several calls came in, many more than usual. By the end of the afternoon they were flooded with calls. When Jeff signed off at four, the three of them were glowing with pleasure, the broadcast had gone so well.

Father and son, still warmed by the success of the broadcast and slightly embarrassed by this new found relationship, walked home together for dinner. The two men entered the house in high spirits. Edie was setting the table and noted with surprise, and a rush of pleasure, the warm relationship that had developed between father and son. When Alice, the young wife, brought the roast to the table she, too, noticed the change. Jeff, forgetting the strain between his wife and himself kissed his wife on the cheek and sat down at the table. Alice looked at her husband, actually looked at the man for the first time since the death of the child. Edie, too, looked more kindly on her self-absorbed spouse and remembered how charming the man could be, when he wanted to be. At the end of the week long visit the atmosphere in the young Lombard household had evolved from a dispirited one to a warm and loving one.

✳✳✳✳✳✳✳✳✳✳✳✳✳

Ralph Krumsky was delighted to be traveling with Betsy Landers. They were both planning to spend the holidays with their families, and they were taking the same train up north; Ralph to Utica, New York and Betsy to Lawrence, Massachusetts. Ralph had not given up hope of winning Betsy over. Until that moment arrived, however, he derived great pleasure in bathing in the warmth of her presence. Betsy sighed inwardly; if only he were older and more settled and if only he wasn't an actor.

On the train they sat side by side. They were comfortable enough with one another so that conversation wasn't really necessary. Betsy sat reading a novel, Thomas Wolfe's "Look Homeward, Angel." In the Strand book shop Ralph had picked up a second hand copy of a collection of early American plays and he found them fascinating. As they sat next to one another riding north they might have been taken for a married couple, though the husband looked a little younger than the wife.

They both got off at Utica, Betsy to change to the train across the platform. Ralph hesitated for a moment then boldly bent over and kissed Betsy on the lips. He blushed slightly as he said, *See ya.* Betsy smiled as she watched the husky young man hurry down the platform toward the stairs, tightly clenching his bulky, brown leather suitcase, probably afraid of being reprimanded for taking liberties.

Utica no longer seemed like home anymore, Ralph thought as he rode in the taxi to his parents' house in the suburbs. It stopped being his home the day he left for college. New York City was his home now. Utica was a part of the past, even then it consisted of only remnants. His brother and sister had left the nest. His brother was an assistant professor at Syracuse University. He taught history and philosophy. His sister was married and lived in California with her husband, who was an architect. His parents both taught at the local high school. Both siblings would not be home for the holidays. His brother had to spend the time with his fiance's family in Nebraska. His sister and her husband couldn't afford the air fare, and promised to be home for Easter.

His friends seemed like strangers now. His closest friend never went to college. Hal had a full time job, working in the local department store and didn't seem that close anymore. They did get together a couple of times, but Hal didn't seem that interested in him anymore. Ralph used to confide in him about his dream of having a little theatre of his own someday. Hal used to be excited about Ralph's show business aspirations, but not anymore. He seemed to be completely involved in local goings on, in local friends. Ralph's other friend, John, was in Ohio at the university there. He was a year and a half younger than Ralph, and he wasn't expected home for the holidays.

TOURING WITH STALIN

There was a family get-together with a few relatives, which was pleasant enough. The rest of the time the young man spent taking long hikes and reading. One day he'd like to produce a season of those early American plays, he decided.

****

Betsy loved her parents dearly and had pleasant memories of her childhood in Lawrence. Her parents were part of a large, close knit immigrant family. They came over from Frankfurt in the early twenties. Her father worked in one of the textile mills. He was a sweet, gentle man. He smoked a pipe and he loved opera. Her mother was a rather stern, down-to-earth woman. She was deeply distressed that her daughter was divorced and alone. No grandchildren there, apparently.

Her brother was much younger than she was. He was a senior in high school and was planning to go to college. He had expressed interest in theatre but was discouraged by his mother and by the struggle his sister was experiencing. He wasn't sure what he wanted to do. Betsy tried to encourage and support him. She felt more like his mother than his sister. Her three close friends were all married. Two of them had children. The third was pregnant.

Mary's pregnant, you know.

Yes, Mother, I know.

All right, I'm not gonna say a word.

Can I count on that?

That was the only fly in the ointment when she visited home. She loved children, and she envied her friends and she still hoped that one day she might experience motherhood. And, after all, she wasn't even thirty. Actually it was almost a year and a half away. And then when she sat down and talked with her friends, they all envied her. How exciting it was to be on television, to be on the stage. What a glamorous life she must lead! And, of course, it was, when one was working.

And, believe me, raising kids is not a bed of roses. I'd trade places with you any day, said her friend Alice, who had three, two boys and a girl and they were all over the place.

So, actually, every time she visited home she ended up with

a renewal of faith. She had chosen the right path. The theatre was something she could never give up. And suppose she did miss out on motherhood, apparently it was not all that it was cracked up to be.

****

Peter Thomas detested his parents. Well, maybe that wasn't quite the right word. He had contempt for them, utter contempt. Two phonies. His mother with her artificial airs. *I wouldn't live anywhere, but the East Side. I took a job just to keep from being bored to death. And, at least, at Bloomies one meets the creme de la creme.* She had had dreams of being an actress and claimed that the birth of Peter put a halt to a very promising career. Peter suspected that she hadn't tried very hard. As far as he knew, except for an appearance on some amateur hour at some local club, she never appeared anywhere. Della put all her show business dreams in her darling baby boy. For a while Peter did well, but as he left his childhood, jobs came fewer and far between. Della, disillusioned, soon lost interest in her son's career.

His father, a handsome man who smoked a cigar and wore splashy jewelry and odious shaving lotion, had big plans in real estate. He was always *looking over some property,* while he worked as a waiter at the Carnegie Deli. In public his parents made a great show of affection. They were both very good at putting on a show. In private there were continual bitter squabbles.

The holidays were a series of noisy parties and a lot of drinking. Peter got drunk twice and had sex with a call girl he would drop in on once in a while...when he could afford her.

****

Nat Brenner had given up the room he'd been renting in the city and was forced to spend the holidays with his family across the river in New Jersey. Ever since his divorce the young man continued more and more to bury himself in his work. Life in the real world was something he was not prepared to cope with at the moment, and he wasn't looking forward to all this free time. The work was all. The writing first and foremost.

He was still trying to learn how to write a play. He was

now on the thirteenth draft of the play he was working on while on tour. And the acting, of course. That paid the bills, or, at least, was supposed to pay the bills. And now that those reviews had confirmed his talent as an actor, there was no reason why he couldn't become a star. He'd joke about it to his sister, who looked at him with skepticism, but actually he was quite serious. It was just a matter of being at the right place, at the right time.

His mother and his sister were both disappointed in him. His sister discovered that her idol was all too human, divorced and struggling as an actor no less. His mother thought he ought to have been a teacher. *You'd make a good teacher. There's still time. You could go back to college and then get a job as a teacher.* His father, as usual, said nothing. He supported the household and on Sundays would take the family for a visit to various aunts and uncles.

Nat nursed a broken heart, and was now wary of women. You had to be able to afford them, apparently. His wife had wanted a child. The very thought horrified him. He couldn't even support himself. But he was human. He did need love...sex...love. There was one blonde actress he was attracted to and sort of dated, but he kept it casual. He made it clear. He was just a friend. When Herb floated the belief that the young man was probably gay, Nat was actually relieved. Not that he was physically attracted to Betsy. She was kind of scrawny, but he did like her and during a long tour...he might become attached to her and he might possibly come to find her attractive, and that was something he didn't want. He wasn't really ready for a relationship. In addition to the fact that Betsy was actually just another actress, and he'd just been burnt by one.

Nat's family sojourn wasn't particularly rewarding, and he looked forward to returning to work, to writing his play, to glorying in his performance.

****

Alvin Gorman spent the holiday in New York City all by himself. He hadn't been in New York very long and hadn't made any real friends. The few friends he did have were in Los Angeles.

175

TOURING WITH STALIN

His parents were in Los Angeles as well. He was not welcome there, ever since his father caught him kissing another young man. He finally came out to his parents. Actually he didn't have much of a choice. His father tried to be understanding. It was a sickness and you just go to a doctor, a head doctor and you'll be cured. Alvin was faced with the choice: family or to be true to himself. He chose the latter.

He didn't say good-bye to his stern looking father who was very angry, nor to his older brother, who had always found Alvin a bit of an embarrassment. He did say good-bye to his mother who was conflicted. It was hard to choose between ones husband and ones child, and homosexuality was a sin. Her eyes were moist as she gave him a farewell kiss. He moved out of the house and into the local "Y."

In New York, where he was hoping to find some stage work in addition to television, he'd stayed at a rather shabby hotel in the Broadway area. He decided, however, that the "Y" would be a more congenial place to spend his holiday break. It turned out to be so congenial that when it was time to rejoin the tour, he was reluctant to leave.

The spectacular opening of the show trials in 1936 with the testimony and execution in August of the two star Bolshevik witnesses, Kamenev and Vinoviev, was followed by the execution of Martemyan Ryutin, a prominent leader on the right. This performance, however, proved an embarrassment. Ryutin actually refused to confess to having committed a crime *when I am completely innocent.* He was shot ignominiously.

Next in line was Yagoda, who shared with Yezhov, control of the NKVD. Yagoda was a big disappointment to Stalin. He showed too much respect for veteran revolutionaries. Instead of torturing them, he coddled them. He was weak. Besides which, he knew too much, and he had to go.

Yagoda was exposed to the same routine that many prominent doomed Bolsheviks experienced. He was fattened for the kill. He was given an apartment in the Kremlin and had the impression that he had a free hand in regard to the NKVD. Knowing the Boss's fondness for things aristocratic, he outfitted the upper echelon of the NKVD in elegant dress uniforms of white and powder blue with a gilded dagger on their belts, just like the ones worn by the officers of the tsars navy. There were fancy dress balls, the men in tuxedos and impressive uniforms, the women in long elegant dresses, masks and costumes borrowed from the Bolshoi. Yagoda was in his glory.

Then in September, Yagoda was demoted to People's Commissar For Communications and Yezhov was made sole commander of the NKVD. Yagoda finally began to get the message. All he could do now, was to wait for the axe to fall.

With Yezhov in complete charge the NKVD began to be invigorated. The organization became an army of hundreds of thousands, with branches throughout the country. Salaries were increased to the point that they were higher than anyone's in the government. A network of unpaid informants was established. These people all received some sort of reward, especially promotions in their line of work.

Informing became the thing to do. People were falling all over themselves to point out suspicious characters, traitors, miscreants. Members of a family would inform on one another. No one was sacrosanct, not even members of the Party, including those on the Central Committee. There was a special department created for keeping an eye on them, and then there was a special department created to keeping an eye on the individuals in the special department.

From January 23, 1937 through January 30, 1937 the trial of the "Parallel Trotskyist Center" took place. These were former followers of Trotsky. They had since distanced themselves from him, but, no matter. They had to go. The star of this event was a former favorite of Lenin, Yuri Pyatakov. Pyatakov had been heroic in his efforts for the revolution. He happily testified against his old comrades, Zinoviev and Kamenev. His performance in a supporting role was so effective that he was deemed ready to star. He was given a very colorful scene to play in this new production. Flying in a German plane, he testified that he met Trotsky in Oslo. The fact that there was no record of any foreign plane landing in Oslo at the time, was really of no importance. Pyatakov was under the impression that his life would be spared because of his star turn. He was disappointed. He was rewarded for his excellent performance by a bullet in the back of his head.

Next in line for a starring role was Karl Radek, who'd been a close associate of Trotsky. He was allowed to write an article for Izvestia demonizing his former hero. The next thing he knew he was the central figure in the next act. When Bukharin, Stalin's close friend, heard of this he wrote to the Boss on behalf of Radek, to no avail.

Radek, however, was a clever man. He took one look at the script he was handed and said it was nonsense. He could do better than that. He went on to write an inspired "confession" condemning himself and his cohorts. The German author, Leon Feuchtwanger, a refugee from the Nazis who was present at the trial, spoke admiringly about the way things were conducted in that court. As a result of his brilliant presentation, Radek received a sentence of ten years in prison, while the others were condemned to death.

Eventually, however, Radek was killed while serving his prison sentence.

Abroad, the trials were looked upon with skepticism, which Trotsky helped to encourage. The Boss invited eminent figures to visit the country and help bolster its image. H. G. Wells, Bernard Shaw, Emil Ludwig, Romain Rolland returned from their visit full of praise for Stalin. Leon Feuchtwanger, in particular, was given the deluxe treatment. He marveled at Stalin's accomplishments.

Suddenly the trials came to a halt. They were just slowing things up. The arrests continued, as black cars patrolled the streets of the city picking up members of the Party and their families. With no big fuss the victims were quietly stood up against the wall and shot. People were terrified. It was dangerous to trust anyone. One even lied to ones diaries. Torture became the name of the game. Stalin signed a message stating that "the application of physical pressure by the NKVD has been authorized by the Central Committee since 1937."

Torture was broken down to a system. It began in the initial overcrowded cell, airless and unbearably uncomfortable, stifling in the warm weather. The elderly and the fragile were eliminated early. Then there was the vicious beating by the interrogator. One official's wife was whipped to death. Boxes of nails were used in various ways. There were kicks and blows. One chemistry professor was driven to madness. He assumed the personality of his prosecutor and began to vilify himself.

After the prisoner had been properly disciplined, he was given cigarettes and asked to think about what he might add to his confession. Most prisoners were then executed. If, however, the victim was to appear in court, he was carefully rehearsed. Any deviation from the text was threatened with further torture. During all this the prisoner was reminded that it was all for the good of the Party. At this point this was something positive to cling to, and there was always the possibility that one's life might be spared.

Finally it was Yagoda's turn. Ironically he was forced to confess to the poisonings he had so efficiently carried out for the Boss...Gorky, for one, and a number of others. Before his death

Yagoda lapsed into a dreamlike state. Now and then he wept. His collection of bullets was passed on to Yezhov.

It was also necessary to get rid of all the veterans of the NKVD, who were possibly appalled by what they had to resort to. Young, fresh blood, free of sentiment, was what was needed. Yezhov was most diligent in removing the old timers. Former agents found themselves in prison cells shoulder to shoulder with those they'd pursued. Lined up against the wall they were shot, after which there was the trip to the crematorium. Their ashes, mixed in with the ashes of their former victims, were buried in a common grave.

At the end of 1936 the new constitution was adopted. It promised freedom of speech and civic rights for all. The writing of the constitution had been entrusted to Bukharin and Karl Radek. Radek was gone. Bukharin, one of the few remaining men who'd been close to Lenin, mourned the death of "dear Karl." He was proud of what the two of them had accomplished...and he was still alive.

MAY 1952

Playwright Clifford Odets testifies before HUAC, and names former communist associates. Playwright Lillian Hellman appears before HUAC, but invokes the Fifth Amendment and refuses to identify others as communists. She is subsequently blacklisted in Hollywood. Actor John Garfield is found dead of a heart attack that his friends believe resulted largely from agitation caused by his blacklisting.

BACK ON THE ROAD

As he sat in the van on Broadway and Fifty Seventh Street, waiting for the cast to reassemble, Herb Volpe felt as if he were living in a dream. Nothing seemed real. Was he a grown man about to become a father? Did he have a wife who was pregnant and, at times, behaving erratically? Was he an actor touring the country, for the fourth and last time, in charge of a company of actors? Where was he heading, and why? What did he want out of life? Was it fatherhood? Was it stardom, or was it just peace and quiet?

He needed a rest, but he wasn't really tired. Yes, it was peace that he needed, peace with himself. He felt weighed down by responsibilities. Everyone depended on him: his pregnant wife, the cast of Darkness At Noon, Stanley, the producer, his widowed mother. She was living alone, she was independent and he worried about her. *Look after your mother,* were his father's last words. But she refused looking after. And now there was this new life, waiting to be born, a son. He was sure of it. Another burden.

He thought about his father, a big bear of a man. Could he be there for his son, the way his father had been for him and his brother? Could he be as patient and as loving as his father had been, even when he was ill? He missed his father. Why do the good die young? Suppose something happened to him? Who would take care of his wife and his son? On the road, day after day, anything could happen. There was that time they were on this icy road in the wilds of Kansas. The van suddenly spun out of control. He held onto the steering wheel, and sat helplessly as they whirled round and round and round and finally landed safely in a snow bank. It could have been...fatal.

Good morning.

Oh, hi, said Herb.

It was Nat Brenner, bright and cheerful, as usual. A pang of envy shot through Herb. Oh, that he, too, could be that carefree! Nat stashed his suitcase and typewriter in the trunk, and took a seat in the van behind Herb.

How's the wife?

She's okay, said Herb. He could not, for the life of him,

understand why he felt uncomfortable with Nat. Maybe it was this childlike quality, that seemed unseemly in a man, and Nat must be pushing thirty. Well, he was certainly late twenties. Middle twenties?

How old are you? asked Herb.

I'm twenty nine, said Nat. *Why?*

I was just wondering, said Herb.

Of course all actors were blessed or cursed with this childlike quality, but Nat was so goddamned cheerful, so..so what? So optimistic? *How were your holidays?* asked Herb, forcing himself to be concerned about this man who, after all, he was responsible for, in a way.

Okay, said Nat and, apparently, there was nothing more to be said.

They were joined by Betsy Landers.

Good morning, said Betsy.

Herb and Nat returned her good morning. She placed her suitcase in the trunk and sat down in the van next to Nat. Nat noticed, to his discomfort, that Betsy looked rather attractive. Had she done something to herself, or was he just getting horny? That's all he needed, to fall in love again. He must remember to steer clear of Betsy.

Art was easy, compared to Life, that is. If only one could bury oneself in the cocoon of make believe. At least he had rid himself of that shy, thoughtful persona and developed that bright Midwestern mask of congeniality; the mask of the happy fool that all actors must assume, the cheeriness that concealed the problems, the insecurity, the facade that was so convincing that he was beginning to believe it himself.

And why not? He was in charge of his life, and everything was possible. Aim for the top, and if one fell short, one could still make a splash.

Betsy regretted sitting next to Nat. She couldn't understand this wall he erected between them. She felt that there was a sweet, friendly soul beneath it all, and wondered whether she was to blame for this barrier, which made her so uncomfortable. Maybe he was gay after all. She wanted nothing more than friendship, congeniality.

She turned her attention to Herb. Herb recounted all the problems Helen was encountering in pregnancy. He revealed that she had finally gotten to make the record which had been planned for years. It was a collection of arias and art songs.

Can we get to hear it? asked Nat.

I brought one along. I thought I'd play it for those that might be interested, said Herb.

She has a beautiful voice, said Betsy, who had attended a recital Helen had participated in.

After the initial exchange, a silence ensued. The three of them sat contemplating the road ahead; the series of venues, a huge theatre like the one in Kansas City or the school auditorium in Athens, Ohio; the series of hotels, small and shoddy, or the occasional motel, cold and impersonal. And then there was the schedule, a series of one night stands, sometimes one right after the other. There were the endless hours sitting in the van driving from one town to another, the discomfort, the boredom.

Despite it all, thought Nat, there was the performance, stepping onto a stage and engaging the audience. You were their host, and they were your guests. You were taking them on a journey to a place they'd never been to before. There was the hushed silence during the love scenes between the imprisoned Bolshevik, Rubashov, played by Herb, and his meek, devoted secretary, Luba, played by Betsy; or the dramatic conflict between the young ruthless, Bolshevik, Gletkin, played by Alvin Gorman, and the moderate veteran, Ivanov, played by Ted Lombard; or the occasional, nervous titter at the sexual references during his scene as the half demented Prisoner 402. One time several indignant members of the audience stamped up the aisle and out of the theatre. This was, after all the "Bible Belt." And afterwards there was the glorious satisfaction of doing the job one was put here on earth to do. One was ten feet tall, and one could stride down the street with the knowledge that one was endowed with special powers. One was not an ordinary mortal.

Herb's heart sank when Betsy broke the silence and said she'd received a call from the television producer, Arnold Handsman. Arnold was in the throes of creating a new soap opera. He hoped to go into production sometime in the spring. He asked Betsy to keep in touch. Herb grew gloomy at the thought of continuing the tour without the sweet face of Betsy to light up his day. He decided to call Helen **every** night, despite the expense.

Ralph Krumsky arrived, bright-eyed and bushy tailed, ready to resume his first professional job. He warmed to the sight of Betsy, looking lovelier than ever, and Herb, who was so much more outgoing than his father, who was rather stiff and pedantic. He was now back home, with his real family. Betsy smiled at Ralph and the young man's heart leaped up in hope.

Ted Lombard greeted Herb warmly. After acknowledging the others briefly, he sat next to Herb, in the front seat, and the two of them exchanged news about their respective holidays. Ted was aglow with the memory of the breakthrough in his relationship with his son. He told Herb how impressed he was with the boy's know-how, his intelligence, his cool, how they bantered with each other during his son's radio broadcast.

Herb expressed his concern about the problems his wife was going through with her pregnancy. He accompanied her when she went to register for a class for pregnant mothers. Apparently they went through all these exercises in preparation for giving birth. He was asked if he would be joining his wife. Many men did accompany their wives, he was told. He noticed Helen's eyes when he told the instructor he'd be out of town for the next few months. She couldn't conceal her disappointment.

Paul Thomas did not try to hide the fact that he was not particularly happy about rejoining the tour. He threw his suitcase into the trunk. He acknowledged the others with a curt nod, took a seat in the rear of the van, then settled into the corner of the seat and sat looking gloomy. He didn't want to be here, and he certainly didn't want to be back with his family, his real family, that is. As a matter of fact, he wasn't quite sure where he wanted to be.

Herb looked at his watch. It was two fifteen. The call time was two. Alvin Gorman was usually the last one to appear, but he was never more than a few minutes late. He remembered that he didn't have a phone number for Alvin. Alvin hadn't been sure where he was going to stay. He thought about going upstairs to the office to see what contact number Stanley had for him, but decided to wait another five minutes.

He was about to get out of the van when he cited Alvin striding down the block. Mr. Gorman was not alone. He was accompanied by a slim young man, fashionably dressed. The two men stood in front of the van, exchanged a few words and kissed. Alvin got into the van and, without a word, climbed into the back seat next to Paul. Paul, who'd observed the amorous exchange with great discomfort and some disgust, moved away from the new occupant, as if the disease might be catching. Alvin looked out the window of the van and waved to the young man. The young man, who'd stood watching Alvin climb into the van, waved back and departed.

Are we ready? asked Herb of no one in particular.

There was no response. Herb put the van in gear, stepped on the gas and the American Drama Theatre touring company of the Arthur Koestler novel, "Darkness At Noon," as adapted for the stage by Sidney Kingsley and edited by Stanley Warren, was back on the road.

STALIN

The historic purge was about to come to its dramatic and poignant climax. Nikolai Bukharin, beloved family friend, and particular favorite of Nadya, Stalin's late wife, had always been on the other side of the aisle. He was a Rightist.

The first hint of the man's doom came in February 1936, when an article severely critical of Bukharin appeared in Pravda. Immediately after that, strangely enough, Bukharin, accompanied by his wife, was allowed to leave the country. He was part of a delegation sent to Paris to retrieve the archives of the German Social Democratic Party, the party that Hitler had destroyed. Bukharin, free from the restraint one endured when living at home, made some comments he would later come to regret. Speaking to an associate he referred to Stalin as *"a vicious little man, not a man but a devil."* Speaking to William Bullitt, the American ambassador to the USSR, he spoke of *"the strange, pro-Hitler sentiments which were getting more and more a hold of Stalin."* Since Paris was a city rife with NKVD spies, these comments were bound to be sniffed out.

The second warning shot was fired while Bukharin was on vacation in Central Asia, shortly after his return from Paris. His name, along with other Rightists, were accused of complicity in the Kirov murder trial. One of the Rightists mentioned had the good grace to commit suicide. As soon as he got back from his vacation Bukharin denied his complicity. He swore to his allegiance to Stalin and claimed that he had long ago broken ties with the others mentioned. He wrote letters to the prosecutor, Vyshinsky, and to Voroshilov, a member of the Politburo, protesting his innocence. Voroshilov washed his hands of the obviously condemned man, wanting nothing to do with him.

Interestingly enough, an announcement appeared in Pravda stating that the investigation into Bukharin and Rykov, an associate of his, had been halted. What was not printed, however, was that the investigation would be continued in secret. Bukharin, anxious to clear his name once and for all, begged to be heard. He even wrote a poem extolling Stalin, which he submitted to him. He was not heard, and Stalin advised him not to print the poem.

TOURING WITH STALIN

Finally in December of 1936, at a Central Committee meeting, Yezhov, currently head of the NKVD, openly accused Bukharin of counterrevolutionary activity. Stalin, seemingly concerned, urged that one must not jump to conclusions. In between sessions of the Central Committee, however, former associates were brought from their prison cells to accuse Bukharin and Rykov of their complicity. Bukharin, growing hysterical in the process, defended himself.

Amid all this Stalin was elevated to the realm of immortals. At the eighth Congress of the Soviets the long awaited constitution, drafted, ironically, by the doomed Bukharin, was put up for discussion. The acclaim for the Boss was almost an ecstatic religious event. From the ordinary citizen to the famous author, Boris Pasternak, there was unbounded enthusiasm, elation, joy. Bukharin, alarmed by this idolatry of Stalin, wrote to him complaining about an article in Pravda comparing the Rightists to Trotskyists and saboteurs. The newly elected saint wrote to the editor pointing out that the investigation into Bukharin had been temporarily postponed. The editor took the Boss's subtle hint and continued to cast accusations at Bukharin.

In January of 1937 Bukharin began to receive reports of his culpability which were extracted from Rightists prisoners subjected to "interrogation." Panic stricken, he wrote letters to the man he continued to refer to by his youthful name, Koba. He asked to be seen. He was not. Later in the month he was dismissed from the staff of Izvestia. He continued to receive reports, twenty of them, about his guilt. He continued to write letters to his friend, all to no avail. When they started to evict him from the Kremlin he phoned Koba. *You tell them to go to hell,* said his friend. Bukharin was given a brief reprieve. He refused to attend the next meeting of the Central committee if the charges against him weren't dropped. He questioned why he was no longer listed as Comrade Bukharin. He went on a hunger strike. The meeting was postponed.

Meanwhile attention was focused on Sergo Ordzhonikidze, a prominent official and long time comrade of Stalin who had been under surveillance for some time. One by one Sergo's close associates were arrested, his brother among them. One of them, who'd been promised his life, was shot. Sergo phoned Stalin and vented his fury. He'd always been vociferous. Stalin empathized. They might even come and arrest him, complained the Boss.

Early the next day the two men were alone. They met and talked for hours. Afterward Sergo seemed quite calm. The rest of the day went smoothly. He conducted business as usual. He got home after midnight and retired to his bedroom. A short time later a shot was heard. His wife found him in his underwear covered with blood. The man had obviously committed suicide. The idea, of course, that someone might have slipped in, a guard perhaps, and been responsible was ridiculous.

Stalin's grief was genuine. After all, they'd been through a great deal together. It wasn't his fault that the man had to go. Sergo had even come to the defense of one of his associates he should not have defended. Sergo's wife was wise enough not to express any suspicions. Her husband had shot himself. Other relatives were not that circumspect. There was no reason on earth for Sergo to have committed suicide. Those that expressed their suspicions found themselves in prison.

Bukharin wrote a heartfelt letter to Koba grieving the death of dear Sergo. No reply from Koba was forthcoming. If only dear Bukharin had the good sense to end it all and save the state a lot of trouble. Either Bukharin refused to take the hint or he just didn't get it. When he and Rykov appeared at the postponed meeting they were put under arrest. Members rose at the meeting demanding that the two men confess. Bukharin rose and angrily defended himself. The Boss evenhandedly and magnanimously suggested that a committee be formed to decide the proper steps to follow. Lenin's widow and sister were included as members of the committee. When Bukharin was accused of lying when he said that Lenin died in his arms, he turned to the widow and the sister and asked them to confirm the report. The two women remained silent.

The committee decided that the NKVD would conduct an investigation. The investigation was short and to the point. When Bukharin and Rykov turned up for one of the sessions they were surrounded by agents of the NKVD. They were formally under arrest. It had been decided that the two men knew about the terrorist activities. They were escorted to the Lubyanka prison. The Boss then delivered a virulent speech advocating the "liquidation of Trotskyists and other double dealers."

The incarceration of Bukharin and Rykov was followed by a deluge of arrests. Traitors were found everywhere. Yezhov reported 141 arrests of members of the Electrical Industry. There were complaints that 141 was a very small number. Yezhov assured the politburo that many more were to follow, and that the majority of those arrested were shot. The reply was greeted with cheers. After all, one had to demonstrate ones loyalty in some way. 228 members of the Department of Education were arrested.

Voroshilov, the Commissar for War reported, happily, that there were few saboteurs in the army. He was told that the army was no exception. If there were so many saboteurs everywhere else, there must be, at least, that many in the army.

The army now became Stalin's next victim. Since Trotsky had been in charge of the army, the army was of paramount importance. Up to this time 47,000 officers had been ousted. Most of the generals who remained were war heroes, legendary figures. No matter. Links were found to Hitler. A conspiracy was uncovered. One general signed a confession on a paper which had reddish brown spots on it. The reddish brown spots turned out to be blood. One general was given the opportunity to shoot himself. The others were shot post haste. One war correspondent and war hero had a long interview with the Boss. His audience went on for three hours. As he was leaving Stalin asked him if he had a gun, and if he planned to use it. The man replied that he had no intention of using it. Several months later the man was arrested and shot.

Over one hundred officers were called in from the provinces, found guilty of conspiracy and shot. The destruction of the army, which began in 1937 continued through 1938.

While in prison Bukharin was found guilty of complicity in the military plot. From his cell he wrote forty three letters, revealing all the major events of his life, his love affairs, his devotion to the Boss. He noted on the envelope that the letter be shown to no one before it reached Stalin. After reading the letter Stalin passed the letter around, inviting comments. Bukharin and the letter were uniformly vilified.

At first, he refused to give in. Eventually, like all the rest he confessed his guilt. Unlike the others, however, Bukharin was not tortured. There was no need. The sensitive poet tortured himself.

In his final letter, he acknowledged that for the sake of their shared ideal, the purge was necessary. He asked to be allowed to take poison instead of being shot. He asked to be allowed to say goodbye to his wife and his son before the trial. None of his requests were granted. He was allowed to write a farewell letter to his wife. He asked her not to be bitter, but to remember the greater good. The wife was in prison at the time and didn't receive the letter until fifty years later.

During the trial it was concluded that Bukharin and Rykov had conspired with the Trotskyists and the German spies. Yagoda, the former head of the NKVD, was also one of the stars of the trial. He, along with several doctors, were found guilty of poisoning various comrades. One of the accused retracted his confession. The next day he retracted his retraction. It was reported that the Boss watched the entire trial from behind a curtain.

Bukharin not only confessed his guilt, but overdid it so enthusiastically that it was evident that the whole trial was rigged. A defense for Bukharin was organized, but came to nothing. The author, Romain Rolland, wrote to Stalin for clemency. The letter was ignored. The feeling abroad was mixed. Some looked to Stalin as the last bulwark against Hitler. After the death sentence was passed Bukharin offered an eloquent appeal. Yagoda also petitioned for clemency, to no effect. Bukharin was the last to be shot.

It was at this time Stalin's mother grew gravely ill. He continued to correspond with her. He sent her a shawl and some medicines. In the summer of 1937 his mother died in her apartment. It was too dangerous to journey to Tiflis for the burial.

TOURING WITH STALIN

The area was in upheaval. He did not attend the funeral. Most of those closest to him were now deceased.

JUNE 1952

Soviet jets shoot down a Swedish air force plane over international waters in the Baltic Sea.

ALVIN GORMAN

Despite the fact that the national tour of Darkness At Noon had five more months to go, somehow there was the feeling that the end was in sight. Eight months was a long time to be out on the road, but the holidays had been left behind. In addition to that they were soon to lose their leading lady. The tight knit family was beginning to unravel. The tour which, at one time, felt as if it was going to go on forever, no longer seemed eternal. One became aware of a light at the end of the tunnel. There were all those things to look forward to.

Betsy Landers waited impatiently for the call she'd be receiving from the television producer, Arnold Handsman. There was going to be a major role for her in the new soap opera he was producing, and she would shortly bid a fond farewell to a job which she had been hesitant to undertake to begin with. She'd regret leaving her co-workers behind, yes even that strange Alvin Gorman, and she'd look back fondly on those adventurous three months. And then there was Herb. She'd miss him, but she looked forward to putting some distance between them. The relationship was both rewarding and disturbing at the very same time.

Herb Volpe was anxiously looking forward to the birth of his son, still sure that the child was going to be a boy. It had to be, he was wishing hard enough. Though, of course, he would love it just as much if it were a girl, maybe even more so. And he would soon be back home with, what now, he could call a family. What would the child look like? Of course, all babies looked alike, didn't they? But would it resemble Helen? Would it resemble him, God forbid? He hated his large nose and squinty eyes. Maybe it would resemble one of his parents. His mother was quite attractive.

Nat Brenner was rather reluctant to face the end of the tour, and the uncertain future that would follow. What a great joy it was to be able to work on his play every morning (a play, now in its twenty first draft and no end in sight) and then, after that, being able to look forward to performing in the evening in a role he'd triumphed in, in spite of being fired...almost fired...on opening night. (He kept wondering what Stanley Warren's reaction was when he saw those glowing notices, and realized how mistaken he'd been.) But the tour was really a stop gap, wasn't it? He was anxious to return to New York with those reviews in hand, and find immediate success as an actor, because success as a playwright lay in the future, the dark, dim future. He was going to become a star. Why the hell not?!

Ted Lombard had mixed feelings as well. This was to be his last tour and, reluctantly, perhaps, his last time on a stage. He promised his wife, Edie, they would put down roots in L.A. and he would concentrate on getting television and film work. But first he was looking forward to a long visit with his son, with whom he had recently bonded...after all those years.

As far as Paul Thomas was concerned, the length of the rest of the tour was a relatively short one. Paul had made up his mind. He was saving his pennies. No drinking, no spending. In four weeks time he'd have enough money put aside. He would give in his notice, return to New York and try to figure out what he was going to do with the rest of his life.

Alvin Gorman and Ralph Krumsky were actually quite content with the status quo. Alvin was well aware of the fact that a role like the villainous Gletkin was a rarity for an actor who was told, time and time again, he was hard to cast; and Ralph looked forward eagerly to each performance. He learned so much every evening, so much from Herb, from Betsy, from Ted from Nat, and even from Alvin...from everyone in the cast, except for Paul. Paul's attitude really puzzled him. What was he doing here? And why? Didn't he realize how lucky he was to be paid for going on stage in front of a paying audience, for living the life of a professional actor?

Occasionally there was the pleasant surprise of the company running across another touring company, of running across some fellow actors, some familiar faces, a reminder of what a wide spread family show business was. In Duluth, Minnesota there was a production of "Mister Roberts." The manager of the company invited the cast of "Darkness" to a performance. Herb recognized some of the cast, actors he'd sat with in the Horn and Hardart automat, bullshitting about this and that. He went backstage afterwards and went out for a beer with them.

An acquaintance of Betsy's played one of the nurses. Betsy was disappointed to see that this acquaintance of hers, whom she'd never seen on stage before, and really didn't know that well, was not a very interesting actress. She decided not to go backstage. The woman wasn't aware of the fact that Betsy was in the audience, and, besides, what can you say to someone who is really dull?

In Texarkana, Texas they ran into a film company that had recently completed shooting a movie...starring Marlon Brando and directed by Elia Kazan. It was called "Viva Zapata!." It was thrilling to see the very first screening of a fascinating movie. They were invited to the party afterwards as well. The refreshments were meager and, unfortunately, Marlon Brando and Elia Kazan were nowhere in sight.

There was the occasional crisis as well. The flu made its way through the cast. The worst one affected was Nat Brenner. He could barely walk. He slowly made his way to the theatre. Actually it was a high school auditorium. Half dead, half alive, he took his place on stage. Happily the role of Prisoner 402 did not call for any movement. Nat conducted his entire performance from his prison cell, and there was a chair to sit on when he was not involved in the action. Just speaking his lines, however, was an enormous effort. He was proud of his speaking voice, which he'd worked so hard to cultivate, and had been praised in one of his notices, and he was concerned about being heard. He found that if put all his energy into projecting one key phrase, or even one key word he could put across the meaning of his speeches. This was a lesson to be treasured, a lesson in stage technique. "Sweet are the uses of adversity," Nat remembered. Shakespeare, "As You Like It," the good Duke in exile.

In Clarksville, Tennessee Herb had to deal with a rather unpleasant incident.

He'd just finished a long phone conversation with his wife, Helen. The pregnancy was going well, so well that she'd actually fulfilled a concert engagement. Dressed in an elegant muumuu she sang at a church supper. Herb lay half asleep, half awake, picturing Helen in the elegant muumuu when the phone rang. Somehow or other the ring seemed rather loud and ominous. When he picked up the phone and said hello the responding voice sounded unfamiliar.

Herb?

Yes, said Herb. *Who is this?*

It's Alvin.

Yes, Alvin? What is it?

I'm in prison, said Alvin. *I've been arrested for...loitering. Can you come down and get me out, please?*

A policeman came on the phone and told Herb where the lockup was. Herb put on his clothes and walked over to the prison which was only a few blocks away. He found Alvin looking distraught and embarrassed. The bail was fifty dollars. Alvin had only twenty dollars on him. Luckily Herb had the thirty dollars needed. They paid the bail and walked back to the hotel. Alvin explained that he had to be in felony court at noon the next day. This meant starting out two hours later than planned, which didn't disturb Herb as much as the fact that he might lose a cast member to the jailhouse in Clarksville.

Felony court? asked Herb. *Did you commit a felony?*

I don't know, said Alvin. *I just started to talk to this man, and he turned out to be a detective, and then he said that I was under arrest.*

For talking to him?

Well, he insisted that I was trying to pick him up, said Alvin.

Where was this? asked Herb.

Not far from this bar, said Alvin. *Actually it was near this public toilet. I just happened to come out and, he was standing there and I thought he wanted to talk to me.*

I see, said Herb, beginning to get the picture. *You tried to pick him up.*

Alvin said nothing.

What's the penalty for this? asked Herb. *Do you know?*

Alvin shook his head.

They continued in silence.

When they got into the elevator in the hotel Alvin turned to Herb, looking rather woeful. *We don't have to tell anyone, do we?*

No, said Herb. *I better come with you though, in case there's a problem. There's bound to be a fine, at least. How much money do you have?*

I have about eighty dollars, said Alvin.

I've got about a hundred or so, said Herb. *If worse comes to worst I can take some money out of the box office. I haven't sent it off yet.*

Thank you, said Alvin. *I'll pay you back, of course.* Then, looking rather pitiful, he added, *I'm sorry to cause you all this trouble.*

They were standing in the hallway, in front of Alvin's room. Herb stood looking at the man, and seeing him for the first time, the open wound, the bitterness, the confusion. He felt sorry for the poor slob.

Don't worry about the money, said Herb, and returned to his room. He had a hard time falling asleep, concerned about what might happen in court the next day.

Alvin lay awake all night reviewing all the fatal steps leading to the mess he was in.

STALIN

In spite of the blood bath Stalin bestowed on the country during 1937, the people were surprisingly cheery and optimistic. There were victory marches to demonstrate how great things were. The Kremlin was all lit up bright and shiny. Workers were inspired to work harder. There were statues of the two gods that had brought us to this state of Nirvana, the god Lenin and the god, Stalin. They could be found in the central square of all the parks. How wonderful it was not to have to worry about one's conscience. One was part of a collective conscience. What if the apartments were overcrowded, what if one had to stand in line to get into the bathroom. What a small price to pay!

Arrests continued unabated. When one's neighbor was whisked away during the night, one looked away, and went on with one's business. The people arrested were obviously guilty of something. Why else would they be arrested? How lucky we were! The NKVD was looking after us, making us safe from all those insidious traitors!

The black cars continued to glide quietly through the streets of Moscow after midnight. There were still the knock at the door and family members quietly disappeared, unless, of course, a shot was heard from within and the government had one less problem to deal with.

For a time the operation was conducted by a troika, a three man team that functioned super efficiently. They rounded up the villains. No questions were asked, no trial was conducted. A shot in the back of the head and the work was done. When Stalin lost interest in the troika those dedicated workers found themselves following the same path followed by their victims.

The Old Guard disappeared one by one. Even the Boss's personal bodyguard joined the long line into oblivion. He'd committed the fatal sin of having been associated with the past. Stalin tirelessly scanned the lists of the condemned. He signed 366 such lists. They included 44,000 names. Once in a great while one or two names were scratched off. Boris Pasternak was one.

Foreign ambassadors with ties to the past were not forgotten. They were called in, assigned other duties and then eliminated. Some were astute enough not to answer the call. This did not, however, mean that they were safe. The NKVD had its agents everywhere. People died mysteriously in Nice, in Switzerland, in Washington, DC, shot or poisoned. One ambassador was wily enough to make a bargain with Stalin. If he were left in peace, he wrote, he would not divulge all he knew. His letter was never answered, but he survived...and he kept his word. His memoirs were published only after Stalin's death.

Prominent scientists found themselves incarcerated. Their prison, however, was quite comfortable. They were supplied with all the amenities. In addition they were provided with all the equipment they needed to go on with their work.

Nor was the Comintern neglected. It was important to export socialism, but not by those with ties to the past. They had to make way for fresh blood, men who were not antagonistic to fascism. Hitler was on the rise, and the Boss had his eye on an alliance with this rising force.

Members of the masses were routinely rounded up and converted into slave labor. Government projects flourished as people were worked to death. Nor were members of the Boss's family able to escape, like a brother-in-law, a niece, the husband of his mistress who was actually his sister in law. The mistress was replaced by an attractive young housekeeper, who worked for Stalin for years. It was rumored that the young housekeeper had become his wife. There seemed to be a consensus, at any rate, that she had become his mistress.

By the end of 1937 Stalin had reached the unattainable. Capitalism had been vanquished. An agrarian society had been transformed into an industrial one, and everything was in the hands of the state. He had a young army whose loyalty was unquestionable. In regard to the Party, half a million new appointments were made to replace the vacancies. Ninety percent of the new members were under forty. When the Boss now entered a meeting the entire membership rose to its feet. This was followed by a prolonged ovation with calls of, *Long live Comrade Stalin!* and *Hurray for Stalin!*

TOURING WITH STALIN

More and more the Boss began to resemble the tsar. Lenin would have been astounded to find, attending the Bolshoi, a group of cossacks wearing uniforms with the colors of the old regime. The new textbooks proposed that the Russian tsars had made a significant contribution to the country's history. In 1938 a new Party history was published denigrating the early Bolshevik leaders, now vanished, and deifying the Boss.

In 1939 Stalin had a change of heart or, perhaps, he'd come to the conclusion that enough was enough. 327,000 condemned men were released. They included military men, scientists, engineers. One of the men released, Sergei Kavtaradze, a comrade of Stalin during the days that the Boss was a terrorist tells an interesting story.

Sergei spent an evening with Stalin who was in a mellow mood. In his light tenor voice the Boss began to sing an old favorite Georgian song. *I sought my sweetheart's grave, but could not find it.* Suddenly Stalin stopped and murmured, *Poor, poor Sergo.* He resumed the song then stopped again and murmured, *Poor, poor Lado.* Then there, was *Poor, poor Alyosha.* He went on to mourn all the Georgian friends he'd eliminated. *They've gone, they've gone...not one of them left,* he mourned with tears in his eyes. Sergei started to sob and clung to his old friend. Stalin pushed him away. In a fury he muttered, *They've gone! Not one of them left! You all wanted to kill Koba! But it didn't come off. Koba killed all of you instead, sons of whores!* Then he ran out of the room, kicking his bodyguard, who didn't get out of the way quickly enough.

It was now time for the finale. The instrument of the terror itself had to be eliminated. Yezhov, who succeeded Yagoda as head of the NKVD was arrested. He'd been found guilty of being part of an espionage ring. He'd been in cahoots with Polish and German intelligence. In addition to that he was planning to overthrow the Boss. He was tortured and, at first, tried to deny the charges. He did not deny, however, using his position to take sexual advantage of men and women. During his ordeal, the man became unhinged. He suspected his wife of conspiring against him. His wife denied the accusation vehemently. He ended up poisoning her. His last words were, *Tell Stalin that I shall die with his name on my lips.* On February 4, 1940 he was shot. His death was followed by the death of many of his personnel. There had to be a clean sweep.

Before the bloodbath ended, however, it took with it some notable talents. Isaac Babel, the brilliant writer, for one, as well as a couple of scientists and poets. The great theatrical impresario, Vsevolod Meyerhold, was beaten mercilessly and, as he lay bleeding, one of his interrogators urinated on him. A plan to put Babel, as well as Pasternak and Shostakovich on trial was abandoned. It was decided that artists were too temperamental, and could not be relied on to follow the blueprint. Babel and Meyerhold were quietly shot. Meyerhold's wife, who protested his innocence too loudly, was murdered in her apartment. She was stabbed again and again. Her cries went unheeded by her neighbors. Lavrenti Beria, who succeeded Yezhov as head of the NKVD, moved into the vacated Meyerhold apartment with his mistress.

In February 1939 Stalin celebrated his sixtieth birthday. The Bolshoi Theatre produced Glinka's "A Life For The Tsar," a favorite of the Romanovs. The text was adapted to suit Stalin, who inspected the new version himself.

The Boss was now alone, without a wife. He resented the family ties of his associates. They deprived him of their company. The wife of Kalinin, the president of the Supreme Soviet, was sent to a camp. Molotov and Stalin's secretary were deprived of their wives who languished in prison. The stag dinners went on late into the night.

In 1940 Beria, now the head of the NKVD, presented the Boss with the gift to surpass all gifts. Trotsky, living in Mexico, took a bright young man into his confidence. While they were alone the young man produced an axe and split the great man's head in two. The Boss was now the last remaining veteran of the October Revolution.

JULY 1952

The U. S. bans the Soviet periodical, "Amerika," along with the Soviet information bulletins.

ALVIN GORMAN: PART TWO

The bar Alvin dropped in on turned out to be a big disappointment; dark, dreary, inhabited by three older men, and all three of them rather unappetizing. Even the bartender was gross. Alvin had his Tom Collins and decided to take a brief walk before returning to the hotel. And there was this public toilet. No harm in taking a look. As he was relieving himself, he turned to find this very interesting looking man standing at a nearby urinal. He smiled at the man. The man looked rather friendly. As he left, the man sort of nodded. Was it an invitation, or a courteous leave-taking? Alvin waited a few seconds then stepped outside. The man was standing there, lighting a cigarette.

Nice night, said Alvin.

Actually it was rather chilly and windy.

The man nodded.

Do you live around here? asked Alvin.

Why do you ask? asked the man.

Alvin said nothing. He was puzzled. The man seemed interested. Maybe he was shy.

I'm staying at the hotel down the block, said Alvin. *I'd invite you up, but it might look strange at this hour.*

Why would you invite me up? asked the man.

Alvin smiled, not quite sure how to answer the man.

Okay, buddy, said the man, *you're under arrest. I'm a detective.*

Arrest? said Alvin. *What for?*

Lewd behavior, said the detective.

You must be kidding, said Alvin.

A second man appeared from nowhere.

Are you gonna come quietly? said the first detective, *or do we have to handcuff you?*

Alvin said nothing. The two detectives escorted Alvin to the police station. There he was led into an office where a policewoman took his picture. Then she took a roller and spread ink onto the tips of his fingers, after which she pressed his fingers onto a chart in order to record his fingerprints. He was then led into a large room and told to take a seat.

TOURING WITH STALIN

How long are you gonna keep me here? asked Alvin.

Till tomorrow noon, said the first detective, *when you'll appear in felony court.*

I'm on tour with a show, said Alvin. *We're supposed to leave at noon tomorrow.*

Tough shit, said the second detective.

I'll like to make a phone call, said Alvin. *I'm allowed to make a phone call, ain't I?*

Sure you can make a phone call, said the first detective. *Have you got a dime?*

Alvin dug into his pocket and found he had a dime. He called the hotel and asked for Herb. They rang Herb's room, but there was no answer. Alvin returned to his seat, unsure as what to do next. The two detectives were seated at a table, smoking. A third man entered the room and eyed Alvin.

What have we got here? asked the third man, probably another detective.

We got a little birdie here, said the first detective.

Not another one, said the third detective.

And he's on tour, said the second detective.

On tour? asked the third detective. *How sweet!* He turned to Alvin. *Are you in show business?*

Alvin nodded.

Maybe he can do a dance for us, said the third detective. *Can you dance...what's your name?*

Alvin.

Alvin what?

Alvin Gorman.

Can you dance, Alvin?

No.

He looks like he could use some exercise, said the second detective. *Why don't you take a few laps around the room, Alvin.*

You heard what the man said, said the third detective. *Get moving.*

Alvin rose and started to trot around the room. The third detective joined the other two at the table, and lit up a cigarette.

After a moment the second detective looked over at Alvin circling the room and wondering how long this was going to last.

Is that the fastest you can run? asked the second detective..

You heard the man, said the third detective. *Pick up those feet.*

Alvin ran faster. The room was rather warm and Alvin began to perspire. Whether it was the heat or the tension he couldn't say, but he began to feel wobbly. He bumped into a chair and almost collided with the wall. The detectives looked up. Alvin started up again. The detectives looked at one another.

Take a seat, Alvin, said the first detective. *Relax.*

The second detective came over to Alvin and sat down beside him.

Care for a cigarette? he asked, offering him one.

Alvin shook his head.

Where's your manners? said the third detective. *The man offered you a cigarette.*

Alvin hesitated and said, *I don't smoke.*

That's okay, said the second detective. *Alvin's a little nervous. Have you got any friends in town, Alvin?*

No, said Alvin.

Don't you know anybody in town? asked the second detective.

Not really, no, said Alvin.

Don't you guys keep in touch with one another? asked the third detective. *Sort of a little network.*

Not that I know of, said Alvin.

You must have some friends, persisted the second detective.

I'd like to try the phone again, said Alvin. *I've got to let the company know where I am.*

Let him make his phone call, said the first detective.

Thank you, said Alvin. He rose, started for the phone, then stopped, turned and asked, *Do I have to stay here all night?*

Not if you've got fifty dollars to post bail, said the first detective.

Thank you, said Alvin. He reached into his pocket and found that he had no change. *I don't have a dime,* said Alvin.

Here you are, Alvin, said the second detective. *The phone call's on us. See how nice we're treating you.*

Thank you, said Alvin.

He approached the phone, praying that Herb would answer. When he heard Herb's voice, he heaved a sigh of relief. The sound of Herb's voice reminded him of who he was, and where he was, and the realization that there was another world out there and that this nightmare would come to an end...eventually, that is. There was still the threat of jail. Suppose he had to miss a performance. Who could possibly stand in for him? And what if word got back to Stanley. He'd be sure to be fired, wouldn't he? Oh, God! What a mess!

STALIN

Now that Lenin's dream had been realized within the country, it was time to fulfill the ultimate goal. Hitler had come to power, and echoed the Soviet goal, "Tomorrow the world!" And Stalin was convinced that tomorrow had arrived.

Stalin made preparations for war. The Red Army was being re-armed. The grand new Moscow Metro was built, specifically, to be able to act as a bomb shelter in case of an air raid. When Hitler annexed Czechoslovakia this simply fell in with the Boss's plans. Let Hitler pave the way and then conquer Hitler. The Boss conferred with France and England while secretly extending a hand to Der Fuhrer. The Soviet ambassador to Germany was a Jew. He was replaced. The two titans, supposedly enemies, were slowly becoming, on the surface at least, close allies.

The wily Stalin offered to help Czechoslovakia if France and England came in with him, knowing full well that this would never come to pass. Thus, in Western Europe Stalin became the hero. Then, using England's appeasement of Germany with the Munich agreement as a betrayal, he was able to justify his approach to Hitler. On the other hand, with the Western Allies committed to come to the aid of Poland, Hitler needed a Russian ally. Ribbentrop was sent to Moscow. Stalin spent three hours with the German ambassador. A secret treaty was signed with Molotov, the Russian Foreign Minister, representing Stalin. The Boss gained access to the Baltic States, Bessarabia and Poland. The event was concluded with a lavish feast. Ironically Stalin had Ribbentrop drink a toast to one of Russia's Jewish ambassadors, while the Jewish ambassador had to drink a toast to Hitler.

As expected, Hitler invaded Poland. This paved the way for Stalin to enter the conquered country, taking back part of the land lost after the Revolution. The purpose of the Russian presence, of course, was to preserve the peace by protecting the Belorussian and Ukrainian minorities. When Ribbentrop returned to Moscow Stalin was able to acquire all the Baltic States, including Lithuania. He also acquired certain very valuable Polish oil fields, with the understanding to sell oil to Germany.

A secret meeting was supposed to have taken place between

Hitler and Stalin after the fall of Poland. The fate of Finland was supposed to have been the topic. To everyone's amazement little Finland led the attack against Russia. Fighting on their own familiar grounds the Finns were victorious. Even so, they had to cede certain areas to Russia.

Meanwhile, Hitler continued his conquest of Europe. Denmark, Norway, Holland, Luxembourg and finally France fell beneath the German juggernaut. After each conquest Stalin sent a note of congratulations, and with each note he acquired more territory. After the Baltic States he turned his attention to the Balkans, gaining territories held by Romania. The NKVD went to work in these newly acquired territories. Freight car after freight car carried fresh slave labor to the Gulag.

The war between Germany and England was now heating up. The furious battle was in the air. Inspired by the indomitable Churchill, the British were beginning to win that battle. Molotov was sent on a quick visit to Berlin. Hitler and Stalin assured each other of their mutual support.

In March 1941 Stalin received the astonishing word that Hitler would attack Russia between May 15 and June 15. For many reasons he pooh-poohed the idea. For one, Churchill's prediction of an early May invasion of Russia by Hitler backfired when, instead of attacking Russia, the Fuhrer attacked the British on the island of Crete. For another thing, Stalin reasoned that if the Germans were to invade Russia the army would have to be supplied with winter clothes. No preparations were being made for a winter attack. Not that Stalin was not preparing, on his part, to conquer Hitler, and acquire all the countries his ally, and former enemy, had so conveniently lined up. The plan was to liberate all these occupied countries.

Stalin was actually gearing up for a major war with Germany. The military was being glorified. One could achieve no greater honor than to be a soldier and fight for one's country. Composers wrote songs glorifying a Russian victory. Pravda published articles extolling war. Airborne troops were being trained in unprecedented numbers. A new air raid shelter was being built for the Kremlin.

On the other hand Russian embassies in Belgium, Norway and Greece, countries opposed to Hitler, were shut down. Yet in a speech Stalin gave at the Red Army Academy he spoke about taking the offensive. That part of the speech, however, was omitted when it was published in Pravda.

On May 15, 1941 Georgi Zhukov, Chief of The General Staff, urged Stalin to take the offensive, since Germany seemed ready to strike. His suggestion was supported by a number of Russian officers. Stalin preferred to believe that the time wasn't ripe yet. To reassure Hitler of his good faith, he pulled back certain divisions, with the intention of eventually moving them back again. On June 18 he received reports of the movements of German fighter planes. The reports also stated that Hitler was appointing certain men to govern Russian territories as soon as Germany occupied them. The Boss was still skeptical. Hitler would be mad to make such a foolish move.

Hitler, however was mad enough to make such a foolish move. Aware of the fact that Stalin was planning an offensive, he was counting on the element of surprise. A blitzkrieg would give him the advantage. Members of the German Embassy began to leave for home. Stalin took this as a scare tactic.

Meanwhile, he occupied himself with a fascinating archeological and scientific expedition. There was a plan to excavate the body of Tamerlane, the Eastern conqueror, and reconstruct his face to see what he actually looked like. On the evening of June 19 a newspaper crew gathered at the floodlit mausoleum. An old attendant warned that a disaster would occur if the tomb of Tamerlane was desecrated. The tomb was opened. The skull of Tamerlane was held up for the cameras, and the film was flown to Moscow for the Boss to view.

On June 21 a German deserter reported that war would begin at dawn. Reports of German troop movements came from the field. The Russian troops were put on alert. At 9:30 PM Molotov cornered the German ambassador and asked for an explanation.

None was forthcoming. The man just seemed embarrassed. The Politburo went into session. Afterwards Stalin and his chief aides retired to his dacha eating and drinking. At 12:40 AM Molotov sent a telegram to the Soviet ambassador in Berlin, instructing him to question Ribbentrop. At 3:30 AM German planes bombed Belorussia. At 4:40 AM German planes bombed Kiev and Sevastapol. Zhukov, the Chief Of Staff, put in a call to Stalin. He asked that the Boss be awakened at once.

What? Right now? Comrade Stalin is sleeping, said the guard on duty.

Wake him up immediately, said Zhukov, *the Germans are bombing our cities.*

Three minutes later the Boss was on the phone. He summoned Molotov and the entire Politburo to the Kremlin. Three days after Tamerlane was exhumed Russia was defending itself against a German attack.

AUGUST 1952

Stalin receives China's premier, Zhou Enlai, in Moscow.

ALVIN GORMAN: PART THREE

Herb Volpe was deeply disturbed by Alvin's arrest. He compared his own situation to Alvin's. Society welcomed his passion for his wife. He remembered the first few weeks of his marriage, the joy of turning over in bed to find one's lovely partner. There she was every single night. She was there in the middle of the night, or early in the morning...or any time at all. It was all perfectly legal, and it was so glorious it was sinful.

Yet Alvin's love life was marked by shame. Herb didn't understand the idea of romantic love between two men. He could understand the sex. Men deprived of woman might turn to one another for gratification, like in a prison or in the army. He remembered, at the age of twelve, meeting secretly with four of his friends in the basement. What a strange miracle it was to discover that that thing between one's legs was capable of so much more. It seemed perfectly natural to share this discovery with his friends. He remembered admiring a handsome man and then feeling guilty about it. The human animal was, after all, a mystery. And if two men loved each other, why the hell not?

Several of his theatre friends were openly gay. Gay. Not exactly the right word he thought as he pictured Alvin's woeful expression when he picked him up at the police station. He now understood Alvin's dilemma, the reluctance to reveal his inner feelings, the determination to isolate himself, the intensity with which he threw himself into that very virile role he was playing, and he dreaded accompanying Alvin to court in the morning.

Actually it was noon. He respected Alvin's wishes to keep the unpleasant incident a secret from the rest of the cast, and he'd have to think of a reason to start off two hours later than planned.

At a quarter to twelve Herb met Alvin at a coffee shop three blocks away from the hotel. Alvin was seated at the counter when Herb arrived. He was wearing a shirt, tie and jacket and looked like he was going to his execution.

What did you tell the cast, asked Alvin, *about starting late?*

I didn't tell them anything, since nobody asked, said Herb. *I was prepared to tell them I was expecting a call from Stanley at the hotel.*

TOURING WITH STALIN

Alvin paid for the cup of tea he'd been nursing, and they started out for the courtroom, which was in the town hall. It was five minutes to twelve when they arrived. The visitors' section of the courtroom had like five or six people. Herb took a seat in the third row on the aisle. Alvin sat in the first row. Ten anxious minutes later the judge entered and everyone rose. The judge took his seat. He shuffled through the papers in front of him. He was a very composed middle aged man, and was rather prim looking with wire frame glasses.

The first case involved a heavy set, sheepish looking man accused of beating his wife. Apparently he was a repeat offender. This was his fourth time up. The man mumbled something incoherently.

I don't want to hear a word out of you, said the judge. *Thirty days, and I wish it could be more.*

The man was led away, looking resigned.

Alvin was called up next. The detective who Alvin met in front of he public toilet appeared from nowhere.

What's the charge? asked the judge.

The detective, with a perfectly straight face, told the judge that Alvin had signaled him while in the toilet, then met him outside where he invited him up to his room to perform a sex act. Alvin stood aghast at the false, lurid picture painted by the detective. How could someone lie like that? Alvin felt sick to his stomach and gave up. What was the point? It was his word against an officer of the law.

Is this true? asked the judge.

Alvin nodded. He felt numb all over.

I didn't hear you, said the judge.

Yes, said Alvin.

I still didn't hear you, said the judge.

Yes, said Alvin a little louder.

What? Are you a man lover? asked the judge, spitting out the last two words as if they were so vile it was difficult for him to let them pass his lips.

Yes, said Alvin to himself. That's what I am, a man lover,

and that's certainly nothing to be ashamed of. Actually it's something to be proud of. What's more precious than love?

The judge went on to comment about Alvin being in the company that gave a very impressive performance the night before, adding that Alvin was a disgrace to his profession. He dismissed Alvin with disgust. *One hundred and twenty five dollars, or thirty days!*

Alvin started to follow the clerk to another room. Herb caught up with him and slipped him the money he needed to supplement what he had. Alvin paid the fine, was given a receipt and met Herb in the lobby.

Thanks, said Alvin.

They walked back to the hotel in silence. Alvin wondered whether Herb believed the detective. But, of course, Herb did since he was foolish enough to admit it. He debated telling Herb the exact truth, and decided there was no point. Besides, the intention was there, even if the details were false.

As they approached the hotel they caught sight of Paul Thomas coming out of the hotel with his suitcase. Paul went directly to the back of the van and was out of sight. Herb assumed they hadn't been seen and, respecting Alvin's request for secrecy, told Alvin to go on ahead. As Alvin approached the hotel he was greeted by Paul.

Out for a walk? asked Paul.

Yes, said Alvin and entered the hotel.

Paul lit a cigarette and lingered in front of the hotel. A few minutes later Herb came walking down the street.

Out for a walk? asked Paul slyly.

Herb ignored the question. *Ready to go?* he asked.

All loaded up, said Paul.

He watched Herb enter the hotel, sighed and shook his head. The company left for Nashville at eleven thirty. Paul was strangely quiet for the rest of the day. If he had respect for anyone in the company it was Herb. There was usually some sort of inconsequential banter between them, but that night he pointedly avoided Herb.

Alvin, too, was unusually subdued. His performance was lackluster. After the curtain came down, Herb walked over to Alvin and, to everyone's surprise, put his arm around Alvin's shoulder. While the rest of the cast looked on in surprise, Herb led Alvin aside.

You mustn't let it get you down, said Herb.

I know, said Alvin. *I'll be all right.*

We're going to have some drinks at the bar in the hotel, said Herb *Why don't you join us?*

I don't think so, said Alvin. *Thank you.*

When Herb entered the dressing room alone everyone looked up.

Has Alvin got a problem? asked Paul.

We've all got problems, Paul, said Herb, and started to remove his costume.

Some more than others, said Paul.

Alvin entered the room and proceeded to change. Paul picked up his jacket and walked out of the dressing room, slamming the door behind him.

What's the matter with him? asked Nat.

Herb didn't answer. He finished dressing and left calling out to Nat, Ralph and Ted, who were still changing, *See you later.* Alvin changed quickly and as he stepped out the door he turned, smiled weakly, and said, *Good night.* The three men looked at each other questioningly. *Whatever his problem is,* said Nat, *it's sure an improvement.*

He wasn't up to snuff this evening, said Ralph.

Maybe it's someone he ate, said Ted with a wicked grin.

Ralph and Nat looked at Ted in surprise. Ted always had this air of old world respectability. This was a raunchy side of Ted they hadn't been aware of.

The entire company, except for Alvin gathered in the bar half an hour later. Even Nat, who usually went right to bed, since he got up very early to work on his play, showed up. Everyone expected some sort of an explanation. After the beers had been ordered and served Herb offered a toast to Ted's son and daughter-in-law. They were expecting another child. This was a particularly important event, since they had recently lost a child. There was a moment of silence as everyone took a sip of their beers, then Nat looked at Herb and spoke up.

We're all of us waiting, said Nat.

For what? asked Herb.

What's Alvin's problem? asked Nat.

As if we didn't know, said Paul.

Actually, I'd like to know what your problem is, Ralph said to Paul.

Alvin's going through a very difficult time, said Herb.

Is there anything we can do? asked Betsy.

No, said Herb. *Just go about our business. He'll work it out.*

Paul set his mug down on the table, rose and announced, *I've gotta take a piss,* then marched off to the mens' room.

After a moment Herb rose quietly and made for the mens' room. When he entered he found Paul alone at the commode. Paul looked up, zipped up and walked over to the basin. He washed and dried his hands and started to leave. Herb was blocking the door.

If you've got something to say, say it, said Herb.

I'm very disappointed in you, said Paul.

Go on, said Herb.

I saw the two of you coming down the street, said Paul.

And you think...? Herb stopped and smiled. *I'm sorry to disappoint you.*

Then it's true? asked Paul.

No, Paul, I am not having a...thing with Alvin, said Herb. *He's going through a rough time and he wanted to keep it private. Is there anything else?*

No, said Paul.

Good, said Herb. He patted Paul on the shoulder and walked over to the urinal. Paul hesitated and left.

Things quieted down after that. Paul tried to dismiss the affair from his mind, but was left with a residue of uneasiness in regard to Herb.

For his part, Alvin nursed his wounds for several weeks.

Eventually he reverted to his own private world, which now contained an island of gratitude for the kindness Herb had shown him.

STALIN

Before he could accept the obvious, that Hitler had beaten him to the punch, Stalin sent Molotov to speak to the German ambassador. Perhaps this was all just a ruse. While they waited for Molotov's report, word came through that the Germans were moving rapidly into the country and finding no resistance. Molotov returned and reported that *The German government has declared war on us.*

Stalin had Molotov make the first address to the people. It ended with words written by Stalin, *Our cause is just, the enemy will be smashed, victory will be ours.*

The Boss created the General Headquarters (GHQ) of the High Command. All thought of world revolution, of international communism was abandoned. It was replaced by patriotism, loyalty to the Motherland. Stalin had recovered from the shock. Who was to blame? Somebody was responsible for this dire situation. He rode on a wave of fury, castigating generals right and left. The army was ordered to attack. Word went out that a Peoples' Militia was being formed. It was voluntary, of course, but those that did not volunteer, were looked down upon.

Moscow prepared for war. Windows were blacked out. Street lamps were extinguished. On June 24 an air raid signal was sounded. People took refuge in the shelters. Reports were received that enemy planes had been shot down. It turned out that the downed planes were actually Russian planes returning from a bombing mission.

Trusting no one, Stalin stuck his nose into everything. It didn't help that reports he sometimes received were diluted. Aides were afraid to tell him how bad the news was. They exaggerated enemy losses. When he lost his temper too often he could sense the resentment. He began to realize that he might be losing his grip. His power was based on fear, and people were afraid, but not of him any longer. That, of course, would have to be remedied, eventually. Eventually heads would have to roll.

There was, however, one stopgap remedy. For two days he was incommunicado. He made no appearance whatsoever at the Kremlin. Nothing was seen of him. It was as if he had disappeared from the face of the earth. Panic began to set in. Had the Boss collapsed? Was he deathly ill? Or had he just given up hope? Finally a delegation was sent to his dacha. They were met by a haggard, gloomy looking man. He had failed the people, he claimed. He had failed Lenin. Perhaps there was someone else much better than he to lead the country to victory. The delegation pleaded with him vociferously. They reasoned loudly, insistently. No one could take his place. He was their leader. He was the Boss, Thus was the Boss reinstated. He was back in the saddle and held the reins once more.

On July 3rd Stalin finally made his address to the people. During his private hiatus, apparently, he resolved on some radical changes. Suddenly a Godless country now welcomed God into its midst. God's name would now be on soldiers' lips as they went into battle. This was a patriotic war, a holy war. Two of his close aides were religious men. One of them had a vision. The mother of God appeared to him. The churches, he said, and the monasteries must be reopened. Priests must be released from prison. The sacred icon of Our Lady of Kazan must be preserved. It must be paraded from city to city. As a result, twenty thousand churches were reopened. The icon of Our Lady of Kazan was paraded through the streets of Leningrad, through the streets of Moscow and then sent to the besieged city of Stalingrad.

Now that he'd solidified his leadership Stalin decided to try to negotiate with Hitler. He ordered Beria to put out feelers. What his motives were, wasn't exactly clear. Was he serious, or was he just bargaining for time? At any rate the effort fell flat. Hitler wasn't interested.

One of his aides mentioned that his first son, Sasha, had joined the army. He asked if the boy should be sent to the front. Stalin replied angrily that he should never be asked questions like that. On July 19, 1941 Stalin received word that Sasha had been taken prisoner. The Germans made the most of it. Headlines, leaflets dropped from the air proclaimed that Stalin's son had surrendered.

The Boss had never been fond of his first born. Sasha

graduated from the Academy and joined the army the first day of the war, and was sent to the front. Stalin had no time to see the boy before he left. Now he hated the child. The boy's relatives on his mother's side suffered from his dislike as well. Both the boy's aunt and uncle were shot. When the Red Cross offered to try to obtain the boy's release he never answered. When the offer came to exchange his son for a German general, he replied that he was not in the business of trading a general for an ordinary soldier.

Gradually, however, it came out that Sasha had acted heroically. He was a prisoner, but an honorable one. The boy had redeemed himself in the father's eyes and the Boss spoke proudly of him. He would sooner die than surrender. This was a decree that the Boss had ordered. No soldier could surrender. Those that did would pay the penalty. Their parents would suffer for it as well. While in prison Sasha demanded to see the commandant. While the guard was on the phone the young man wandered into the forbidden zone. When ordered to halt he kept on going. He was shot. Mortally wounded he kept on walking till he fell on the electric fence. His body hung there for twenty four hours, after which it was dispatched to the crematorium.

His second son, Vasily, was not so noble. Perhaps his childhood was to blame. His mother was a suicide. He hardly ever saw his father, and he was aware of the fact that many of his close relatives had been executed. Though his school grades were not very good he was sent to the much sought after Air Force Training Unit. There he took advantage of his connection and, as a result he was pampered like a prince. Stalin put a stop to the special treatment. After graduation he was sent to train with an Elite Air Force. The report came back that, though he was a capable pilot, he was in danger because of his excessive drinking.

After the death of his brother, Vasily was kept safely on the ground. He mingled with a sophisticated, raunchy crowd and had one affair after another. In restaurants, when drunk, he would shoot at the chandeliers. The game was called "the cut glass chimes." On a drunken spree he wounded himself in the cheek and in one leg.

His father relieved him of his command and sent him to the

front. Occasionally he was allowed aerial combat under heavy protection. His father saw to it that he received promotions regularly. He was promoted to head of Air Force Inspection with nothing to do, but drink. By the war's end, at the age of twenty four, he was a general. The drinking, however, never stopped.

His daughter, Svetlana, at this time, became another thorn in his side. As a child he doted on her. They'd play games in which he was obliged to obey her orders. When the war began she was fifteen. He had to accept the fact that she was growing up, and becoming independent. He was determined to keep an eye on her though and an NKVD agent was assigned "to protect her." The agent never let her out of his sight.

When the enemy was advancing toward Moscow she was evacuated to a nearby town for safety. It was there that she experienced the shock of learning of her mother's suicide, which must have had a great effect on her. When the city was safe she returned to Moscow. She shared a dacha with Vasily's wife and child. Vasily often brought members of his fast crowd to the house. Despite the fact that there was a war going on, the house was alive with the phonograph playing loudly, dancing and drinking.

At one of these parties Svetlana met Alexei Kapler, a film writer and a notorious ladies' man. Kapler was fat, ugly and not particularly talented, but he was a great talker. As a raconteur he could cast a spell. He had recently returned from the front where he'd been sent as a war corespondent. The shy young girl was enthralled by the daring tales he had to tell. In turn, the forty year old roue fell in love with her. They danced, they talked. She told him everything.

After that they met secretly. He'd wait across the street from her school till she came out. He passed on forbidden books to her which, if discovered, could have cost him his life. Finally, under the watchful eye of the NKVD agent Kapler escorted his young love to an art gallery, to the opera to see "The Queen of Spades." Stalin, of course, was aware of all this, but was too busy with the war to pay much attention to it. That was, until the foolish Kapler wrote an article which appeared in Pravda, from which one might deduce that he was having an affair with the Boss's daughter. Stalin was fit to be tied. He managed to control his temper and had one of his guards call Kapler and suggest that the writer undertake an assignment that would take him away from Moscow. Kapler told the man to go to hell.

Kapler and Svetlana continued to date. When they spent some time alone in an empty room the NKVD agent grew alarmed and sent in his report. Kapler was arrested. Stalin confronted his daughter, telling her that the man was an English spy. *I love him,* said the rebellious girl. For the first time in his life Stalin slapped her, twice. Then said nastily, *Just look at yourself. Who do you think would want you?* She stopped talking to him, and their relationship was never the same.

Meanwhile Kapler was thrown into prison. From there he was sent up north for five years, where he was allowed to work in the theatre. He returned to Kiev, where his parents lived, since he was forbidden to enter Moscow. He made the mistake of taking a brief excursion to the city, where he was picked up and sent to work in the mines for the next five years. After a brief return to the Moscow prison, after over ten years of confinement, he was finally given his freedom.

SEPTEMBER 1952

In regard to the Korean War, Stalin and Zhou En Lai discuss the exchange of POWs, peace negotiations, Chinese cooperation with India and Burma, and creation of regional organizations.

It was in Ada, Oklahoma at the beginning of March that Betsy Landers finally heard from Arnold Handsman. His prospective new soap opera fell through. However, he was in a position to guarantee her television work if she returned to New York. She said she'd call him back that evening, or the next morning. After she hung up she sat lost in thought.

Now that the end was really at hand, she began to have second thoughts. The tour had three more months to go. She could save some more money. But that really wasn't an issue. She'd put enough aside, and besides she had some money in the bank to begin with. She did enjoy playing Luba, Rubashov's love interest, more than she thought she would, and she knew Herb would regret losing her. But did he really need her? And did she really need him? How much did they really mean to one another?

They were more than friends. Maybe they weren't lovers. You might say they were soul mates, and as such, he should be pleased to see her move on, and certainly under Arnold Handsman's wing, she would move on. Not that performing in soap operas was her ultimate goal, but she would be comfortable while she continued her assault on Broadway. And besides, acting in a soap opera was acting, wasn't it?

She picked up the phone and rang Herb's room. She arranged to have dinner with him before the show. They chose a restaurant in the area where, they hoped, they would not be joined by members of the company. It was the first time they'd been alone in months.

So, what's up? said Herb.

Arnold called, said Betsy.

I see, said Herb. *Well, I can't blame you.*

Herb obviously believed that the new soap opera had come through. Betsy hesitated at telling him the truth. Angry at herself at the thought of concealing it from him she finally blurted out, *The soap opera didn't come through, the new one, that is.*

She's come to cry on my shoulder, thought Herb. Poor, dear Betsy, if only she'd find someone. That stupid Nat. He'd be right for her, if he wasn't gay, and maybe he isn't, for all I know. But there's something wrong somewhere. Maybe I ought to have a talk with him.

But he wants me to come anyway, Betsy was saying. *He promises that he'll find work for me. What do you think?*

Herb said nothing, since he knew an answer was pointless. Betsy had a mind of her own.

This tour is getting me nowhere, Herb. You're angry.

Don't talk nonsense, said Herb.

I'm letting you down, said Betsy.

Of course, you've got to go. Arnold has connections, and he's on your team.

Herb phoned Stanley the next morning and told him that Betsy was giving in her two weeks notice. Stanley cursed and said, *It's always something.*

And don't send me someone the very last minute, said Herb. He decided not to say anything to the cast until Stanley found a replacement.

Betsy phoned Arnold Handsman the next morning and said she'd be back in town in about two and a half weeks. As the days went by she began to get sentimental about her leavetaking. They were, after all, a family. Of course, she was closer to some more than to others. Herb, of course, and Ted Lombard, who was like a father and Ralph Krumsky, who was like a younger brother.

Ralph was the first one she told. He tried to be enthusiastic about this upward move she was making. He'd given up hope of a romantic relationship, but they were like brother and sister, he thought. He took down her New York address and her phone number. He confided in Nat Brenner.

Did you know that Betsy is leaving? he said to Nat.

Really? said Nat. *I wonder why.*

She's had offers for work in television, said Ralph.

Television?! said Nat, as if it were a dirty word. *Why would she want to do television?*

It's acting, said Ralph. *It's work.*

Nat shrugged. He could understand leaving the show for a movie, or a Broadway show, but television... *I hope she knows what she's doing,* said Nat. He ran into her at lunch in the coffee shop in the hotel the next day. He was sitting at a table eating his soup when she entered. *You're welcome to join me,* he said.

Thank you, said Betsy.

She sat down at the table.

After the waitress took her order, Nat said, *I hear you're leaving the show.*

Yes, said Betsy, *Yes, I am.*

I'm sorry to see you go, said Nat. He could say that now, now that he'd be safe.

Thank you, said Betsy, wondering why he took the trouble. Did he really mean that?

I hope it's a better job, said Nat.

Betsy sat looking at him, as he finished eating his soup. He'd put on a little weight since they started out, and he'd grown a goatee in order to save having to put spirit gum on his face to keep the false beard in place, but he was still an attractive man. She wasn't quite convinced that he was gay, despite Herb's pronouncement.

Ralph said you'll be doing television, Nat continued.

And auditioning, said Betsy. *There are a couple of agents that keep sending me out.*

Well, you are talented, said Nat.

Where is this man coming from, she wondered. He must be gay. *How's your play coming along?* she asked.

I don't know, said Nat. *I keep rewriting and rewriting.*

Maybe you ought to go on to something else, said Betsy.

I hope you've made the right decision, said Nat. He picked up his check. *See you later,* he said, and left.

How come I'm the last one to know, said Ted Lombard, as he joined Betsy at the table.

I hope I've made the right decision, said Betsy.

What have you got to lose? asked Ted. *We'll miss you.*

Thank you, said Betsy. *I'll miss you, too. All of you.*

Ah, yes, said Ted. *All the families I've been a part of all these years. I'll have some interesting memories when I retire.*

TOURING WITH STALIN

You're not going to retire, said Betsy.

If Edie had her way, I would, said Ted.

You're not even sixty, said Betsy.

Paul Thomas heard about Betsy's coming departure one night after the show, when some members of the company were having some beers. He made no comment. She beat me to it, was the thought that crossed his mind.

Alvin Gorman, back in his own private world, was unaware of Betsy's imminent departure until, that is, Herb made an announcement before the show one night, that a new actor would be joining the company. Alvin panicked for one moment. The horrible thought crossed his mind that he was being replaced.

Who's leaving? he asked.

Betsy, said Herb. *She's going back to New York to be a big television star.*

Oh, said Alvin, heaving an inward sigh of relief.

Three days before Betsy's scheduled departure Jane Applebaum arrived. She looked younger than Betsy, much younger. A little shorter as well, solidly built, rather pretty with shoulder length red hair and a few freckles. There was something straight from the shoulder, no-nonsense about her. With Betsy's assistance, Herb ran through her scenes. Jane knew her lines and was completely professional, Herb was relieved to find. But, alas, she was no Betsy Landers.

The girl seemed completely comfortable in her skin and made friends with everyone in the cast. Even Paul and Alvin seemed to take to her, which was a amazing, especially for Alvin. She was so down to earth and unpretentious that it would be hard to find fault with her.

Despite all these positive aspects of her personality she did not have Betsy's special warmth, which was a great relief to Nat Brenner. Jane was safe. She could make a good friend, but he couldn't see himself having an affair with her, and now that Betsy was leaving he realized that Betsy was someone he could be serious about. Or was that because she was leaving and would be out of reach? He resolved to keep in touch with her after he got back to New York. After all, you never know.

In the back of his mind, however, there was still the thought that his ex-wife might come to her senses and come back to him, even though they were now divorced. He still could not understand how she could bring herself to leave him, after all the support he had given her.

Betsy gave her last performance in Alexandria, Minnesota. The performance was an emotional one for the entire company. Herb and Betsy found the evening particularly moving. The lines where Rubashov tells Luba that their relationship can never be more than this, and he takes his leave and tells her that they may never see each other again took on a special meaning. The two of them seldom did see one another; and Herb seemed to be putting a special emphasis on the lines where Rubashov tells Luba that she should find herself a husband and get married.

After the performance the entire company, including Alvin, as well as Jane, gathered in the bar in the hotel. Herb, Ted and Ralph toasted Betsy. After that there didn't seem that much more to talk about. The farewell gathering ended rather abruptly, since the company was starting out very early the next morning. Betsy was planning to take a train the next afternoon to Chicago, where she would catch a plane to New York City. Betsy kissed everyone goodbye, and the cast retired to their respective rooms.

Betsy was up most of the night, wondering what was going to happen next, wondering what turn her life would take. Uneasy as she'd been to take the job, her nights as the love of a Russian commissar slowly became a romantic haze.

STALIN

During July 1941 Stalin and Russia were facing their darkest hours. Stalin's personal affairs had sunk to a new low. His first son, Sasha, whom originally he hadn't been very fond of, turned out to be a hero by meeting what amounted to a martyr's death as a prisoner of the Germans. His second son, Vasily, was a hopeless drunk and a wastrel. His beloved daughter, Svetlana, had defied him and gone her own way, getting involved with men he disapproved of. They were never really close again. Meanwhile the Germans continued their invasion and were now one hundred and fifty miles from Moscow.

In August Stalin finally pulled himself together. He took up the reins and regained his undisputed power by the surest means he knew how...the use of fear, fear inspired by terror. Men had no choice but to fight and die. Deserters were shot. In addition to ordinary soldiers, officers were shot. Commanding generals, three of the highest ranking commanders were executed for cowardice and mismanagement. No one now dared to question Stalin's failure to anticipate the German invasion. Men now died with the words *For the Motherland! For Stalin!* on their lips. The Germans found that the Russian supply of manpower was inexhaustible. One German complained that where there were two hundred divisions to begin with, now there were three hundred and sixty.

In addition to that, Hitler found himself short of supplies. Hoping to gain supplies from the Ukraine, counting on its animosity towards Russia, he judged wrongly. For one thing the brutality of the German soldiers worked against him. In addition to that his attempt to annihilate the Jews stirred up the animosity of the Russian intellectuals who entered passionately into the fray.

In October the Germans resumed their march on Moscow. Fortunately they were slowed up by the autumn rains. Tanks and trucks were stuck in the mud. Then a miracle happened. Snow in October. The temperature fell dramatically. It was so cold the oil froze in their vehicles. Russians were dying but, on the other hand, the Germans were losing their strength, getting weaker and weaker. Nevertheless, by the middle of October, the Germans were twenty miles away from Moscow. Hitler was jubilant.

TOURING WITH STALIN

Stalin decided to evacuate the government to a distant city. It was also decided to smuggle the precious body of Lenin out of Moscow. The news of this decision could have had a devastating effect on the morale of the people so the operation was conducted with the greatest secrecy. A special coffin was put together. A train was found with springs to prevent the jarring of the body, and the temperature in the car had to be just right.

And finally Stalin, himself, made preparations to leave. His daughter, Svetlana, helped pack his books. His dacha was booby trapped to prevent its being looted. The entire family was evacuated. Bonfires were lit to burn the archives. Prisoners were shot. Food in the shops was distributed to the people to prevent the Germans from confiscating them. People sold all their valuables for a pittance. Special trains were lined up to carry out the women and the children.

Suddenly Stalin changed his mind. He appeared abruptly at his dacha, which had been mined and was about to be blown up. The mines were cleared. The lights were turned on. Moscow would not be surrendered. Looters were shot. House managers who abetted the looters were shot. The word was out. Stalin was staying. He'd decided not to give up the city.

Elaborate plans were made to celebrate the anniversary of the October Revolution. Since the Bolshoi Theatre had been badly damaged the celebration would now take place in the Mayakovsky Square Metro Station, which had been decked out to resemble the Bolshoi. Stalin rose to make his speech. This was followed by the traditional concert. Secret preparations were made for a magnificent parade. A hospital was set up in GUM, the mammoth department store. This was in case there was an air raid. As luck would have it a heavy snowfall sheltered the Russian troops as they marched by preventing the incursion of enemy planes. The troops marched defiantly and triumphantly directly from the streets of Moscow to the front.

The defense of Moscow continued under General Zukhov. The German soldiers, victims of the freezing cold, continued the siege. Russian soldiers fell right and left. Zukhov demanded more troops, begged for more. Stalin refused to supply them. He held in abeyance a large striking force. Then, at the very last minute, when the Germans were at their weakest, he unleashed his own blitzkrieg. The German attack was halted. The back of the German invasion was broken, and Hitler would never again gain the upper hand.

As far as the defense of Russia was concerned this might be called Stalin's finest hour. He organized his military operations with a clear mind and a firm hand. Millions may have died in his ruthless handling of his forces, but if the Germans had been victorious more people would have met a worse fate.

After rescuing Moscow the Boss turned his attention to the defense of the city that bore his name. Stalingrad had been almost leveled. But in December 1942 a counterattack was launched and the German forces were destroyed. German prisoners, haggard and filthy were marched through the streets of Stalingrad.

The bitterest encounter took place in Leningrad. In July 1941 the city was cut off and a siege took place that lasted ninety days. The German army placed women and children in front of them as a buffer. Russian soldiers were reluctant to fire. The order came down to level the enemy, voluntary or not. There was no electricity in the city. No pure drinking water. People were starving to death. They froze to death, dropped in the streets and died. Skeletal men volunteered to fight then fell down and died. The blockade was eventually broken after the loss of countless lives. Perhaps the rescue could have come sooner, but the Boss had his reasons. And besides, Hitler's command read, "We have no interest in preserving any part of the population of that large city."

After Hitler's invasion of Russia, England became, reluctantly, Stalin's ally. Stalin now clamored for a second front, but Churchill kept putting him off. After Pearl Harbor which, incidentally, according to Stalin's intelligence, Churchill knew of in advance and neglected to inform Roosevelt, in order to draw America into the war, Stalin sent the Jewish Litvinov to America as ambassador. The Yiddish Theatre and Yiddish poets suddenly found themselves in favor. Mikhoels, the famous Yiddish director, was enrolled in collecting money from wealthy American Jews. Another of his missions was to raise American support for a second front. Litvinov arranged for American shipments of war supplies as well as food parcels to Russia.

In 1943 Churchill paid a visit to Russia, where he was greeted royally. The two men seemed to have much in common. The Englishman still refused to open a second front, heading his armies south for Africa instead.

Left to his own devices, with the support of Allied weapons and food supplies, Stalin built up a massive military force. In the spring of 1943 he dissolved the Comintern. The message was that Russia had no intention of involving itself in European affairs. In preparation for extending his influence deep into the European continent, Stalin did his utmost to give the impression that Bolshevism, as such, had come to an end.

OCTOBER 1952

The Supreme Court rejects the Rosenbergs' appeal of their conviction for stealing atomic secrets for the Russians, and eight New York City teachers are fired for alleged communist activities.

JANE APPLEBAUM

The arrival of Jane Applebaum as Betsy Landers' replacement seemed to remind everyone that the national tour of Darkness At Noon had less then three months to go; ten weeks to be exact. Had they really been out on the road for over five months? In no time at all, their private sheltered theatre world would dissolve, disappear and become a memory.

Herb Volpe looked forward to greeting his lovely wife with his newborn son, now due in less than four weeks. He'd picked up a small, portable phonograph and each night he'd play one selection from the record Helen had recorded. His favorite was the aria, Un Bel Di, from Madame Butterfly. Sometimes it made him tremble, he was so moved by the emotion of the song. The loveliness of the voice, the vision of the beauty of his wife's face often brought tears of joy to his eyes. How proud he was as he played the record for the cast and watched them listen so intently and then shower his wife with praise!

Ted Lombard looked forward to a visit with his son and his pregnant daughter-in-law. He wondered how he could have been so blind for all those years, how he could not have seen what a remarkable young man he and his wife, Edie, had produced. But then, again, he reasoned, maybe the boy had had some growing up to do as well. Maybe they both had matured with the years.

Nat Brenner was reluctant to leave this comfortable cocoon, the ability to get up in the morning and attack his typewriter, then ride in the van relaxed and peaceful, having done a morning's work, and then look forward to giving an assured performance in a role he had made his own, a role which was praised by the critics, a role with which he could manipulate an audience and make them titter, shock them and move them. What a glorious world he lived in, and certainly when he showed his reviews to the New York agents, to the New York producers he was bound to get more work. But, of course, he still had to master the craft of playwriting.

Ralph Krumsky continued to enjoy his first professional acting job, as well as the adventure of travelling across the continent of America and seeing the country he lived in for the very first time. And when the tour ended and he settled in New York, Herb promised to show him the ropes.

Paul Thomas did not have ten long weeks to wait. The following week he planned to hand in his two weeks notice. He might look back, in years to come, with fondness on this tour. At the moment, however, there was not one bit of sentiment for the tour or for the company, for that matter. He couldn't wait to get out and decide what to do next.

And Alvin Gorman refused to think about what was coming next, because he dreaded what was coming next. When, again, would he find a role he was so suited for? He might even approach Stanley about going out again next year.

And what of Jane Applebaum, the newcomer to the cast? First of all, the job was a life-saver. Jane was a free spirit, and sometimes, in pursuing ones freedom, one forgets that one must eat and pay ones bills. She was twenty three, and one was getting a little too old to run home for refuge when things got a little hairy, especially when one's parents were getting a little impatient with their daughter's "la vie boheme."

The first shock she provided the cast with was her ability to communicate with Alvin. They actually talked to one another like ordinary human beings. She saw nothing odd about Alvin, and Alvin, for his part seemed to welcome being treated as a normal person. She treated Herb with respect, but certainly was not in awe of him nor did she express any admiration. He was just another actor she was hired to play opposite. Ted Lombard wasn't quite sure what to make of this young lady. She certainly had spirit, and she certainly was an attractive young thing. Ralph also found her rather puzzling. She reminded him of the fast girls in his class at the university. Paul found her rather amusing, and Jane, for her part didn't quite know how to figure Paul out, nor did she find him particularly interesting. Nat admired her spirit, found her safe because he was not physically attracted to her and the two of them, coming from a Jewish background, seemed to speak the same language. They bonded rather quickly.

What puzzled Nat about Jane was her cavalier attitude

towards everything, especially her career as an actress. She seemed to be above all that. And then there was her obvious disinterest in what anyone thought of her. Being a free spirit, thought Nat, was all well and good, but what did she want out of life? Surely adventure couldn't be the be-all and the end-all. One ought to have a specific goal in mind, thought Nat. He began to be concerned about this wild creature. She could be heading for a lot of trouble.

One day at breakfast in a hotel coffee shop he sat studying her nose. It was perfect.

It ought to be, said Jane. *I paid for it.*

Ever since his ex-wife had a nose job, which improved her appearance immensely, Nat had contemplated having his nose done. Not that his nose was as bad as his wife's...she'd been cursed with a schnozzola. Actually he thought his nose gave him sort of an aristocratic look. On the other hand, he felt that it prevented him from being cast as a romantic lead.

Jane described her operation, which took place in the office of a plastic surgeon in Brooklyn. It hadn't been that much of an ordeal and, most important of all, it hadn't been that expensive. Nat took down the name of the plastic surgeon, and made up his mind that, when the tour came to an end, he was going to have his nose done.

Jane appeared to be full of surprises. Her businesslike attitude towards those around her tended to antagonize people. Here was this petite, pretty girl acting as if she were...what, exactly? As if she were in charge of things. Herb had the feeling that this newcomer could run the company as well as he could, maybe better. Ted Lombard wondered where this assurance, in one so young, came from. It turned out that little Jane was actually a veteran. She'd been in the business since she was a child.

The only one in the company that showed his resentment openly was Paul Thomas. There seemed to be a minor ongoing skirmish taking place between the two of them, Paul being the aggressor. He adopted this attitude of sarcasm toward Jane. Wherever possible he'd slip in a snide remark. The matter came to a head one night at a bar after a performance in Kansas City. Most of the cast had turned in. Jane, Paul and Nat were the only ones left. Paul, as usual, had drunk too much and was feeling no pain. He was questioning Jane's taste in people, Alvin Gorman, for one.

You don't like Alvin? asked Jane.

I don't know Alvin, said Paul, *and I don't want to know him, and I think the feeling is mutual.*

That's understandable, said Jane.

You like Alvin? asked Paul.

More than I do you, said Jane.

Maybe you're more tolerant than I am, said Paul.

And you're in show business? said Jane.

Being an actor, said Paul, *does not mean that one has to lose one's sense of decency.*

I quite agree, said Jane.

What do you know? said Peter.

I know it's a mistake, said Jane, *to pass judgement on people, when you know nothing about people.*

I know a queer when I see one, said Paul.

Do you really? asked Jane. *I've slept with a woman. Would you call me queer?*

I wouldn't put it past you, said Paul, *but I don't think you have.*

Suit yourself, said Jane. *I'm ready for bed.*

Jane rose and, without saying good night to Paul, left the bar accompanied by Nat. *He really pisses me off,* said Jane as they walked back to the hotel. As they started for their respective rooms Nat said, *Was that true? That you slept with a woman?*

Why? asked Jane, *Are you shocked?*

I'm not shocked, said Nat. *I'm just surprised.*

Jane invited Nat into her room. They sat down and Jane went on to tell Nat about the affair she had with a beautiful, exotic movie star when she was in Hollywood. Nat listened in fascination. The story, coming from this sweet innocent looking girl, seemed preposterous, but he didn't doubt her veracity. What wasn't she capable of, and where was she heading?

He wandered back to his room, lost in thought. He wished

he had the courage to face life that boldly, but he was a prisoner, a prisoner of the goals he'd set for himself, to be a great playwright and to be a star. But suppose his imprisonment meant cutting himself off from life experiences, depriving him of material he might need for his art? It took Nat a long time to get to sleep that night.

Jane, for her part, looked forward to the company's coming engagements on the West Coast. Who knows? Her return there might engender some interesting developments.

In 1943 Churchill, Roosevelt and Stalin met in Teheran. Stalin was a day late for his first meeting with the American president. Churchill's and Roosevelt's styles were quite different and Stalin did his best to take advantage of this.

Presenting him with the Stalingrad Sword, Churchill proclaimed, *Marshall Stalin can take his place beside the major figures in Russian history.*

Stalin replied, *It is easy to be a hero when you are dealing with people like the Russians.*

In 1944 the Allies opened the Second Front. While they landed in Normandy the Boss took over Poland, Hungary, Romania, Yugoslavia and Czechoslovakia. A Communist dominated army conquered Greece.

On October 9, 1944 Churchill, along with Eden, but without the presence of Roosevelt, quickly arranged to meet with Stalin in Moscow. A heated bargaining took place. In exchange for Romania Stalin traded Greece and Italy. The Balkans were divided by percentages giving the greatest percent to the Boss. This was a gentleman's agreement, sealed with a handshake, and worth the paper it was written on, since Stalin knew that Roosevelt would not accept these secret deals. When Churchill tried to meet secretly with Hitler, the Boss let the American president know and the attempt was aborted.

When the Germans surprised the Allies in the Ardennes, Stalin came to the rescue. This valiant effort had its rewards when it came time to negotiate the division of the European Continent. As the war neared its end Roosevelt and Churchill were Stalin's guests in Yalta, where they were housed in the Livadia Palace, the favorite residence of the last tsar. The disarmament of Germany and the establishment of the United Nations were dealt with and, of course, the partition of the continent of Europe.

Stalin insisted on Poland but, before this could be accomplished, there was a rather embarrassing matter that had to be cleared up. Reminded of the incident in 1918 when the Czechoslovak prisoners revolted, Stalin secretly ordered the massacre of the twenty thousand Polish officers held near the

TOURING WITH STALIN

Soviet frontier. The Polish Government in Exile demanded an explanation. Where were all those officers? The first explanation was that they had all escaped. That excuse didn't hold water when mass graves were discovered. The explanation then was that the prisoners had been transported and captured by the Germans.

Stalin succeeded in establishing a Communist Eastern Europe. His ambition, however, didn't stop there. He joined in the war against Japan and had his eye on Asia as well.

At the end of 1944 the Boss received a visit from DeGaulle. Stalin's sense of humor came to the fore.

He proposed a toast to one of his trusted aides ....*a brave man. He knows that if the trains do not arrive in time,* he paused, then added sweetly, *we shall shoot him.* The Boss then proposed a toast to an air marshal ....*a good man. Let's drink to him. And if he doesn't do his job,* Stalin smiled and concluded, *we shall have him shot.* Finally the Boss laughed and said, *People call me a monster but, as you can see, I make a joke of it. Maybe I'm not so horrible after all.*

DeGaulle was nonplussed. But then remarked, afterwards, *In his behavior you caught a glimpse of something resembling the despair of a man who has reached such heights of power that he has nowhere to go.* And then DeGaulle remembered Stalin saying, *In the long run, death is the only victor.*

Now that the war was coming to an end attitudes that were useful temporarily had to be eliminated. God and the Church were no longer needed as a source of inspiration. But first and foremost nationalism had to be eradicated. In the Caucasus 37,103 Balkars were put on trains and settled elsewhere. 478,479 people, consisting mainly of Chechens and some Ingush were shipped to Siberia. In the Crimea 225,009 people, consisting of Tartars, Bulgars, Greeks and Armenians were shipped to the East. There was no resistance, per se, but there were a number of incidents where people had to be rooted out, and there was bloodshed.

The Jews had been useful during the war. Since American interests were involved that question had to be handled delicately. The idea was to establish a Jewish Socialist Republic in the land vacated by the Tartars. "A California In The Crimea" was the slogan thought up to find favor with the American Jews.

When victory arrived the Boss gave General Zukhov the honor of accepting the German's unconditional surrender. He also allowed the general the privilege of inspecting the victory parade. Such a windfall should have alerted the hapless hero.

The end of the war left the country in ruins. In addition to that graves of Russian solders were everywhere. The army reported the death of 8,668,000 men. The number of civilian casualties came to sixteen million. Stalin now had to deal with men returning from war with the skill to kill. Criminal gangs sprang up. Many soldiers were homeless and destitute. Many were crippled and disfigured. Something had to be done to pull the country back into shape. The answer, as usual, was terror.

Prisoners returning from German camps were sent to Soviet camps. They had disobeyed orders. They did not die fighting. 126,000 Russian officers were stripped of their rank and sent to these camps as well. Civilians followed the same fate. Those returning from Germany, after being deported there by the Germans, were sent to Soviet camps. One woman rushed to the railing of a bridge, threw her child into the river, then followed after it. Former enemies of Stalin, who had fought in the White armies then fled to Czechoslovakia, Yugoslavia, Bulgaria, Romania and Hungary were now sent back to Russia and then directly to the camps.

In July 1945 the Boss set out for the peace conference to be held in Potsdam. Seventeen thousand NKVD agents guarded the route of the train.

NOVEMBER 1952

Writer-director, Abe Burrows, voluntarily testifies before HUAC. He denies membership to the Communist Party. He avoids directly identifying party members, but acknowledges that he assumes certain individuals, whom the committee identifies, had been members.

PAUL THOMAS

Two weeks after Betsy Landers handed in her notice, Paul Thomas did the same. Paul was certainly not as popular as Betsy, but he was an integral part of the company, primarily because he was always a part of the gathering at the nearest watering hole after a performance. He could be counted on for that and also for too often imbibing more than he could handle. The family bond seemed even more fragile now, not that Paul would really be missed that much. At first one was drawn to his pleasant, boy-next-door face, until one was faced with a cool, not very likeable disposition. No, he would not be missed that much, but his departure meant that there would be a new body in the seat at the dinner table...or more likely the bar stool.

Actually there were only seven more weeks to go, but lots of things can happen in seven weeks, thought Herb as he phoned Stanley to tell him of Paul's imminent departure. Stanley just sighed and said not to worry. He'd have someone out there in plenty of time. Herb's reluctance to see Paul leave was primarily due to the fact that Paul was not a troublemaker, per se, and who knew what his replacement would be like?

Aside from Herb, the one most deeply affected by Paul's departure, oddly enough, would be Nat Brenner. They did have that history that could not be eradicated. During the rehearsals Nat thought he'd found a soul in step with his own. They established this banter to which they both looked forward. The banter continued for the first month of the tour, but then it began to sour. They were, actually, of two different and opposing minds. Not exactly enemies, but the two young men could never be friends. Nat was an optimist. Paul was a pessimist. But Paul's pessimism was actively destructive. Not only that, Paul's pessimism sent him to the bottle. And there was that one night when he returned to the hotel polluted and threw his shoe at the chandelier, showering the hotel room with fragments of glass.

Though Nat lamented the extra money he would have to pay for a single room, he felt he had no choice. Paul was really a dangerous man, a danger to others as well as a danger to himself. From that time on Nat gave Paul a wide birth, something that Paul, for the life of him, could not understand. He chalked it up to the fact that Nat was strange, to begin with.

Ralph Krumsky, the friendliest member of the company gave up on Paul pretty early in the run. Ted Lombard and Betsy, during her presence in the cast, treated Paul with polite circumspection. Jane Applebaum, the newest member of the company, sized Paul up pretty quickly and all but ignored him, after their run in, that is, about Alvin's sexuality.

So the feeling of life being transitory was caused by the departure of a second member of the family, not by the identity of the departee. Actually even Alvin Gorman's departure would have been a greater source of regret since Alvin, bless his heart, was a source of sly, gentle ribbing, as one sat in the van waiting for his habitual dilatory arrival. *Here comes Alvin now,* or *Let's be patient. Alvin does have more baggage to carry,* were some of the humor flavored comments. These were not really mean spirited remarks, but rather fond ones about a family member one didn't really understand, but tolerated and finally accepted.

As the day for his departure grew nearer, Paul began to assess the experience. The only one in the cast, oddly enough, he had respect for was Jane. She had a head on her shoulders and seemed to know where she was going. Either that, or when she found out where she was going, nothing was going to stop her from getting there. There was a spirit worth emulating, rather than Nat Brenner's nonsensical romantic view of life's thorny journey.

And yet there was something about Nat Brenner's attitude that really annoyed him. Perhaps it was the uneasy feeling that maybe, in the long run, Nat was right. Maybe optimism was the only road to take, the only road that gave one enough fortitude to solve life's insoluble problems. Then again this blindly positive outlook on life could lead either to madness or to becoming an utter fool...like Nat Brenner. Of course, there was Betsy, whose attitude was somewhat similar to Nat's, but then again, that was sheer luck, wasn't it? She was probably on her way to success in television, but, then again, she just happened to know the right person at the right time, which only went to prove his point.

TOURING WITH STALIN

Where was one to find a role model? Certainly not Herb, who was definitely a loser. This tour was about as far up as his career was likely to go, or Ted Lombard, a has been who never really was. And then back home in New York, his mother, with her phoney airs, a liar and a cheat, whom he suspected of being unfaithful to his father, a vain egotistical ne'er-do-well. There ought to be someone to look up to.

Or did he have to force himself to look inside himself, and give himself a harsh evaluation. He was not particularly talented as an actor, yet show business was all he knew and, frankly, the only thing that really interested him. Okay, okay. There were other aspects of the business that he might have a talent for...production, marketing, casting. Good God, there were all sorts of avenues to pursue! He heaved a sigh of relief. That was it. A road he could journey down, aspects he could investigate.

But not New York. He needed to get away from New York. He did have a couple of friends in L.A. Okay, okay, they were more like acquaintances, but it was a place to start. One of them might put him up for a week or so, until he had a chance to look around.

Two days before Paul's departure the company was joined by a young man named Albert Fenwick. Herb, accompanied by Paul, put the young man through his paces.

On the evening of the following day Paul Thomas boarded a plane for L.A., where he hoped to find a new career, but one related somehow to show business, and Albert Fenwick took his place as Prisoner 403.

STALIN

When Stalin reached Potsdam he was met by President Truman and Clement Atlee. Roosevelt was dead and Churchill had been defeated. The business of dividing Europe was one of the primary considerations. In addition to winning most of Europe, by joining in the war against Japan, the Boss was able to come openly to the aid of Mao Tsetung, and gain a foothold in Asia. The division of Europe continued later in London at a session of The Council of Foreign Ministers. Molotov took over in London, coached secretly from behind the scenes by the Boss.

At the Potsdam Conference Stalin was informed by Truman of the successful creation by the United States of an atomic bomb. Truman was rather surprised that Stalin took the news so casually. But the Boss, from 1943 to 1946 had been receiving intelligence reports from the United States and, for quite some time, had been participating in the race to create an atomic bomb. On August 29, 1949 the Soviet Union tested its first bomb. In 1951 they created one twice as powerful. The Boss was now ready to expand the Communist realm even farther.

In February 1946 Stalin gave a speech attacking capitalism which American politicians took as a threat. They queried George Kennan, an official in the American Embassy in Moscow. Kennan, who hated communism, advised that the Russians were determined to destroy the American way of life, and that communism was the greatest threat America had ever faced. He went on to say that the Soviets had to be stopped.

On March 5, 1946, at the invitation of President Truman, Churchill appeared at Westminster College in Fulton, Missouri where he received an honorary degree. In his now famous speech he pointed out that an iron curtain had descended on Central and Eastern Europe. Moscow had taken over, not only all of Europe, but had reached out deep into Asia as well. The English speaking countries had to unite and, through the United Nations, stop the spread of Communism and prevent another world war.

This was all the Boss needed. The gloves were off. He tightened the reins on Czechoslovakia, Hungary, Romania, Poland, East Germany, Bulgaria and Yugoslavia, installing in these countries puppet rulers. Under Stalin's direction the Communist Information Bureau coordinated policy and sent funds and instructions to Western Communist Parties.

There was one fly in the ointment. Josip Tito of Yugoslavia had a mind and ambition of his own. He tried to take over Albania without consulting the Boss. On his own he concluded a mutual security pact with Bulgaria. In addition to that he tried to establish a confederation of his own within the Soviet orbit. Tito was summoned to Moscow. Rather than risk his neck he sent comrades to represent him. Though, supposedly, the differences were resolved, the Boss thought Tito would be much more valuable as an enemy. Yugoslavia was ousted from the fold.

Tito was an excellent excuse to revive the threat of fear. The first target was the army. During the war generals became used to having their own way. The Boss took to monitoring their phone conversations., and he got an earful. Colonel General V. Gordon, who commanded the defense of Stalingrad and was promoted to commander of the Volga Military District, vilified Stalin in a phone conversation with his wife. Gordon and his wife were both shot.

But that was only the beginning. Other officers followed the same fate. The main objective, however, was General Zukhov who had risen far too high and was not exactly in Stalin's camp. An air marshall testified that he had approved planes to be used that were defective and that General Zukhov had used these planes. Zukhov had accepted gifts from an officer who had acquired these valuables by looting Germany. Still not enough evidence was gathered to take on a war hero like Zukhov, so the war hero had to wait his turn.

The Boss turned his attention to the intelligentsia. The first victim was the film maker, Eisenstein. His film, "Ivan The Terrible, Part I" had won the Stalin prize and was considered a masterpiece. The Boss watched Part II with the Minister Of Cinematography. The minister came out of the screening almost unrecognizable. He couldn't speak for the rest of the day. Apparently he'd gotten an earful from Stalin who considered the film to be "a nightmare."

Anna Akhmatova, a famous poet, and Mikhail Zoshchenko,

a popular satirist, came under fire, but the Boss decided to show clemency. For the present they remained untouched. In a February 1947 Central Committee edict Prokofief and Shostakovich were vilified. Prokofief wrote a letter of apology which was read at a meeting of Moscow composers, at which the Central Committee edict was applauded. Prokofief locked his door and burned his copies of the books of Nabokov and copies of the magazine, "America." The Boss magnanimously decided to let the composer off with just a warning. Prokofief's first wife and mother of his two sons was arrested and ended up in a camp. Prokofief's health was greatly affected by the blow. Shostakovich, for his part, hastened to write music that he was sure would meet with the Boss's approval.

Peter Shirskov, a famous academician and Soviet hero was happily married to Zhenya Garkusha, a beautiful young actress. The two were madly in love. For no apparent reason the wife was arrested and sent to the gold mines, where life was extremely harsh. The woman died at the age of thirty three. In order to keep people in check, the trick was to use the relatives. Even Stalin's own relatives were not sacrosanct.

His sister-in-law Zhenya Alliluyeva had spurned Stalin's advances and, after her husband's death, remarried another man. She'd been spreading rumors that her husband had been poisoned. Suddenly the word was out that, yes, the husband had been poisoned...by his wife, who was secretly involved with another man. The woman was sent to a camp. His second wife's older sister was also sent to a camp. She came back mentally ill, and kept hearing things.

Next on the list were the aides closest to the Boss. Most of them were mere puppets. Two young men, however, N. A. Voznesensky and A. Kuznetsov were bright and able, and the Boss thought of them as possible replacements. He was, after all, getting on. This, however, was a very dangerous position for a man to be in. These two men were quite capable of acting on their own. Now that the war was over this was definitely not an asset. The two of them, as it happened, often worked in tandem. They made the mistake of not informing the Boss about organizing a Russian trade fair in Leningrad. They were accused of bidding for "demagogic popularity." Kuznetsov was deprived of all his offices. Vosnesensky came off lucky. He was merely reprimanded.

Molotov, the Boss's second in command was now in Stalin's cross hairs. Molotov was a remnant of the previous alliance with the West, as well as the pact with Hitler, issues best forgotten. Molotov's wife happened to be Jewish. This fell in nicely with Stalin's plans.

DECEMBER 1952

S117, a Soviet Schuka class submarine was lost due to unknown causes. All forty seven crewmen died in the incident.

ALBERT FENWICK

Herb Volpe was not in a good mood to begin with. His wife was in the final weeks of her pregnancy. He was on the phone with her every night. Helen was irritable. She wasn't getting much sleep, because she had to *get up every other minute* to go to the bathroom. And then there was that one night when her mother answered the phone. Helen was in labor...at least she was in great pain. When they got to the hospital it turned out that Helen was experiencing false labor contractions. Though the contractions were painful, alas, they were non productive...and exhausting.

Herb wasn't getting much sleep either, worrying about his wife. And then there was getting up early, driving the van for hours and hours in all sorts of weather, and then arriving at a venue, uncertain about what sort of a crew he'd be supplied with to put up the scrim, set the lights, and run the show, and then finally giving a performance. And this routine had been going on week after week, month after month for almost seven months. He often felt that he was not giving his best. It was hard to keep a performance fresh when one was tired and anxious. And there were six more weeks still to go. They loomed like six more years.

And he was really pissed off with Stanley about the replacements in the cast. He didn't expect a Geraldine Page or a Helen Hayes, but he was really scraping the bottom of the barrel. He didn't blame Jane Applebaum. She was young and eager. But that was it. She was too young, and inexperienced. Not that she wasn't professional. She read her lines intelligently, but the warmth and the nuances he'd received from Betsy Landers were sorely missed. You don't cast a girl in a role that should be played by a woman.

And now there was Albert Fenwick. Now Paul Thomas was no Laurence Olivier, but he did have some vitality and he was reasonably professional. Albert Fenwick was a cipher. He was presentable, it's true. That is to say, he wasn't deformed. He was of medium height. His color was...nondescript. His hair was not quite brown and not quite black. It was short and lay there, on top of his head. His features were symmetrical, but undistinguished. If you passed him in a crowd you wouldn't even notice him. There was no expression on his face, and not very much in the delivery of his lines. His performance, to put it mildly, was lifeless. Thank God the two roles he played were minor ones, and with him playing them they were even more minor. Herb was grateful for the support he was getting from Nat Brenner and Ted Lombard and even Alvin Gorman, whose performance had calmed down somewhat.

The only other person deeply affected by Albert Fenwick's arrival was Ralph Krumsky. The two roles Ralph had, that of the guard and a brief cross as a torture victim, were not really very satisfactory. It's true that, at the beginning of the tour, he was quite content with what he had. He was just grateful to be a part of a professional company six months after getting his college degree. But when he got wind of Peter Thomas's departure it occurred to him that Peter's roles, that of a prisoner and a young Bolshevik, were much more interesting. He debated about approaching Herb and asking him if he could possibly take over Peter's role. But Herb had so much on his mind that he didn't want to add to Herb's problems. But then again, I mean, after all he did know almost every word that Peter spoke. It might actually make things easier. When he finally did work up the courage to speak to Herb it was too late. Herb had already spoken to Stanley, and Stanley had already hired someone.

What was the problem? asked Ralph. So they switched the roles when the replacement got here. But Herb reminded Ralph that the replacement would arrive with his lines already learned. Besides he just couldn't countermand Stanley's decision. Ralph wanted to press the point that all Herb had to do was to speak to Stanley and urge the switch, but he decided to drop the subject, seeing how irritable Herb was.

Ralph sighed resignedly, and waited to see what this replacement would be like. He wanted to get a good look at the man who would be taking over the roles that he now coveted. When Albert Fenwick arrived, Ralph had to admit that, physically, the young man was better casting. Ralph knew that he really did look a little too healthy to be a veteran of a Soviet prison. But then, when he heard Albert's rather lifeless delivery, he grew resentful...and he grew restless. Maybe he'd gotten everything there was to be gotten from this first professional job. Maybe it was time to move on. He began to look forward to what turn his life might take at the end of the next six weeks.

As a matter of fact the arrival of Albert Fenwick enforced the feeling engendered by the arrival of Jane Applebaum, Betsy Landers' replacement, that the Darkness At Noon company was a makeshift gathering soon to be dissolved.

Albert Fenwick, for his part, was completely unaware of the repercussions set off by his arrival. He was still in a daze at this windfall. People never cast him in anything, especially in a speaking role. He was quite content to be part of the ensemble. There was always extra work in a film shooting in New York, or on a television show. The soap operas went on and on, and there were scenes in restaurants or at a party or in a hospital waiting room. And then there was extra work in a commercial, which paid very well indeed. But he did sort of hanker to do some stage work. After all, that was his dream originally.

He wandered into Stanley Warren's office that miraculous day just to leave his picture, because he knew that they'd soon be casting their summer season of Equity shows in the Catskills. It's true he was non-Equity, but he knew of several people who had gotten their Equity cards through a Stanley Warren production.

It just so happened that Mr. Warren, himself, came out of his private office just as Albert came through the door. (Unbeknownst to Albert, Stanley had just gotten off the phone with an actor, the third actually, who turned down going out with Darkness At Noon for six weeks as a replacement.) The receptionist was nowhere to be seen so Albert took the bull by the horns, introduced himself to Mr. Warren and offered him his headshot.

Come into my office, said Mr. Warren.

Albert followed the great man into his private office.

Sit down, said Mr. Warren.

TOURING WITH STALIN

Albert sat down in the large, comfortable leather chair. He couldn't believe his luck.

What have you done? asked Mr. Warren, tossing Albert's headshot onto his desk.

Albert listed several television shows he'd appeared on, neglecting to mention the fact that he appeared on all those shows as an extra.

Read this, said Mr. Warren, and he handed Albert a script, pointing to a specific speech.

May I look it over? asked Albert meekly.

Yes, of course, look it over, said Mr. Warren.

Albert studied the speech and, to his amazement, found himself reading it with more energy, more vitality than he ever thought he possessed. Mr. Warren stopped him halfway through the speech, and offered him the job, right then and there. When salary was mentioned Albert nodded vigorously, and kept on nodding when per diem was mentioned and transportation et al. Then came the question he dreaded.

Are you Equity?, asked Mr. Warren.

Albert hesitated. Before he could make up his mind whether to tell the truth or not, Mr. Warren continued.

You'll have to join, of course.

Albert nodded, afraid to utter a word, afraid to move a muscle, afraid that he might wake up from this dream.

Contract in hand, plus a copy of the Darkness At Noon script, he walked out of the office in a daze. He made his way to the Equity office and placed a small down payment on his membership and first year's dues. Then he took the train to his home in the Bronx where he lived with his aging parents who ran a candy store on Moshulo Parkway. He informed them that he would not be able to help out in the store for the next two months, not even on week-ends. He was going out on tour in an Equity production. His parents sighed. What could they do? They'd given birth to a foolish boy, and his sister had moved to New Jersey, and they were lucky if they saw her and their first grandchild once a month.

TOURING WITH STALIN

Two days later Albert, for the first time in his life, boarded a plane which took him to Des Moines, Iowa where, as he stepped off the plane, he was met by Herb Volpe, the leading man and manager of the Darkness At Noon company. Mr. Volpe was a vigorous, bear of a man who shook his hand and seemed very gracious. That evening Albert watched the performance from the front of the house, and he was most impressed. The acting was very good. This was really a first class company, and he began to feel very insecure.

He hadn't really done that much stage work. In high school, of course, and in community theatre, where he'd played a number of supporting roles. The following morning, he was able to get through the first rehearsal without any mishaps and everyone seemed very polite. Maybe he'd be fine, after all.

Three days later he gave his first performance in front of an audience, and he couldn't believe how calm he was. He said his lines and did everything right, and no one had any criticism whatsoever. He was still cautious, however, and he still couldn't believe his luck, and he just hoped that nothing would go wrong and that he could actually play a role in this wonderful company for six long weeks.

The exigencies of the war had engendered too much freedom within the country. Stalin felt that his authority was threatened. Now that the war was over the reins had to be tightened. The Jews, for one, were no longer useful. They were near the top of the list. The first target was the Jewish Antifascist Committee, with its close ties to America. This organization, however, had strong ties to the Jewish actor, Mikhoels, who was very popular. So Mikhoels had to go.

The report states that the actor was invited to a party by the secret police. A car was sent to his hotel to pick him up. He was taken to the grounds of a suburban dacha where he was murdered. Afterwards his body was taken to a deserted road. It was laid on the ground and run over by a truck. To make sure that no information could be leaked, the agent who took Mikhoels to the "social gathering" was also eliminated, and Mikhoels was buried with great honors.

The decision to attack the Jewish Antifascist Committee was postponed however. In January 1948 the nation of Israel came into existence. The Boss thought he might gain a foothold in this new nation. Golda Meir, Israel's first ambassador, was greeted warmly. An article was commissioned which proposed that the USSR had no "Jewish problem." The Jews were simply part of the Soviet people. The existence of Israel was needed only because of the capitalist countries which were rife with anti-Semitism.

A crowd of fifty thousand gathered in front of the synagogue where the Jewish ambassador attended a Jewish New Year service. The crowd called out lovingly to her. She responded with, *Thank you for still being Jews.* At a reception Polina Molotov, Molotov's wife greeted Meir in Yiddish with, *I'm a daughter of the Jewish people.*

Stalin soon saw, however, that his efforts to establish a foothold in Israel had failed. America beat him to it. At the beginning of 1949 the Boss finally launched his long delayed attack against the Jews. The object of the campaign was referred to as "homeless cosmopolitans." Apparently these "homeless cosmopolitans" had stolen the credit for all the great scientific discoveries from Russian scientists.

The late Mikhoels was now denounced as a spy, an agent for Russian Zionists. He was linked to the Jewish Antifascist Committee. The chairman of the Committee was summoned. The Meir demonstration was proof enough that thousands of Jews were potential traitors. The Committee, with the support of America, was planning a Jewish takeover of the Crimea was the accusation. The entire Committee was arrested.

Polina Molotov was arrested as well. She was accused of conspiring with Meir and being part of the attempt to take over Crimea. She was also accused of being a cohort of the spy, Mikhoels. When Stalin first revealed to the Central Committee that Polina was a traitor, and moved that she be ousted from the Party, Molotov abstained. However he quickly came to his senses. He blamed himself for not restraining his wife, and not recognizing her threat to the country. He divorced her. Polina was interrogated and sent to a camp. In that same year, 1949, Molotov was relieved of his post as Minister of Foreign Affairs.

The disposal of Voznesensky, Stalin's former deputy, which had been held into abeyance was now put into effect. Agents were sent to Stalingrad to dig up the dirt. Voznesensky was accused of falsifying accounts. He was dismissed from all the posts that he held. He spent his time at home writing a textbook. Suddenly he was summoned to the Boss's dacha where he was embraced by Stalin. The Boss drank a toast to him. He was wined and dined. He returned to his home euphoric, and was promptly arrested.

In 1947 two thousand Party officials were arrested. Voznesensky, along with several others, were put on trial. They were all found guilty and sentenced to death. After the sentence had been passed secret agents draped white shrouds over the condemned, and carried them out of the courtroom. One hour later they were all shot.

The trials, arising from the same Stalingrad inquiry, continued through 1951 and 1952. A special prison was built in Moscow which was to hold party officials. A super trial was now in the works. Molotov, Beria, Malenkov and numerous other members of the Politburo were slated to be trotted out. This would all be capped by dragging in the military as well, all those generals that fancied themselves as heroes.

JANUARY 1953

Convicted atomic bomb spies, Julius and Ethel Rosenberg, appeal to President Truman for a stay of execution. Truman declines to act.

JANE APPLEBAUM

It took Jane Applebaum about a week or so to find her place in the company, to adjust to her associates. None of them presented any problems and none of them, unfortunately, offered prospects for romance. The one that first caught her eye was Nat Brenner, but Nat, for some reason or other, didn't seem very interested, romantically that is. He was, however, the one person in the cast with whom she bonded. They seemed to have the most in common. He was as ambitious and as determined as she was, and she enjoyed his sense of humor which she envied, and which she was rather in awe of, and he wasn't just another actor. He was a playwright as well, which made him much more interesting.

Having settled down to the routine, Jane tried to learn as much as she could from the actors in her first Equity company whose work she respected; Herb Volpe, with whom she had most of her scenes, Nat and Ted Lombard. As she rode in the van she looked eagerly out the window drinking in the scenery. She was up early in the morning, at breakfast before all the others, except sometimes Nat who returned immediately to his room to write. After breakfast she roamed through the strange streets of each new city, drinking everything in. She was young and alive and wanted to remember it all. Each day was a different adventure, and who knew what was in store around the corner? The very next minute? What a fascinating and varied country this was! Could she ever satisfy this insatiable hunger she was cursed or blessed with?

It occurred to her that she might jot down some of her experiences and send them to the show business paper she'd worked on for several months in New York. She put in a call to Andy, the man who hired her, and he said he'd speak to the editor. Andy called back the next day and said that the editor might be able to include her reports in his column, but that he couldn't pay her for them. She decided that the credit was worth the while, so she set to work each evening, jotting down some notes about the different cities, about the different hotels, the interesting personalities she ran into. At the end of the week she'd written a human interest story about one of the hotels they'd stayed at, which was run by an old couple who'd been in show business. She borrowed Nat's typewriter, typed up the story and sent it in. The following week she received a note from the editor and a check for ten dollars. Nat was very impressed and bragged about it to the rest of the cast, who were equally impressed...and a little in awe of this strange, pretty young thing.

By this time she was beginning to get a little restless. There were three more weeks to go. She couldn't decide what her next step would be. There was New York and there was Los Angeles. Her family was in New York, but she'd just recently broken free from her family. Her original dream had been the movies. She'd spent almost a year, seven months to be exact, on the West Coast but grew impatient when she couldn't even land an agent. Maybe she ought to try it again. Coming off a national tour might give her some clout.

On her free nights she'd usually go to the local movie theatre, often accompanied by Nat. She'd appeared in a commercial for Oreo cookies a couple of years ago and earned her Screen Actors Guild card. At the movie she'd ask for the theatre manager. She'd show the man her SAG card and say she assumed his theatre extended professional courtesy. The man, slightly confused, would look at the pretty young girl and the eager young man who accompanied her and nod reluctantly. Nat would trot into the theatre behind this enterprising young lady with untold resources, and enjoy the movie even more because it was free.

The Darkness At Noon company was given a breather in Oklahoma City. They were going to stay there an extra two days. In the afternoon after their performance, which took place in a former movie theatre, Nat sat cutting out the review which contained some very flattering comments about his performance. He noticed an ad for a dinner theatre production of William Inge's "Come Back, Little Sheba," featuring the movie star, Shelley Winters and Oscar Stratford, a rather dapper character actor and veteran of many movies. He clipped out the ad, showed it to Jane and they decided to try to get into the theatre with their Equity cards. Actually there was the policy of professional courtesy among Equity companies on the road.

TOURING WITH STALIN

An hour before curtain time Jane and Nat appeared at the dinner theatre, which was located in a large hotel a few blocks from the one they were staying at. Jane sent word back that she'd like to speak to the company manager. While they were waiting for the company manager Jane noticed a program at the reception desk. She picked it up and glanced at it.

I know the stage manager, said Jane.

Great, said Nat.

The company manager was a rather businesslike woman, but as soon as Jane introduced themselves as member of the Darkness At Noon company, and Jane added that she was a friend of Roger, the stage manager, the woman suddenly became a benign mother hen. She seated the two actors at a table not too far from the stage. Dinner was being served and the company manger said, *You can help yourselves to coffee and dessert, if you like. It's on the house.*

Thank you, said Jane.

Thank you, said Nat.

It was theatre in the round. That is to say, the tables were placed in a circle around the playing area. The two actors settled in and prepared to enjoy the show, as well as the free food. The production was a most impressive one. Shelley Winters was cast perfectly as the sweet, rather simple woman married to a man her intellectual superior. Oscar Stratford as the alcoholic abusive husband was a little stiff at times, but it seemed to suit the role. Jane was more enthusiastic about him than Nat was, and was dying to meet him. She thought him *extremely sexy.*

The two actors went back stage after the performance. Jane and Roger, the stage manager, fell all over each other. Nat asked if he could see Shelley Winters and tell her how much he enjoyed her performance, but the star wasn't seeing anyone. Jane was eager to meet Oscar Stratford. Roger left to inquire if Mr. Stratford would receive her. He returned to say Mr. Stratford would see Jane, but just for a minute. Roger led Jane off. Nat found a chair and sat down to wait. Ten minutes passed. Twenty minutes passed.

After half an hour Nat got up, uncertain as what to do. Just then Jane appeared.

I'm sorry, said Jane. *You go on ahead. I may spend the night with Oscar.*

Oh? said Nat, trying to hide his surprise.

Jane kissed Nat on the cheek and disappeared. Nat returned to the hotel, marvelling at the many surprises his young colleague was capable of. Oscar Stratford was more than twice Jane's age. What in the world did she seen in that man?

Nat thought he might see Jane at breakfast in the hotel coffee shop. No sign of her. He returned to his room and to his typewriter wondering all the while what was happening with Jane. He was having lunch in the coffee shop when he spotted her entering the hotel lobby. He jumped up, dashed to the door of the coffee shop and called out. Jane stopped, turned and walked quickly over to Nat.

I can't talk now, said Jane. *I just came back to change. Oscar's waiting for me.* And she was gone.

Fascinating, thought Nat. He remembered his ex-wife's timidity where sex was concerned. He actually had to marry the girl in order to get her into bed. He marveled at this young girl's boldness and he wondered where this would lead her. Wasn't it dangerous to open oneself up like that? Or was it just sex? He supposed women were capable of sex without love, just as men were. Of course, his experience had been pretty limited.

It wasn't until rather late that night and he was getting ready for bed, when Jane knocked on his door and came into his room, that the story unfolded.

I wish I smoked, Jane began, *or drank. Sex is my only vice, if you can call it a vice.*

What do you see in this man? asked Nat.

Jane looked dreamily into the distance. *He's very sweet,* she said, *and sort of lost. And very gentle. But he drinks.*

And he's much too old for you, said Nat.

He wants me to marry him, said Jane. *And he has a wonderful sense of humor...and a son my age.*

TOURING WITH STALIN

You're not going to marry him, are you? asked Nat.

Don't be ridiculous, said Jane. *It was just one of those things. As soon as I stepped into his dressing room, and we looked at one another...it was like electricity. I could hardly speak, and he just looked at me. Finally I said, "I enjoyed your performance."*

And what did he say? asked Nat.

"Won't you have a seat?"

And then what?

He offered me a drink, said Jane. *There was a bottle of Scotch on the dressing table in front of him. I told him I didn't drink.*

And then what? asked Nat. *I mean you were there for almost half an hour.*

I don't remember, said Jane. *I don't remember what we said. It didn't matter what we said. It was the electricity between us. And then he asked me if he could take me to dinner.* Jane stopped and looked dreamily into the distance.

And?

What? asked Jane.

Where did you go for dinner? asked Nat.

His hotel room, said Jane.

For dinner?

He called room service, said Jane.

Sounds very seedy, said Nat.

It wasn't seedy at all, said Jane. *As a matter of fact, it was very impressive, very elegant. And we had champagne.*

I thought you didn't drink, said Nat.

I had one glass of champagne, said Jane. *I couldn't say no.*

And then you spent the night, Nat concluded.

He was a wonderful lover, said Jane. *So tender. And afterwards...he wept.*

He wept?!

He was overcome, said Jane, *with emotion. He called me his darling little girl.*

Sounds vaguely incestuous, said Nat.

Don't be so cynical, said Jane.

I'm sorry, said Nat. *I'm sorry. Well, are you going to see him again?*

Yes, of course, I am, said Jane, *as a friend. He's going to help me find an agent. I've decided...at the end of the tour I'm going to stay in L. A.. I'm going to be a movie star.*

It does help to know someone, said Nat.

He fell asleep in my arms, said Jane. *It was as if I were the parent, and he was the child. It was unbelievable.*

Unique, to say the least, said Nat.

As a writer, you're really very insensitive, said Jane.

I just hope...

What? asked Jane.

You don't end up, said Nat, *being hurt.*

But that's what life is, my dear, said Jane. *And if you're afraid of being hurt, you might as well just die...right then and there.* And then Jane rose, sighed, smiled a Mona Lisa smile and left the hotel room, closing the door softly behind her.

Nat sat lost in thought. This child, this pretty young thing, he decided, was really a wise old man.

STALIN

Stalin was now in his seventies, and it was time to think of his successor. His first son, Sasha, had died in the war. The Boss's relationship with his daughter was on rocky ground. There was her first scandalous affair with the journalist, after which she married the handsome son of an intellectual family. The only trouble this time was the young man was Jewish. The Boss refused to receive him. Svetlana gave birth to a son, after which she divorced her husband, of her own free will. She then married a man Stalin approved of, but the father-daughter relationship never regained the closeness it had while she was growing up.

The Boss still mourned the death of his second wife and was still bitter about her suicide. He found himself alone now, except for his younger son, Vasily, whom he was fond of. Until his death, however, Vasily was to be a thorn in his side. As the Boss's favorite the young man rose rapidly up the ranks. At the age of twenty seven he was in charge of the air arm of the Moscow Military District. He organized the spectacular aerial displays and mock air battles. Supposedly he piloted one of the planes during the demonstration. Actually he sat in the bombers seat next to the officer who handled the controls.

He drank heavily. He divorced his wife, taking over the custody of the children. The mother had to visit the children secretly. He married a famous swimmer, for whom he built an entire sports complex. The marriage ended soon after that. He continued to drink and drive, sometimes on the wrong side of the road. He womanized shamelessly and spent lavishly, using government funds.

He made an attempt to follow in his father's footsteps. He insisted on interrogating a terror suspect personally and made a fiasco of it. He married for the third time, the daughter of a war hero. The woman was something of a termagant and treated the children badly. Stalin's hope that the young man's third marriage might be his salvation was quickly dashed.

Vasily often found himself in hot water. He was a great hockey fan. He created his own very successful team, which received all sorts of special privileges. The team, while traveling, was held up by a storm. Vasily phoned the pilot and ordered him to continue the flight, despite the dangerous weather. The pilot took off, as instructed. The plane went down, and all eleven men were killed. The Boss had to hush it all up.

And then there was the young man's run-in with Beria, the Minister of Interior. Vasily's football team wasn't doing too well. He remembered Nikolai Starostin, a famous trainer and decided that there was the man to rescue his team. Unfortunately Starostin was in a prison camp. The heir apparent picked up the phone and had Starostin flown to Moscow. The trainer was greeted by the Boss's son, toasted with a glass of champagne and reunited with his family. Beria struck back. Starostin, while visiting with his family, was informed that he had to return to the camp. Vasily was furious. From then on he kept the trainer by his side night and day. He slept with a pistol under his pillow.

But Starostin missed his family. One night, when Vasily had fallen asleep in a drunken stupor, he sneaked out of the house and returned to his home. The next morning the trainer was met by two agents who put him on a train headed for the prison camp. Vasily was furious. He had his men stationed at the train's first stop and Starostin found himself back in Moscow again. Vasily phoned Beria and taunted him. Finally Daddy had to step in. Starostin was sent back to the prison camp. Heir apparent or not, one could not defy the government.

It all came to a head in 1952. Vasily had been drinking so heavily that he had to be relieved of being in charge of the air display. He showed up at the reception in a disgraceful state and was a great embarrassment to the Boss. Vasily was relieved of all his positions and sent to the Military Academy as a student. Stalin, however, was well aware why his son buried himself in drink. The young man knew that when his father was no longer there to protect him he would find himself in deep trouble.

The Boss's final years were lonely ones. Deprived of a family, his political associates were forced to take its place. After a long day's work they had to appear at the Boss's dacha for a long nights eating and drinking. Sometimes the gathering went on till dawn. There was a sideboard laden with food. Servants would clear away the dirty dishes, discard them, and replace them with fresh ones. All the food was labeled to indicate that it was poison free. A doctor was also on hand to make sure the air, as well, was free of poison.

Portraits of members of the Politburo hung on the walls. Members would sit beneath their portrait, grateful that their portrait was still there on the wall, since many of those portraits had been removed, together with the man who'd sat for the picture. The guests were forced to drink too much. Dirty jokes were exchanged, as well as silly practical tricks. Someone was pushed into the pond. A tomato was placed on a chair just before someone sat on it. As long as the Boss was in a good mood, however, it was worth all the trouble. They knew they were safe.

After the guests left Stalin would putter in the garden. His hands had begun to tremble and, sometimes, he would cut himself. If a doctor was called to dress the cut, the doctor's hands would tremble out of fear. The Boss would sleep for a few hours in the morning. He liked to toboggan on the grounds, but that soon stopped because his rheumatism was getting so bad.

He confined himself to one room, sleeping on the sofa his housekeeper had made up. He would have his meals at his desk. There was a portrait of Lenin on the wall, under which a lamp burned continually. He would often chat with his guards, simple, uneducated men. He would talk about the past and tell them stories, as if they were his best friends.

He was still, however, the butcher he'd always been. Members of his bodyguard would be eliminated every so often. They knew too much. Even his personal bodyguard would vanish and be replaced. Actually, the Boss was making plans for the future, plans for what would turn out to be, his last hurrah.

As a prelude to his swan song, Stalin published two pamphlets dealing with Marxism and the economics of socialism. He used a ghost writer, but the ideas were his and he did do very careful editing. The works, of course, were highly praised. In these works he proposed that a war between the capitalist countries was inevitable. He hinted that finally the war between the imperialist countries and the communist countries was also inevitable. He was quoted as saying privately, *The First World War delivered one country from capitalist slavery, the Second World War created the socialist system, and the Third will finish imperialism forever.* The Boss now had the atomic bomb and he was ready.

He was now also ready for his final bloody campaign. On October 16, 1952 he made a passionate address at a meeting of the Central Committee in which he vilified Molotov and Mikoyan, another one of his top aides. He then offered to resign his position as Secretary General. Everyone, of course, protested and "persuaded" him to stay on.

A famous Russian author once said, *'Anti-Semitism makes your vodka stronger and your bread more appetizing."* And what better way to unite a country than to find a popular common target? It now appeared that a sinister Jewish conspiracy had been at work way back since the days of Trotsky. Zionists had infiltrated the highest offices. Molotov's wife, for example, had recruited her husband.

But this Jewish conspiracy was not confined to Soviet Russia. Jews were rooted out in Bulgaria and Czechoslovakia, where a number of officials were put on trial and shot. The head of the NKVD was a victim as well. On January 13, 1953, a group of doctors, apparently, were found out to be poisoners. As an after thought, his own doctor was added to the list. All of these doctors just happened to be Jews.

The Boss was now more alone than ever. He seldom saw his daughter. The faithful Molotov, Mikoyan and a number of others were no longer in attendance. They were under the sentence of death. The anti-Semitism was being stepped up. It was not unusual for a Jew to be beaten up in the street.

There were now rumors that the Jews would be loaded onto trucks and shipped off, the same way they were in Nazi Germany. Actually, the rumors were not far off. There were actually plans to shift the Jewish population to Siberia. The Jews were to serve as an excuse for his war with the West. The international Jewry were the agents of that evil plague, capitalism. March 5, 1953 was actually the date on which the Jews were to be loaded onto the trucks and shipped out of Moscow. March 5 turned out to be a red letter day, but for another, unexpected reason.

FEBRUARY 1953

Eisenhower rejects the Rosenberg's bid for a stay of execution, despite an appeal from Pope Pius XII.

HERB VOLPE

It was Spring. The first week in May. The world was in bloom. It was the perfect time of year for a woman to give birth, thought Herb Volpe. Yet that stubborn child of his remained attached to its mother's womb, and refused to budge. Was this an omen in regard to his son's nature? Of course, women can be stubborn as well. Perhaps this was a warning to prepare him for the fact that his firstborn was going to be a girl. Or perhaps the child refused to show itself because it was ashamed...it was badly disfigured. He should be home, holding Helen's hand.

He often challenged himself to choose. Which would he be able to give up...his career or his marriage? He now went through that ridiculous torment once again. How could he give up a part of himself, his wife, to be exact? They were one, two parts of a whole, an inseparable team. They couldn't exist, one without the other. On the other hand, what sort of a husband, what sort of a man would he be without his life's breath, the theatre, to be exact? How can you be a husband and an actor as well? Was it worth it? It was vanity, wasn't it? Vanity?! What a worthless, pointless, unanswerable debate?!

By this time it was difficult for Herb to go out on that stage and give, what he considered, a decent performance. After seven months, he had nothing new to give; there was nothing new to find in his character. People were paying good money, coming to see the show for the first time...and what did he have to offer? Nothing! He was stale, stale, stale.

He wished that Betsy Landers was still playing Luba. She always picked up the scene when he was down. She always challenged him. Jane did her best, but she was green. There was no chemistry between them. He felt he was out there, all by himself.

He was alone and Helen was alone and he cursed the theatre, he cursed his role, he cursed the play and he cursed himself for being a goddamned fool. He was ready to call Stanley and tell him he couldn't go on any longer. All right, it was only three more weeks, less than three weeks. But his wife was two weeks late. She should have given birth almost two weeks ago.

Maybe they'd have to take the baby by caesarian. Maybe they'd have to cut her open. Oh, God!

And thank God for Ted Lombard. At least Ted understood. He was the only one in the company he could turn to. Ted would engage him in a game of double solitaire after the show. *I always find it relaxing,* said Ted. Sometimes Ted would organize a game of poker, usually with Ralph Krumsky, Albert Fenwick and Jane Applebaum. Nat Brenner might sit on the sidelines for a while, then return to his room to do some reading before he turned in.

Herb now took to calling home twice a day; early in the morning and just before show time. He stopped calling late at night since Helen was going to bed early to try and get some sleep. Though she tried to conceal it, he sensed that she was getting worried.

On the first day of the third "late week" Herb put in his morning call. There was no answer. He tried again an hour later, still no answer. He spent the rest of the afternoon in a daze. Obviously she was in the hospital, and in labor...or they were operating on her. He was sure his mother-in-law would call as soon as there was news, and he tried to relax. Late in the afternoon he went to the theatre and supervised the set up, then returned to the hotel to await the call. Ted Lombard joined him, pulled out the cards and they sat playing double solitaire.

At six in the evening the two men went to the restaurant across the street for a light dinner. Herb just had a bowl of soup. As they entered the lobby of the hotel and headed for the elevator the woman at the desk called out that Herb had a message. It was from his mother-in-law. She left a number for him to call.

The two men took the elevator to the third floor and walked quickly to Herb's room. Herb picked up the phone and dialed the number. He reached St. Luke's Hospital. He asked for the extension he'd been given. A nurse answered. Herb gave his name and asked for his wife or his mother-in-law. He held the phone while the nurse went to get them. Five long minutes later he heard his mother-in-law's voice.

Herb?

Yes? said Herb.

She's fine, said his mother-in-law. *She's fine and so is the baby. It's a boy, a big healthy boy. He weighs seven pounds and eleven ounces. He's big.*

Herb sat down.

Herb, said his mother-in-law, *are you there?*

Yes. Yes, I'm here, said Herb. *Can I talk to her?*

There's no phone in the room right now, said his mother-in-law, *and besides she's resting. She had a hard time. She'll call you tomorrow.*

Do you have my number? asked Herb.

Yes, yes, we have the number, said his mother-in-law. *And she said not to worry, and she loves you.*

She's all right, you say? asked Herb.

She's fine, said his mother-in-law. *She's fine.*

Thank you, Millie, said Herb, and he hung up. He turned to Ted. *It's a boy,* said Herb. *He weighs seven pounds and eleven ounces.*

Congratulations, said Ted.

Where are those cigars? said Herb. He rummaged in his suitcase and pulled out a box of cigars he'd bought in Kansas City. He opened the box and offered Ted a cigar. The label read, "IT'S A BOY!"

You guessed right, said Ted.

Good Lord, said Herb. *Look at the time.* It was five minutes to eight.

Don't worry, said Ted. *They can't go up without you.*

The two men started out the door. They were at the elevator when Herb said, *Hold it!* He ran back to his room and returned a moment later with the box of cigars. They walked rapidly to the theatre, and arrived ten minutes before curtain time. The cast was in a panic.

It's a boy! Ted announced.

There were shouts of *Congratulations!* and *Right on!* Everyone crowded around Herb and shook his hand. The new father handed out cigars to everyone, including Jane, who said. *Don't think I'm not gonna smoke it.*

Ralph Krumsky, who doubled as stage manager took it upon himself to come out on stage and make an announcement.

Ladies and gentlemen, we're sorry for the delay. The fact is our leading man has just become a father, and it's taken him a little while to recover.

There was wild applause and laughter.

We'll be going up in just a few minutes, Ralph continued.

There was more applause as Ralph left the stage. The performance that night was as good or better than it had ever been. Alvin Gorman, who was usually too melodramatic, was right on, perhaps for the first time. Albert Fenwick, who was usually a cipher, showed some vitality in his role as Prisoner 403. And the audience response at the curtain call was heartwarming. Ted pushed Herb forward a second time and Herb took an extra bow. This time several members of the audience stood up and applauded, which had never happened before.

Back in the dressing room Ted announced, *I'm buying the first two rounds tonight.* The entire cast turned up at the bar next to the hotel, which was a first. Jane went around collecting ten dollars from everyone to buy a present for the baby. To her surprise Alvin gave fifteen.

I'm only asking ten, said Jane.

I'm aware of that, said Alvin.

Herb slept late the next morning. He forgot to set his alarm. When he woke up he panicked. Then he remembered that Helen was fine and that he was the father of a baby boy weighing seven pounds and eleven ounces.

He packed hurriedly and found the cast all loaded up, and sitting in the van, ready to go. Suddenly he felt a surge of warmth for these six people he was in charge of. They were really six strangers, and yet he felt so close to them. He saw so clearly their faults and their assets, their problems together with the gifts they had to offer, some richer than others. He put the van in gear and started off, his mind was in a whirl.

TOURING WITH STALIN

There would be no more touring. He was a father now, and his little family came first, even if he had to go back to part time work for that accounting firm. And then there was his son, Brutus Volpe, named after the noblest Roman of them all, and his favorite role. As the van sped along the highway, he looked ahead into the glorious sunshine and the cloudless sky of this lovely May morning, he dreamt about the future of the boy he'd given seed to. What would he be like? And what could he do to shape that boy's life? Less than three weeks to go.....

STALIN

At 11:00 PM on February 28, 1953 Stalin, Beria, Malenkov, Kruschev and Bulganin drove to the dacha from the cinema after watching a movie. Stalin was *sprightly and cheerful*. At dinner they discussed arranging a trial for the accused Jewish doctors. At 4:00 AM when the guests left, Stalin was *pretty drunk...in very high spirits*. He was supposed to have said something rather unusual that evening. *I'm going to bed,* it was reported he said. *I won't be wanting you. You can go to bed, too.*

For a man as concerned about his safety as Stalin was, this was peculiar indeed. To add to the mystery, less than a month before that Stalin had dismissed one of his longtime personal guards. The fact that this devoted, trusty caretaker was accused of treason, however, was not that unusual. He joined the ranks of millions in the Soviet Union, among them the Boss's most intimate companions, who were summarily jailed and shot..

At 10:00 AM, the morning following the evening of the usual camaraderie, the guards heard no movement in the Boss's room. At 11:00 AM, still no movement. The guards began to be concerned. The Boss was always up by eleven. 1:00 PM. 3:00 PM. Hour after hour went by. The guards were alarmed by now. There was an argument about who should venture into the room and possibly incur the Boss's wrath. No one had the courage. Finally at 10:00 PM one of the guards, who usually delivered the mail, picked the mail up and walked down the corridor. He made sure his footsteps could be heard since the Boss was wary of anyone *sneaking up* on him.

The guard placed the mail on the desk in the office. The door to the small dining room was ajar. The guard saw the Boss lying on the floor. His right arm was raised as if he were trying to gain someone's attention.

The guard ran over. *Comrade, Stalin,* he asked, *What's wrong?*

The guard noticed that he'd wet himself.

Shall I call a doctor?

Stalin made an incoherent noise, a sort of buzzing sound. His pocket watch, which read 6:30, and a copy of Pravda lay on the floor beside him. It appeared as if he may have made an attempt to reach a table nearby, which held a bottle of mineral water, and then collapsed. When the guard tried to question him, he started to make strange sounds. It sounded as if he might be snoring. The guard broke out into a sweat. Suppose he'd be accused of disturbing the Boss's sleep? He trembled as he picked up the phone and summoned the other guards. They lifted the Boss and placed him on the sofa.

One of the guards put in a call to Malenkov, Beria's assistant.

Stalin lay on the sofa making these strange snoring sounds. They decided to move him into the large dining room, where there was more air. They placed him on the roomier sofa. He looked cold. They covered him with a rug.

Half an hour later Malenkov called. He couldn't locate Beria. Half an hour after that Beria rang.

Don't tell anyone about Comrade Stalin's illness, he ordered.

When Beria and Malenkov finally showed and learned that Stalin was now lying on the sofa in the dining room snoring Beria was furious.

What do you mean by starting a panic? Don't bother us and don't upset Comrade Stalin.

Beria preferred to believe, at least outwardly that nothing was amiss. He and Malenkov left.

A while later the guards phoned again. They seemed to think the Boss's sleep was not an ordinary one.

Kruschev arrived at 8:00 AM, the next morning.

How's the Boss doing? he asked.

Very poor, came the reply. *Something's happened to him.*

The doctors will be here right away, said Kruschev.

Thank God, said the guard.

By this time Stalin had been lying there for thirteen hours unattended. The doctors arrived between 8:30 and 9:00 AM, strange doctors who had never attended the Boss before. Stalin's personal doctors were in prison, accused of treason. These new doctors were terrified of doing something wrong.

The dentist removed the false teeth, and was so nervous he dropped them.

They tore open his shirt and proceeded to examine the patient. They concluded that he'd had a brain hemorrhage.

A crowd began to gather.

Svetlana, Stalin's daughter was summoned, as well as his son, Vasily.

Vasily was drunk, as usual. He kept shouting, *they've killed my father. They've killed my father.* And then he left.

The doctors applied leeches and x-rayed the Boss's lungs. An artificial respirator was brought in. The young technicians gazed openmouthed at their fallen leader. The machine was never used.

On March 2, 1953 Moscow Radio's chief announcer read the official bulletin on Stalin's illness. Meanwhile Beria, Malenkov and Kruschev returned to Stalin's government office. They were joined by other government officials. They proceeded to divide the Boss's power among them. Beria and Malenkov then went back to the dacha.

The final diagnoses was "a hemorrhage to the left cerebral hemisphere resulting from hypertonia and sclerosis."

What's the prognosis? asked Malenkov.

Death is inevitable, came the response.

Stalin groaned every once in a while. Once he seemed to be looking around and recognized people.

How do you feel, Comrade? someone asked.

There was no reply.

The face was a blank.

On March 5 Stalin was given all sorts of injections.

Bulletins were written.

The Boss's eyes remained closed. When they opened briefly Beria rushed over and kissed Stalin's hand.

Svetlana, who was present at the time described his final hours. "Father's death was slow and difficult. His face was discolored and different. The death agony was terrible. It choked him slowly as we watched. At the last minute he opened his eyes. It was a terrible look, either mad or angry and full of the fear of death. Suddenly he raised his left hand and seemed either to be pointing upward or threatening us all. Then, the next moment, his spirit, after one last effort, tore itself from his body. Beria was the first to rush out into the corridor and, in the quiet of the room where we were standing in silence, we heard him say in a loud, undisguisedly triumphant voice, *'Bring my car'*. Valechka Istomina, Stalin's housekeeper and possible mistress, with her round face and snub nose rested her head on the deceased's breast and wept loudly."

At the Kremlin, the Central Committee held a meeting to legalize what had already been agreed upon.

When the body was carried out on a stretcher someone noticed a bruise on the Boss's body, as if someone had pushed him.

There was no bruise. There could be no bruise. Nobody pushed him, came the retort.

The embalming was carried out in the special laboratory of the Lenin Mausoleum. He was laid to rest in a military uniform with the medals of Hero of the Soviet Union and Hero of Socialist Labor, in addition to other ribbons and medals.

All the guards were dismissed and dispersed to various areas out of Moscow. They were told by Beria, who seemed to have taken charge, *Take your family with you.*

Three of the guards wanted to remain in Moscow.

If you don't want to be there, you'll be there, said Beria, and he pointed to the ground.

Stalin lay in state in the Hall of Columns. Thousands came to pay their respects. Moscow was so crowded, and the mob was being hemmed in so forcefully by the police, that thousands were crushed to death.

After the funeral Beria, who had been destined for extermination, made some sort of sardonic remark and laughed uproariously.

MARCH 1973

Georgi Malenkov becomes Soviet premier and party secretary. Nikita Krushchev replaces Malenkov as first secretary of the Soviet Communist Party.

THE FINALE

For the cast of the Darkness At Noon tour the final week was like sitting in a waiting room, waiting to go through customs. It was as if one were returning from a voyage abroad, a voyage that went on for eight long months. When one returned to home base, wherever that might be, what could one expect to find?

Of course, Jane Applebaum and Albert Fenwick had only been gone for a few weeks, so the workaday world would probably not hold many surprises. But the veterans of the tour, Ralph Krumsky, Alvin Gorman, Ted Lombard, Nat Brenner and Herb Volpe were all slightly apprehensive in regard to what they might be facing when they set foot on home soil.

Ralph Krumsky became extremely sentimental as the tour wound down. He looked upon his fellow actors with great affection. They were his comrades during his baptism of fire, during the exciting eight months he became a professional actor; even that odd fish, Alvin Gorman and even Albert Fenwick, who took over the roles he should have been given, would be remembered kindly; and Ted Lombard, that colorful veteran, and Herb Volpe, his mentor, his idol, and Nat Brenner, whom he couldn't quite figure out, but respected as a talented actor.

He made a point of approaching each colleague and getting their phone numbers. Alvin looked at Ralph askance when Ralph approached him. He ended up giving Ralph two numbers, the number of the phone in the apartment he subleased while he was out of town, and the number of his phone service. As a matter of fact, most of the actors in the company were flattered by the attention and the interest, except for Jane Applebaum. She said she couldn't give Ralph a phone number because she wasn't sure where she'd be staying. She would be going to L. A., and probably be staying in a hotel to begin with, or maybe with a friend. She wasn't sure which, and she really didn't seem very anxious to satisfy Ralph's request. Ralph wasn't the least bit offended. That was Jane, a unique and provocative young lady.

As far as his next step was concerned, that was all settled. He'd be living in New York, pursuing stage work, or film or television, and Herb was going to show him the ropes. He picked up a copy of the New York Times at a newsstand when they stopped over in Los Angeles hoping to scan the list of apartments for rent, only to find the edition he purchased didn't have the New York classified section.

Alvin Gorman was torn between returning to New York, his current residence, or moving back to Los Angeles. There was more film and television work in Los Angeles, it was true; but then there were memories there of his faithless lover whom he kicked out, but seemed to find irreplaceable. Deep down inside was the premonition that, perhaps, the juicy role of Gletkin, the fanatical Bolshevik he'd been playing for the last eight months might just turn out to be the highlight of his not very illustrious show business career.

Ted Lombard, the oldest veteran of the lot, was looking forward to entering a new and gratifying stage of his life. His family relationship was richer now than it had ever been, primarily because of the unexpected bonding with his son, Jeff. He would definitely settle with his wife in Los Angeles, and pursue film and television work, which would please his wife, Edie, no end. He'd saved quite a bit during the eight months tour and, of course, he could collect unemployment for twenty weeks, so financially he was in great shape. But first he and Edie would spend a week in Colorado with his son and his daughter-in-law who, he was delighted to learn, was pregnant.

Nat Brenner looked forward eagerly to the next step in his blossoming career. Finally a member of Equity, and on his way to stardom, he still brooded and fumed about the wife who deserted him, walked out on him...he who was better looking than she was. Still bitter, he would start to pick her apart. She'd been gaining weight and her body was not as gloriously sleek as it had been originally. All right, so the nose job had improved her appearance, but she was still no beauty. Actually, you might say, she was becoming matronly. Yes, that was it, she was becoming rather matronly and she wasn't even thirty, and God knows what she's going to look like in a few years from now, when she woke up and found that she'd married that moronic idiot he was sure she was going to marry and she would find that the glamor that he, Nat Brenner possessed, had gone out of her life, and after he had his nose job he'd be playing romantic leads, a combination of Laurence Olivier and John Barrymore...and maybe a dash of Cary Grant thrown in for good measure!

He sat pasting all the glorious notices he received on a sheet of paper, denoting the city and the date of the review. This was to become a glorious flyer which would knock them dead when he returned to New York, the city he was determined to conquer, first as an actor and eventually as a playwright. Of course, he still had to write that masterpiece. After twenty three drafts of "The Sophisticates" he decided it was going nowhere and he put it aside. It was time to move on to a new play, start fresh again. Frustrating, it was true, after all that work, eight months of draft after draft, but he was sure he'd learned something in the process.

Herb Volpe was mentally and spiritually back home in his apartment on the upper West Side of Manhattan. He spoke every morning with his wife, who was making a rapid recovery from a very difficult birth. She was doing so well that she was returning to her church choir job at the end of the month. Her mother was staying with her, at least until Herb got back.

Not that he was ever reckless, but he drove the van even more carefully now, especially that time when they descended the Pacific Heights along the Northern coast of California. The entire cast watched fascinated through the window as they rounded the dangerous hairpin curves of the narrow road, taking in the breathtaking view of the coast and the surf beating against the rocks far below.

The first performance of the final week was in Bakersfield, California, which was not too far from Los Angeles. The cast had the luxury of one whole free day in the West Coast show business capitol, and they took full advantage of it.

Ted Lombard brought Herb along to meet his wife, Edie, and the three of them spent a pleasant afternoon together. They put in a call to Herb's wife, and Ted and Edie got on the phone and met Helen, via long distance.

TOURING WITH STALIN

Nat Brenner contacted an actress friend of his who had migrated to Los Angeles from New York and, together, they explored the famous Hollywood night spots that Nat had read about. They investigated Grauman's Chinese Theatre and the footprints and handprints of all those movie stars, and then the Hollywood Walk of Fame with the bronze stars for all those famous actors. Then they drove by the Brown Derby restaurant, and had lunch at the famous Ciro's, which wasn't like having a glamorous dinner there in the evening, but it was really something, and they looked in on the legendary Mocambo, which wasn't open until the evening. Nat decided it was a great place to visit, but he couldn't ever see himself moving out to the West Coast where there was no real theatre to begin with.

Alvin Gorman had lunch with an old friend, who was also a good friend of his faithless lover. He learned that "the bitch" had found another sucker, and he felt sorry for that next innocent victim. He also felt sorry for himself, and his friend tried to reassure him that he was lucky to be well out of it. At any rate he now felt certain that he had made the right decision to settle in New York. There were too many painful memories here.

Jane Applebaum opened a bank account and, escorted by Oscar Stratford, who had taken her under his wing and was going to introduce her to a couple of agents once she got settled, checked out a studio apartment in West Hollywood and laid down a deposit. She also met Oscar's son, a charming young man who was really quite amiable, she was relieved to find, not that her relationship with Otto would become more than a pleasant friendship.

Ralph Krumsky joined forces with Albert Fenwick. They took a bus tour through Hollywood. The guide pointed out the glorious homes of all the current movie stars like Clark Gable and Lana Turner and Ginger Rogers as well as the very impressive mansions that had once been inhabited by the likes of those legendary stars like Gloria Swanson, Doug Fairbanks and Mary Pickford and Rudolph Valentino.

At 7:00 PM the cast congregated in front of Grauman's Chinese Theatre where Herb, accompanied by Ted drove up in the van. They all piled in and, as the company headed for Bakersfield, there was a glow of warmth throughout the van, the feeling of a memorable day well spent.

The last five days of the tour flew by. There was the performance the next day in Bakersfield, then one in Albuquerque, New Mexico, one in Columbus, Ohio and the final performance in Oil City, Pennsylvania.

The final performance was sort of a let down. It should have been momentous, something special, but it just seemed to slip by, no worse, but not much better than any of the others. When the curtain came down and they took their final bows it was all so...so uneventful. Immediately afterwards the cast piled into the van and, after Herb saw to it that the scrim was loaded, they headed for New York City.

In less than an hour and a half, they drew up to the corner of Fifty Seventh street and Broadway in front of the building that held the office of the American Drama Guild.

The dissolution of the family was remarkably casual. Everyone was tired, and the enormity of the transition from being a member of a team to being a solo performer was just too much to deal with at the moment. There were the cursory hand shakes. Except for Ralph's previous effort, there wasn't even the exchange of phone numbers. If they wanted to get in touch with each other, all they had to do was to call Stanley.

Ralph and Nat headed for Pennsylvania Station. Ralph took a train to Poughkeepsie, picking up a New York Times on the way. Nat took a train to Newark and his family, where he planned to stay until after his nose job, after which he'd seek out a room, a cheap one, in Manhattan. Alvin took the subway to the apartment in the East Village he'd arranged to sublet. Jane Applebaum took the subway to her family in Brooklyn. As soon as she tied up some loose ends she planned to book a flight back to Los Angeles. Albert Fenwick took the subway to the Bronx where he lived with his family. Herb took Ted home with him. Herb met his son, Brutus, for the first time, while Ted booked a flight leaving the following day back to Los Angeles.

L'ENVOI

Herb Volpe became a successful character actor. He appeared regularly on television, in a number of Broadway shows and in several films. His wife gave up her singing career and devoted herself to Herb and their son, Brutus, who followed in his father's footsteps and became an actor.

Betsy Landers became an established soap opera actor, appeared in a number of Broadway shows and in several films. She remarried, but the union was a brief one.

Nat Brenner survived as an actor. He never achieved the success as an actor that he longed for, but he finally did have some success as a playwright. He kept in touch with Betsy Landers, and eventually proposed. She turned him down.

Ted Lombard worked in television and in a couple of films. His wife died two years after the tour ended. He often visited his son, daughter-in-law and his two grandchildren in Colorado.

Alvin Gorman returned to Los Angeles six months after the tour ended. He appeared on television a couple of times in small roles. Two years later he moved to San Francisco where he opened an antique shop with a friend.

Ralph Krumsky worked successfully in television and on the stage. He established an Off Off Broadway theatre where he produced little known American plays. He hired Nat Brenner for two of his productions. He also produced a boy and a girl, and remarried after his first wife died.

Jane Applebaum married three times and led a wildly colorful and adventurous life, covering the globe and all the many various aspects of show business, including a stint with The Beatles.

TOURING WITH STALIN

Paul Thomas returned to New York. He gave up acting and became a talent agent.

Albert Fenwick continued to do extra work in films and on television. On week-ends he worked in the family candy store. Late in life he married an old classmate. After his father died he took over the candy store, and gave up show business.

CPSIA information can be obtained at www.ICGtesting.com
Printed in the USA
BVOW022347100412

287167BV00001B/2/P